OUTRAGEOUS
THAI

OUTRAGEOUS
THAI
SLANG, CURSES AND EPITHETS

T. F. Rhoden

A book of all those words and phrases that Thais would rather you not
know—and can't find in mainstream dictionaries or books!

TUTTLE PUBLISHING
Tokyo • Rutland, Vermont • Singapore

Published by Tuttle Publishing, an imprint of Periplus Editions (HK) Ltd., with editorial offices at 364 Innovation Drive, North Clarendon, VT 05759 USA and 61 Tai Seng Avenue #02-12, Singapore 534167.

ISBN 978-0-8048-4053-8

Distributed by:

North America, Latin America & Europe
Tuttle Publishing
364 Innovation Drive
North Clarendon, VT 05759-9436
Tel: 1 (802) 773 8930; Fax: 1 (802) 773 6993
Email: info@tuttlepublishing.com
www.tuttlepublishing.com

Asia Pacific
Berkeley Books Pte. Ltd.
61 Tai Seng Avenue #02-12
Singapore 534167
Tel: (65) 6280 1330; Fax: (65) 6280 6290
Email: inquiries@periplus.com.sg
www.periplus.com

Japan
Tuttle Publishing
Yaekari Building 3rd Floor
5-4-12 Osaki, Shinagawa-ku
Tokyo 141 0032, Japan
Tel: (81) 3 5437 0171; Fax: (81) 3 5437 0755
Email: tuttle-sales@gol.com

First Edition
11 10 09 08   6 5 4 3 2 1

Printed in Singapore

Contents

Introduction

One of the more frustrating things about learning a new language is that what you get from a textbook or a language instructor is often not what you'll hear on the street or in everyday life. The Thai language is no exception. This book was designed to help bridge that gap. Whether you're a volunteer, businessman, aid worker, English teacher, diplomat, exchange student, tourist, journalist, or visiting professor—this book's for you!

This book takes a lot of liberty in the way of grammar, both in English and in Thai. The English is definitely American and meant to reflect that accent. The Thai is central and meant to reflect the general "twenty-something" and younger generation. For both English and Thai translations, the goal is to express feeling much more so than to provide a literal translation. This leaves much open to interpretation, and I expect this will help to generate further conversation on how best to use these words and phrases. However, any constructive criticism is welcome in the hope of making the next edition even better.

As for putting these types of words and phrases into action, do I really need to stress caution? It's like the gun salesman reminding his customer, "Guns don't kill people. People do!" There are some powerful words in this book that could easily get you punched in the face—probably worse. So instead of writing *impolite* or *vulgar* next to every other word, I remind the reader to be CAUTIOUS in applying what has been learned here. That said many Thais would seriously object to a book like this being published at all. In a lot of ways a book as direct as this simply just goes against many aspects of Thai culture. I really can't imagine a Thai ever writing something like this text of his or her own accord. But because of the outside-looking-in perspective that I offer you the reader, in this book, you will get the opportunity to really learn some extremely strong language that your Thai colleagues would rather you probably not know. I've yet to come across another book on Thai language quite like this one, so what you've got here is something unique.

I've learned over the years that it's one thing to know how to speak a foreign language, and quite another to sound cool. This book will at least give you a fighting chance. Good luck!

T. F. Rhoden

Usage

One general format will be followed throughout most of the book. A concept, word or phrase will be introduced, and then an example of how that word or phrase could be used will be given. For example, when the word เม้มสตางค์ [máym sà-dtàhng] which means *to hold back money* or *to keep a piece of the pie for yourself* is introduced, it will then be explained or narrated upon and then used in a sentence like below:

- ใง! อะไร กัน เนี่ย ⌃เม้มสตางค์ รึป่าว
  ngai 'à-rai-gun nîa MÁYM SÀ-DTÀHNG rúe-bplòw
  Hey! What is this anyway?! Are you **holding money back**, or what?!

First a sentence or phrase will be written in Thai, placing a space between each word in Thai to help beginners read though the sentence, even though in real Thai writing a space is not put between each word. The second line will be a Romanized transcription of the Thai. Since not everyone can read Thai, this has also been included so that anyone at any level can enjoy this book as well (See Pronunciation Guideon next page.) The final sentence will be a translation into American English. Note that the translation will not always follow the Thai sentence word for word. What's more important here is to get the general meaning so that you can start using these words and phrases even sooner.

Pronunciation Guide

I'm of the camp that nothing represents the spoken Thai language better pho-
netically than the Thai alphabet itself. Like most other books on the Thai language, I recommend that you learn how to read the alphabet if you're ever going to be in Thailand, even if for only a short time. However, to be fair, learning
a new alphabet using completely foreign characters is tough and can take some
time. Simply refer to the succeeding pages for the phonetic equivalent of Thai
characters and the guide on using the different tone marks.

Initial Consonants

Take note of the difference between initial and final consonants. The most
foreign consonants are [dt], [pb], [ñ], ['], and [ng] when these are the initial
consonants.

Thai	Phonetic	English
ก	g	s*k*y
ข ค ฆ	k	*k*ey
จ	j	*j*et
ง	ng	si*ng*
ช ฌ ฌ	ch	*ch*eese
ซ ส ศ ษ	s	*s*ong
ย	y	*y*ou
ญ	ñ	espa*ñ*ol
ด ฎ	d	*d*ate
ต ฏ	dt	s*t*and
ถ ท ธ ฐ ฑ ฒ	t	*t*ea

Thai	Phonetic	English
บ	b	*b*oy
ป	bp	s*p*y
ผ พ ภ	p	*p*ole
ฝ ฟ	f	*f*un
ห ฮ	h	*h*ow
น ณ	n	*n*eed
ร	r	bu*rr*ito
ล ฬ	l	*l*ong
ว	w	*w*ay
อ	'	glottal in Hawai'i

Final Consonants

The final consonants are not nearly as aspirated as they are in English. Because these final consonants are "swallowed," only six distinct sounds remain: [k], [t], [p], [m], [n], [ng], and a guttural stop that follows some vowels.

Thai	Phonetic	English
ก ข ค ฆ	k	ba*ck*
ด ฎ จ ต ฏ ส ศ ษ ถ ท ธ ฐ ฑ ฒ ช ซ	t	ha*t*
ม	m	To*m*
น ณ ญ ร ล ฬ	n	ta*n*
ง	ng	si*ng*
บ ป พ	p	to*p*

Vowels

Notice the distinction between long and short vowels. One key to sounding good in Thai is in mastering this subtle difference. Even though every difference between long and short vowels is not transcribed here, these charts can be referred to for clarification throughout. The more difficult of the vowels below to find an English equivalent to are [ue], [er], [ui], and the subtle difference that occurs between [oe] and [oh]. Listen to a native speaker for a better understanding and try to mimic their pronunciation.

Long Vowels

Thai	Phonetic	English
อา	ah	f*a*ther
เอ	ay	b*ay*
แอ	ae	h*a*d
ออ	aw	l*aw*
อี	ee	m*e*
อาย	ai	l*ie*
อาว	ow	h*ow*
โอ	oe	d*ou*gh
–	oo	m*oo*n
อื อือ	ue	N/A
เอิ เออ	er	similar to m*u*rd*er*
อิว	ui	be*au*tiful

Short Vowels

Thai	Phonetic	English
อะ อ็ รร	u, uh, a	H*u*t
เอะ	ay	l*a*te
แอะ แอ็	ae	b*a*t
เอาะ	aw	b*ou*ght
อิ	i, ih	b*i*t
ไอ ใอ	ai	k*i*te
เอา	ao	d*ou*bt
–	oh	m*o*te
อุ	oo	fl*u*te
อี	ue	N/A
เออะ	er	*ir*t
อำ	am	T*o*m
เอ็	eh	n*e*t

Diphthongs

For diphthongs (two vowels thrown together), it is imperative again to listen to a native speaker pronounce them, as many are hard to transcribe. The more trying ones are [eri], [uea], [ooi], [ueoi], [eho], and [aeo].

Diphthongs

Thai	Phonetic	English
โ-ย	ohe	Chloe
อุย อูย	ouie	Louie
เอย	eri	similar to jury
ออย	oi	boy
อาย	ooi	n/a
เอือย อืย	ueoi	n/a

Thai	Phonetic	English
เอีย	ia	India
อั๊ว -ว-	ua	Kahlua
เอือ	uea	n/a
เอียว	eeo	Leo
เอว	ayo	Mayo
เอิ๊ว แอ๊ว	eho	n/a
แอว	aeo	n/a

Tones

Below is a list of the different tone marks in both Thai and the transliteration that this book uses. There are five major tones in central Thai: *middle*, *low*, *falling*, *high* and *rising*. For the transliteration of this book, unless otherwise indicated by one of the tone marks below, a syllable in the phonetic translation will always be a middle tone. Any other tone (*low*, *falling*, *high* or *rising*) will use one of the tone marks below in the left-hand column. Learning how to read tones in Thai depends on four factors: vowel length, class of initial consonant, syllable ending, and the tone mark used. However, there's not room in a book like this to explain how to read them in great detail. If you don't know how to read tones in Thai yet, the phonetic English system has been transcribed throughout for your convenience. Just look for the mark above the vowel in the phonetic English to know which tone to pronounce (See below).

Tones

Phonetic	Tone Marks	Phonetic Example	Thai Tone Marks
	indicates middle tone	[rao] เรา I, me	
`	indicates low tone	[bpàhk] ปาก mouth	makes a low tone
^	indicates falling tone	[nôon] นู่น over there	or makes a falling tone
´	indicates high tone	[chái] ใช้ to use	or makes a high tone
ˇ	indicates rising tone	[sǐa] เสีย to spoil	makes a rising tone

CHAPTER ONE

Slang Basics

Congratulations on your new purchase and welcome to the exciting world of real, spoken Thai. Throughout the book you'll encounter a side of Thai society that is often not privy to the outsider. Some of it will be fun, some of it will be harsh, but all of it will have a degree of honesty often not welcomed by your Thai friends and colleagues. Why do they call this land "The Land of Smiles?" And what's really behind all those smiles anyway? Well, by the end of this book you should have a better idea, and probably more useful a better way to express those ideas.

But, before we jump into subjects like Sex, Cursing, Booze, Status and the like we need to review some of what I call "Slang Basics." This includes words like *gonna*, *wanna* or the overuse of the words *like* or *just* in English. If we don't learn them in Thai, then you may end up sounding even more like a fool than if you were never to learn any of these words or phrases to begin with. Compare the two English sentences below:

"I find her highly disagreeable. I shall not be attending her after-dinner event. Please tell her I have a previous engagement, or something to that effect."

vs.

"Ughhh! She's such a bitch. I ain't gonna go to her stupid party. Just tell her I got shit to do, or whatever...."

I hope that I don't need to explain the differences between these two sentences. In effect, they both get across the same idea, but the second one sounds like something you might say if you were talking to a friend. It's colloquial, idiomatic, and slangy. Think of the second sentence as our overarching goal for this entire book. This book wasn't written for your development as an eloquent speech writer—it was made to help you not sound like a dipshit in Thai!

Me, Yah and the Rest

Thai is a wonderful language for pronouns. Depending on which pronoun you use for *I*, *you* or *he/she/it*, the entire meaning of a sentence can change. Something rather mundane can immediately become a little more hip. After a while though, you should start to realize that for most of the conversations you'll encounter on a daily basis, Thais forego using pronouns altogether. Leaving out words like *I, you* or *he/she/it* and the rest will make your Thai just sound more authentic. This will give extra effect to those pronouns that you do decide to use. First, for guys or girls, stop referring to yourself in the first person as ผม [pŏhm] or ดิฉัน [dìh-chŭn], respectively, and start using the more laidback เรา [rao] instead. See below:

- เรา กลัว ไอ้ กะเทย
  RAO glua 'ài gà-teri
  I'm afraid of those damn ladyboys.

- นี่ แฟน เรา น่ารัก มั้ย
  nêe faen RAO nâh-rúk mái
  This is **my** girlfriend. Is she cute?

If you are a girl try using ชั้น [chún] or เดี๊ยน [dían] instead of the ดิฉัน [dìh-chŭn] for the first person. It sounds just a little bit cooler than ดิฉัน [dìh-chŭn].

- จาก เค้า เหรอ ชั้น ไม่ เคย ได้ อะไร ซัก นิด เลย
  jàhk káo reř chún mâi keri dâi 'à-rai súk níht leri
  From him? **I**'ve never gotten anything at all.

- มา อ่าน บล็อก เดี๊ยน บ่อย ๆ แล้ว จะ รู้ ว่า มี อะไร อีก มี แต่ สนุก ๆ ค่ะ
  mah 'ăhn blàwk DÍAN bòi-bòi láeo jà róo wâh mee 'à-rai 'èek mee dtàe sà-nòok-sà-nòok kâ
  If you read **my** blog often you'll know what **I**'ve been up to—all I do is have fun!

The standard third person is เค้า [káo] which is just a different spelling to reflect its true pronunciation. Learn Thai from a teacher and they will tell you to spell it and pronounce it as เขา [kăo] even though on the street it's pronounced as เค้า [káo]. This can be *he, she* or *they*. See below:

- เค้า ไม่ ได้ รู้ อะไร เลย
  KÁO mâi dâi róo 'à-rai leri
  She doesn't know anything at all.

- เค้า หล่อ มาก เนอะ
  KÁO làw mâhk nér
  He's really handsome, no?

To be a bit more poetic and get that feeling of *my dear* or *honey* try using เธอ [ter]. You'll hear this a lot in love songs. However, it can be used for either guys or girls (though mostly to refer to women), by teachers who often refer to their students เธอ [ter] in either the second or third person.

- ชั้น รัก **เธอ**
  chún rúk TER
  I love **you**.

- พวก **เธอ** มี ปัญหา อะไร ก็ มา ปรึกษา พี่ ก็ ได้ นะ
  pûak-TER mee bpun-hăh 'à-rai gâw mah bprúek-săh pêe gâw dâi ná
  You guys have any problem at all, just come and see me.

Sometimes to be cute or show innocence, a younger girl or maybe a girl-friend will refer to themselves in the first person as *mouse*: หนู [nŏo].

- **หนู** ขอ ใช้ อัน นี้ หน่อย ได้ มั้ย ฮะ
  NŎO kăw chái 'un-née nòi dâi mái há
  May **I** please use this one?

Like many of the counties surrounding Thailand, the centrality of family in Thai society is reflected in the language. No matter how distant your relationship is with another person, it's very normal to refer to oneself or another as *big brother/sister* or *little brother/sister* in almost any situation. พี่ [pêe] means older and น้อง [náwng] means younger. These terms will often be used at work, school or even just at a restaurant when placing an order. This concept of พี่น้อง

[pêe náwng] also reinforces hierarchy in traditional Thai society in that the younger (the น้อง [náwng]) should always show some level of deference to the older (the พี่ [pêe])—no matter how much of a jackass the older may be. Depending on the context, พี่ [pêe] and น้อง [náwng] can be used in either the first, second or third person.

- พี่ จะ กลับ บ้าน แล้ว เหรอ
  PÊE jà glùp bâhn láeo rǎw
  You're gonna go home already?

- น้อง ๆ เก็บ ตังค์ นะ ครับ
  NÁWNG NÁWNG gèhp dtung ná krúp
  Check please!

A newer adaptation for *I, you* and *she* in Thai comes directly from English— อัย ['ai], ยู [yoo] and ชี่ [chee]. Since all three are just a play on English words not everyone will understand you when you use them, nor will it have the same effect as when a Thai uses them. A Thai would probably just think you don't speak Thai very well. But either way it's good to be aware that they're being used more frequently these days.

- ยู ไป ไหน เนี่ย
  YOO bpai nǎi nîa
  Where **you** goin'?

If pulling out the class card is your game give ข้า [kâh] and เอ็ง ['ehng] a try, meaning *I* and *you*. These two have the feeling of *I'm above you, I'm your master*, or *you're my bitch-ass little slave*. The only time I ever used one of these was when I was getting off a bus in Udorn Thai in the Northeast of Thailand. As usual a swarm of decrepit individuals calling themselves Tuk-tuk drivers had surrounded the passengers trying to exit the bus. After maybe the tenth time of trying to politely refuse their service I finally ended up snapping at the next Tuk-tuk driver to touch me by yelling out, "อย่าถูกข้า!!" [yàhk róo jung] Basically, this translates as, "Don't you dare touch me, you little insignificant nothing!" I was lucky I didn't get punched.

- อย่า ถูก ข้า
  yàh took KÂH
  Don't you dare touch **me**!

If you want to be a little rougher or distance yourself from the person whom you are talking about try using แก [gae]. To be even harsher refer to someone in the third person as *it* in Thai: มัน [mun]. Using the word *it* to refer to someone can start trouble. Both แก [gae] and มัน [mun] can also be used to mean *you*, but watch out cause these then become fightin' words!

- แก ทำ ตัว แบบ นั้น ตลอด
  GAE tam dtua bàep nún dtà-làwt
  He always acts like that.

- ไอ้ มัน พูด ปากหมา
  'âi-MUN pôot bpàhk măh
  That jerk talks like a f—kin' dog!

If you really want to get nasty, nothing does the trick or gets straight to the point like using กู [goo] or มึง [mueng] to mean *I* or *you*, respectively. This can turn the simplest phrase into a f—k-you phrase immediately. However, in the case of a very close friendship Thais will refer to each other as กู [goo] and มึง [mueng], but you won't hear it often, and you definitely won't hear them using it with a foreigner in this manner. The few times I've tried to use กู [goo] and มึง [mueng] as an indication of close friendship it didn't go so well and was strongly discouraged. That said, here are a few sentences to really, really piss a Thai off. This will lead to blows...I promise.

- กู จะ รู้ ได้ ไง วะ มึง บ้า เว้ย
  GOO jà róo dâi ngai wá MUENG bâh wéri
  How the f—k is **my ass** supposed to know. **You**'re a f—kin' retard!

- กู ไม่ เชื่อ มึง
  GOO mâi chûea MUENG
  I don't f—kin' believe **you**!

- แม่ มึง!
  mâe MUENG
  Your f—kin' mother!

Really? Eh? No? Nahh!

Similar to how we might ask, "Ya gonna go?" instead of "Are you going to go?" in English, Thais have their own short cuts for making questions. First off, the all-encompassing question word of ไหม [măi] should really be pronounced like it is on the street with a high tone as มั้ย [mái], sometimes written as มั๊ย. Other times ไหม [măi] might be pronounced as a short มะ [má] or a short ปะ [bpà]. These renditions as opposed to the written form of ไหม [măi], will give your question a more personable, laidback, informal flair. See the examples below and make yourself familiar with มั้ย [mái] in particular since it will be used as the default question word throughout most of this book.

- เรา ขอ เข้า ไป ด้วย ได้ **มั้ย**
  rao kăw kâo bpai dôoi dâi MÁI
  Can I come along, too?

- กิน ข้าว เที่ยง ด้วย กัน **มั้ย**
  gihn-kâo tîang dôoi-gun MÁI
  Ya wanna do lunch together?

- น่ารัก มะ
  nâh-rúk MÁ
  Is she cute?

- แบบว่า อยาก เข้า มหา'ลัย สุด ๆ เลย ใช่ **ปะ**
  bàep-wâh yàhk kâo mà-hăh-lai sòot-sòot châi bpà
  You totally like wanna get into college, right?

The second big way to form a question in Thai is using หรือเปล่า [rŭe-bplào], which is a little more direct than just your simple มั้ย [mái]. Yet, alas, this pronunciation is fairly antiquated as well. Instead say the quicker รึเปล่า [rúe-bplào], or even cooler than that drop the *L* sound in the second syllable to make it รึเป่า [rúe-bpào] or รึป่าว [rúe-bpòw]. Using these requires a yes/no response. Often it's translated as *or not?* in English.

- มี กิ๊ก **รึเป่า**
  mee gíhk RÚE-BPÀO
  Do you have another girl on the side **or not?**

- อยาก รู้ จัง ว่า ถ้า ไม่ เข้า ประชุม จะ มี ผล อะไร **รึเป่า**
  **yàhk róo jung wâh tâh mâi kâo bprà-choom jà mee pŏhn 'à-rai
  RÚE-BPÒW**
  I really wanna know if I don't go to the meeting what the effect's gonna be?

Many questions in Thai are formed by using the word *really*. Colloquially this is normally written as เหรอ [rěr] or รึ [rúe], but in practice the *R* normally comes out as an *L*, and the vowel sound *er* sounds more like *aw*, like in the word *law*. Though I've never seen it spelled this way the final pronunciation would be something more like เหลอ [lěr] or หลอ [lǎw]. See below, these types of more informal questions will often come up in everyday speech:

- ไม่ ชอบ **เหรอ** แล้ว จะ อยู่ กะ เค้า ได้ ไง ล่ะ
  mâi châwp LĚR láeo jà yòo gà káo dâi-ngai lâ
  You don't love her? Then how the heck ya going stay with her?

- เค้า ไม่ ได้ เป็น คน ที่ ใจดี **เหรอ**
  káo mâi dâi kohn têe jai-dee LĚR
  What...he's not a good person???

The formal way to say *Have you yet?* would be to use แล้วหรือยัง [láeo rǔe yung], but on the street Thais will shorten it to รึยัง [rúe-yung] or to just ยัง [yung]. The sooner you start using these shortened versions the sooner you'll start to notice that almost everyone in Thai society speaks like that.

- กลับ มา ถึง ห้อง รึยัง
  glùp mah tŭeng hâwng RÚE-YUNG
  Have you gotten back to the room **yet**?

- พี่ กิน ข้าว ยัง
  pêe gin-kâo YUNG
  Have you eaten **yet**?

The fourth most popular way to phrase a question in Thai is similar to the English *Ehh?, No?, Nahh?* or *Yeah?* This is pronounced as เนอะ [nér] or sometimes as นะ [ná], and sounds very similar to *no?* in English.

- เค้า จ๊าบ นะ
  káo jáhp ná
  She's cute, **yeah?**

- เค้า เมา แต่ ไม่ ได้ ถึง ขนาด ที่ ขับ ไม่ ได้ **เนอะ**
  káo mao dtàe mâi dâi tŭeng kà-nàht têe kùp mâi dâi NÉR
  He's drunk, but not to the point where he can't drive, **no?**

Gonna, Gotta and Dying To

Most Americans today are too lazy to fully pronounce *am going to* or *have got to*. Saying *gonna* and *gotta* just seems to flow so much easier, doesn't it? Thais today are not much different. The slang word for กำลังจะ [gam-lung jà] (going to/about to) shortens to become the two syllable กะลัง [gà-lung].

- **กะลัง** ซื้อ โน๊ตบุ๊ค ช่วย แนะนำ หน่อย คับ
  gà-lung súe nóht-bóok chôoi náe-nam nòi kúp
  I'm **gonna** buy a laptop. Can ya give me some advice?

Other times though they will put the จะ [jà] back into it but with a long vowel instead like จา [jah]. This final product then is the phrase กะลังจา [gà-lung-jah], where the third syllable is stressed over the first two.

- **กะลังจา** โดน แฟน ทิ้ง ล่ะมั้ง
  GÀ-LUNG-JAH doen faen tíng lâ-múng
  I'm probably **gonna** get dumped by my boyfriend here.

To say *just gotta* or *just dying to* as in you have an incredible urge to do something, try using this: ต่อมอยาก [dtàwm yàhk] as apposed to word อยาก [yàhk] which just means *want*.

- เบื่อ แฟน เรา จัง **ต่อมอยาก** มี กิ๊ก ซัก คน
  bùea faen rao jung DTÀWM-YÀHK mee gík súk kohn
  I'm sick of my girlfriend. I'm **dying to** have a fling.

- ต่อมอยาก รู้ จัง!
  DTÀWM-YÀHK róo jung
  I **just gotta** know.

Stuck On, Addicted To or Obsessed With

The phrase มัวแต่ [mua-dtàe] in Thai get rights to the point. It can be translated as *stuck on*, *addicted to* or *obsessed with* and just sounds cool to use.

- ทำไม คนไทย **มัวแต่** เรียน ภาษา อังกฤษ ทั้ง ๆ ที่ พวกเค้า เรียน ไม่ เป็น ชะที่ เลย
  tam-mai kohn-tai MUA-DTÀE rian pah-săh 'ung-grìht túng-túng-têe pûak-kâo rian mâi bpehn sá-tee leri
  Why are Thai **so obsessed with** learning English if they can't learn it for shit?

- แบบว่า แก **มัวแต่** มี ปัญหา กะ ทุก คน
  bàep-wâh gae MUA-DTÀE mee bpun-hăh gà took kohn
  It's like he's **addicted to** having problem with everybody.

I Don't Get Why...

The phrase ไม่เห็นต้อง [mâi hĕhn dtâwng] can be translated as *I don't get why...* or *I don't see why...* This is good for showing your displeasure with someone's actions without having to sound whiny.

- **ไม่เห็นต้อง** เสีย มรรยาท เลย
  MÂI-HĔHN-DTÂWNG sĭa má-rá-yâht
  I don't get why ya gotta be so impolite.

- **ไม่เห็นต้อง** เข้า มา ทำ ตัว งี่เง่า จัง
  MÂI-HĔHN-DTÂWNG kâo mah tam-dtua ngêe-ngâo jung
  I don't see why ya gotta come round here startin shit!

Well..., Uhhhh..., Ummm..., So...

The most basic of all utterances are those *Ummm* or *Uhhh* sounds that can escape our mouths when our brains haven't quite caught up to what it is that we want to say. When you don't know what to say, or you reach a point in a sentence where you can't think of what to say, the slang meaning of ก็ [gâw] or ก้อ [gâw] has an effect similar to *Ummmm...* or *Well...* in English.

- ถ้า เค้า ไม่ ไป ชั้น **ก้อ** ไม่ ไป เหมือน กัน
  tâh káo mâi bpai chún GÂW mâi bpai mŭean-gun
  If he's not going, **then uhhh...** I'm not gonna go either.

- **ก้อออ** ไม่ รู้ อ๊ะ
  GÂW mâi róo 'á
  Well, uhhh...I dunno.

- ในที่สุด **ก็** ตัดสินใจ ปิด เว็บบอร์ด
  nai-têe-sòot gâw dtùt-sĭn-jai bpìht wéhp-bàwt
  In the end I ...**ummm**... decided to shutdown the web-board.

Like...

To use the word *like* in Thai take a crack at แบบว่า [bàep wâh], or use it in conjunction with ก็อ [gâw] from above.

- แบบว่า อยาก โชว์ ให้ นะ
  BÀEP-WÂH yàhk choe hâi ná
  I just wanna **like** show it off.

- คือว่า... **แบบว่า แบบว่...** ไม่ มี ปัญหา ค๊ราบ
  kue wâh BÀEP-WÂH BÀEP-WÂH mâi mee bpun-hah kráhp
  Well, ya see... like, uhhhh.... I don't have problem.

Just

The word *just* as in *just do it!* can best be represented by the Thai word เลย [leri]. As you get better in Thai you'll realize that there are a lot of different ways to use เลย [leri], but for our purposes here I want to stress the colloquial use of *just*.

- ไม่ เป็น ไร ถ้า เรา ไม่ มา ก็ ไป **เลย** ก็ ได้
  mâi-bpehn-rai tâh rao mâi mah gâw bpai LERI gâw dâi
  Don't worry about it! If I don't come then you can **just** go.

- ไม่ เห็น ต้อง ขอ น่ะ เอา ไป **เลย**
  mâi hĕhn dtâwng kăw nâ 'ao bpai LERI
  I don't see why ya hafta ask—**just** take it!

All Those Weird Endings

There's a ton of different ending particles that you can throw to the end of any Thai sentence or phrase and the meaning of the sentence will totally change. The two most common ones for beginners of the Thai language are the super polite ครับ [krúp] and ค่ะ [kà] for guys and girls, respectively. While these are incredibly useful they are also incredibly boring. Nothing—and I mean nothing—will make you sound more like a dweeb then to continue using these for every situation. The Thais will tell you that, "Oh, you're so polite," or "Wow, how cute!" and will discourage you from using what I'm about to teach you, but don't give in! The truth is that they simply don't want you to know too much.

The more of these you learn the more Thais will be wary of you in general. But the flip side to that is that they won't see you as a pushover. I want to help you succeed in the latter.

Since there isn't room in a book like this to go into all the various endings, I want to stress the most important and most slangy. These will help to get Thais to start taking you seriously. The most common particles after ครับ [krúp] and คะ [kâ] are นะ [ná] with a high tone and น่ะ [nâ] with a falling tone. The first one is used to soften a phrase, while the second is used to mildly strengthen a phrase. Sometimes they are also pronounced as long vowels for extra effect as นา [nah] and น่า [nâh]. If you don't already use these regularly, start now! There's no excuse to not have an ending particle of some sort for every phrase you utter. The sooner you start to use these, the sooner you'll start to sound more natural. When you can't think of any others to use—use these two.

- พี่ อยาก ดู นม แป๊บเดียว **นะ**
  pêe yàhk doo nohm báep-dieo NÁ
  Ahhh, come on, I just wanna see your tits real quick.

- อย่า ชี้ **นะ**
  yàh chée NÁ
  Please don't point.

- อย่า ชี้ **น่ะ** มัน หยาบ
  yàh chée NÂ mun yàhp
  Don't point! It's rude!

After those two come the endings ละ [lá] and ล่ะ [lâ]. These can have a host of different meanings, but for our purposes in understanding slang they are mostly used to convey extra feeling. ละ [lá] (sometimes pronounced หละ [là]) is used in this way, while ล่ะ [lâ] can be used to either strengthen or soften a phrase, depending on intonation. ล่ะ [lâ] can also be used to create a short pause after an utterance, or it can sometimes be used in place of แล้ว [láeo] to mean *already*. ล่ะ [lâ] is also occasionally pronounced or written as ล่า [lâh] or เล่า [lâo].

- ถูก **ละ** เค้า ก็ นิยม กัน มาก ใน เมืองไทย
  took LÁ káo gâw ní-yohn gun mâhk nai mueang-tai
  Of course! He's really popular in Thailand.

- อยาก อยู่ กะ ชั้น ทำไม **ล่ะ**
  yàhk yòo gà chún tam-mai LÂ
  Why do ya wanna be with me anyway?

- อยา ลืม ซื้อ เบียร์ ลีโอ **ล่ะ** ใม ใช้ ช้าง หรอก
  yàh luem súe bia lee-'oe LÂ mâi châi cháhng
  Don't forget to buy Leo Beer, not Chang!

- แล้ว ใอ้ เครื่อง นี้ ใง **ล่ะ** ใช้ ใด้ รึเปล่า
  láeo 'âi krûang née nai LÂ chái dâi rúe-bplào
  This damn machine! Does it work or not?!

- พอดี มี ธุระ เหมือน กัน เรา ไป **ล่ะ** นะ
  paw-dee mee tòo-rá mŭean-gun rao bpai LÂ ná
  Just as well I'm gonna head out **already**. I've also got some stuff to do.

- นี่ ใง ของ ของ ใคร **ล่ะ**
  nêe ngai kăwng kăwng krai LÂH
  This here! Who does this belong to?

- แก จะ กอด กัน อยู่ ถึง เมื่อใร **เล่า** ใม่ ใด้ อาย เหรอ
  gae jà gàwt gun yòo tŭeng mûe-rai LÂO mâi dâi 'ai rěr
  Man, how long you guys gonna hug for? You're not shy?

To be a little sterner and make full use of the imperative in Thai, start to use
ซะ [sá] or, in more formal Thai, เสีย [sǐa].

- ทิ้ง ยัย ใป **ซะ** ปวด หัว แล้ว
  tíng yai bpai SÁ bpùat hua láeo
  Dump the girl! She's already a headache.

- ใป **ซะ**
  bpai SÁ
  Get outta here!!

If you want to add the meaning *of course*, *isn't it obvious* or *for sure*, try the
ending participle ซิ [síh]. In more formal Thai this would be rendered as the low
tone สิ [sìh]. Sometimes you'll also hear a short ดิ [dìh] or a short เดะ [dày]. All
of these mean the same thing as ซิ [síh] but are a little bit more slangy.

- ก้อออ มี แฟน **ซิ**
  gâw mee faen SÍH
  Well, yeah, **of course** I have a girlfriend.

- เอา ดิ!
  'ao DÌH
  Yeah, I want it!

Another cool way to indicate the imperative or to say *let's* in Thai is to use the low tone เหอะ [hèr]. Sometimes, though, it is pronounced as the high tone เฮอะ [hér]. Both of these pronunciations come from the more standard เถอะ [tèr]. For most situations though if I want to say *let's*, I normally use the first pronunciation of เหอะ [hèr]. It just sounds the best.

- สนุก จัง เลย ลอง ดู **เหอะ**
  sà-nòok jung leri lawng doo HÈR
  This is awesome fun! You should try it!

- ป๊ะ ไป กิน เบียร์ กัน **เฮอะ**
  bpai gin bia gun HÉR
  Come on! **Let's** go drink some beers!

To indicate that you're unsure of something or to say *probably* or *I guess,* use the particle ละมั้ง [là-múng] or just มั้ง [múng]. These are cool and will make you sound more colloquial.

- มัน โอเวอร์ ไป **ละมั้ง**
  mun 'oe-wer bpai LÀ-MÚNG
  That's **probably** going overboard.

- เค้า เข้าใจ ใน สิ่ง ที่ เรา พูด **มั้ง**
  káo kâo-jai nai sìhng têe rao pôot MÚNG
  I guess he understands what we're saying.

Probably one of the trickiest ending particles to use is วะ [wá]. Similar to how the pronouns of กู [goo] and มึง [mueng] can turn any phrase into a f—k-you phrase, so can the ending particle วะ [wá]. It can, however, also make you sound like you really know what you're doing in Thai since not a lot of foreigners use this. After you've heard a few of your Thai friends use it, give it a try also. They'll discourage you from using it, but I say screw it! If you really want Thais to take you seriously, you'll need to learn how to curse in Thai. The word วะ [wá] is simply a slang basic that you need to master. Also, be aware that วะ [wá] is sometimes pronounced as ฟะ [fá] by the kids today in and around Bangkok.

- เฮ้ย! แก คิด จะ ไป ไหน **วะ**
  héri gae kít jà bpai năi WÁ
  Hey! Where **the f—k** ya think you're going?!

- อะไร **วะ!**
  'à-rai WÁ
  What **the f—k**!?!? / What **the hell**!?!?

- หาย หัว กัน ไป ไหน หมด **ฟะ**
  hăi hŭa gun bpai năi mòht FÁ
  Where **the hell** did everyone go?

One last thing about ending particles is that you can string as many of them together as you want. See the following example:

- ก็ เคย มี ล่ะ นะ ซี
  gâw keri mee là-ná sí
  Well, yeah! I used to have one!

CHAPTER TWO

Quick Greetings

For this chapter I just want to review a few of the different ways to say *hello*. You already got the chance to learn most of the Slang Basics in the first chapter, but it's always good to go over these greetings one more time. I'll start with some of the more normal ways to greet someone and then move on to some of the more casual ways to say something like "What's up?"

Hello, Hi and Hey!

The most common phrase you'll hear in Thailand for a greeting is สวัสดีครับ [sà-wùt dee krúp] or สวัสดีค่ะ [sà-wùt dee kâ]. As mentioned, the ending particle ครับ [krúp] is for guys and the ค่ะ [kâ] is for girls. This phrase can be used with pretty much anyone and at anytime of the day to mean *hello* or *hi*. Sometimes you might just hear the words วัสดี [wùt dee] or วัสดี ๆ [wùt-dee wùt-dee] said quickly. This is similar to the English *hey* or *hi*. This is a little bit more informal than the สวัสดีครับ [sà-wùt dee krúp], but you will hear it around all the same. Another common way of saying *hello* comes from the English language itself. This is the word ฮัลโล [hun loe] and is used whenever a Thai person answers the phone. Often times they will say the second syllable with a rising tone like: ฮัลโล่ [hun lŏe].

- สวัสดีครับ คุณ สมชัย
  SÀ-WÙT DEE KRÚP koon sŏhm-chai
  Hello, Mr. Somchai.

- วัดดี ๆ
  WÙT-DEE WÙT-DEE
  Hey…hi!

- ฮัลโล่ ใคร โทร หา อ่ะ
  HUN-LŎE krai toe-hăh 'à
  Hello? Who's calling?

How are ya?

To ask how someone is doing instead of just saying *hello*, the most common phrase you will hear is สบายดีมั้ย [sà-bai dee mái]. This just translates to *How are you?* Similar to the phrase สวัสดีครับ [sà-wùt dee krúp], you can use the phrase สบายดีมั้ย [sà-bai dee mái] with just about anyone and at anytime of the day. You can also switch the question particle มั้ย [mái] with ปะ [bpá] to ask the more casual สบายดีปะ [sà-bai dee bpá]—just another way to ask *How are ya?* or *How ya doin'?* The best response to this question is just สบายดี [sà-bai dee], which translates to *I'm fine*. For both phrases it's probably good to tack on the ครับ [krúp] or ค่ะ [kâ] depending on what gender you feel like representing. This just adds an extra degree of politeness.

- **สบายดีมั้ย ครับ**
  SÀ-BAI DEE MÁI krúp
  How are you?

- **สบายดี ครับผม**
  SÀ-BAI DEE MÁI krúp-pǒhm
  I'm fine, thank you.

How's it going?

The phrase *How are you?* is a good one but sometimes it's easier or more natural to say something like *How's it going?* or *How's it?* The phrase in Thai is เป็นยังไงบ้าง [bpehn yung ngai bâhng] or เป็นยังไงมั้ง [bpehn yung ngai mûng]. This is a little more informal than asking สบายดีมั้ย [sà-bai dee mái]. I suggest to not use this phrase until you are fairly familiar with a Thai friend or colleague. This can be shortened down even further to the phrase เป็นยังไง [bpehn yung ngai] or even the more common เป็นไง [bpehn ngai]. You will most likely hear this among friends. A Thai national would probably give you an odd look if you used such an informal way to ask how they are, but I think เป็นไง [bpehn ngai] just sounds cooler than เป็นยังไงบ้าง [bpehn yung ngai bâhng]. I think a natural way to say *I'm fine* or *Just good* is to answer with ดี [dee] or ก็ดี [gâw dee]. If you want to make your retort a little more cocky, you can say เป็นยังงี้แหละ [bpehn yung-ngée làe], which can be translated to *Well, it's going...* or *Well, it's like this.*

- **พี่ เป็นยังไงบ้าง อ่ะ**
  pêe bpehn yung ngai bâhng
  How's it going?

- ก็ เป็นยังงี้แหละ
  gâw BPEHN YUNG-NGÉE LÀE
  Well… it's going.

- เป็นไง
  BPEHN NGAI
  How's it?

- ก็ ดี
  GÂW DEE
  I'm fine.

What just happened? What's the deal?

If something just happened or there seems to be something off and you want to know more than just how it is going, you may hear Thais ask เป็นอะไรไป [bpehn 'a-rai bpai]. This translates to *What just happened?*, *What's going on?* or *What's the deal?* This is more direct than the other earlier greetings because you may be inquiring about a particular situation or event. This phrase is often shortened to เป็นไรไป [bpehn rai bpai] in colloquial speech. Another common way to ask *What just happened?* without the phrase sounding like a greeting is to say เกิดอะไรขึ้น [gèrt 'à-rai kêun]. This is everyday speech and you can always add the ครับ [krúp] or ค่ะ [kâ]/คะ [ká] onto the end of any of these phrases to make them more polite.

- เป็นไรไป น่า ทำไม ทำ หน่า บูด จัง อ่ะ
  BPEHN-RAI-BPAI nâh tam-mai tam nâh boot jung 'à
  What's going on? Why just the sour face?

- นี่ เกิดอะไรขึ้น ครับ
  nêe GÈRT 'À-RAI KÊUN krúp
  What just happened here?

Have ya eaten? Where ya off to? Hello!

Another very traditional way to make a greeting in Thai is to ask whether some-one has eaten yet. Most of the time the person asking the question isn't really so much interested in whether you have eaten or not or what you have eaten, instead think of this greeting in the same way that you might start talking about the weather when you meet someone or when an American will say *What's up!* In this sense the speaker really doesn't care so much about the weather nor does he really want to know every new thing that's happening in your life. A simple *Yep, looks like it's gonna rain today* or *Nothin', just hangin'* are good enough re-sponses and the two persons may continue to go about doing whatever it was that they were doing before they bumped into each other and had to exchange pleas-antries. So when a Thai asks you กินข้าวรึยัง [gihn kâo réu-yung] or กินข้าวยัง [gihn kâo yung], which means *Have you eaten yet?*, the best response is กินแล้ว [gihn láeo], which means *Yep, I've eaten.* I think to respond in any other way would just throw the rhythm of the entire conversation off. In fact, these two phases are so common that you'll be forgiven if you begin to wonder whether or not Thais are interested in anything other than the current state of your stomach. Just remember that when you are confronted with กินข้าวยัง [gihn kâo yung], you'll know that nine times out of 10, it just means *Hi!*

- พี่ กินข้าวยัง
  pêe GIHN KÂO YUNG
  Have you eaten yet?

Two other similar phrases that are often used as greetings are ไปไหน [bpăi năi] and ไปไหนมา [băi năi mah]. The direct translation for these two are *Where ya going?* and *Where'd ya come from?* More often than not, these two phrases are used as simple greetings much like กินข้าวยัง [gihn kâo yung] is used to mean *Hi!* Though Thais ask you where you are going or where you have been, it's better to think of these greetings as just your regular *Hello!* I've learned that it's probably best not to give an overly detailed description of where you are going, but instead to just mention something quickly and be on your way. If you can't think of anything to say and you want to be polite just say that you're on your way to the market or that you've just come back from the market like this: ไปตลาด [bpai dtà-làht], *I'm heading to the market* or ไปตลาดมา [bpai dtà-làht mah], *I just came from the market.* You can also just say that you're *going home*, กลับบ้าน [glùp bâhn]. This way you can answer their question without really having to answer it, which I think is what they want anyway. Too much information is rarely good for anyone and will probably just get you into trouble—similar to this book.

What's up?! So what!

Another useful phrase that you will hear often used as a greeting is ว่ายังไง [wâh yung ngai]. This translates most easily to *What's up?* or *What's new?* This is the least formal of all the greetings that have been presented so far. If you are going to use any of these with your good friends I think that this phrase sounds the most natural and casual. Similar to the other greetings you can also tack on the ครับ [krúp] or คะ [ká] to show additional respect. However, if politeness is your goal you are probably just better off saying สวัสดีครับ [sà-wùt dee krúp]. The phrase ว่ายังไง [wâh yung ngai] is often shortened to just ว่าไง [wâh ngai]. This phrase can also be used in a host of other situations, but the translation *What's up?* is probably the most common usage of ว่ายังไง [wâh yung ngai] or ว่าไง [wâh ngai].

- ว่าไง อ่ะ
  WÂH NGAI 'à
  What's up?

The last one for this chapter before we get physical in the next chapter is not so much of a greeting but just another useful phrase you should know. I often hear this one and you should use it whenever you want to be both direct and laconic. The next time someone comes up to you making excuses about this or that use the phrase แล้วไง [láeo ngai]. In this context this phrase means *So what?!* and is just a sharp enough set of words to get your point of indifference across admirably.

- แล้วไง
  LÁEO NGAI
  So what?

CHAPTER THREE

The Physical

Now that we covered the slang basics and greetings we can move on to something a little more fun. Like English the Thai language has a plethora of words to describe how one looks. In this chapter I'm going to give you a broad selection of slangy words. Some of them will be nice, some of them are not so nice, but all of them are cool. As soon as you get the vocabulary down for making the delineation between physical appearances like a girl who's *hot* and a girl who's *homely*, or a guy who's *fine* and a guy who's a *fat tube of lard*, we'll move on to the next chapter for character traits.

Goodlooking, Cute and Hot

There are a lot of different ways to say that someone is pleasing to look at in Thai. The big mistake I see beginners make is overusing the word for *beautiful* in Thai: สวย [sǒoi]. This would be about as lame as it would in English if you were only to use the word beautiful to describe someone who might just be goodlooking, or may be cute, or just pretty, or perhaps totally hot. Here's a list of trendier words to supplement your arsenal.

The easiest way to say someone is goodlooking is to refer to them as หน้าตาดี [nâh dtah dee] as in their face and eyes are nice, or a little more cool sounding is to say that they are ขึ้นกล้อง [kûen glâwng] as in they are *photogenic*. Both of these can be used with either sex. You are probably already familiar with น่ารัก [nâh rúk] or *cute*, so let's learn two new ones. The word จ๊าบ [jáhb] can mean *cute* as well, but this one can also have the feeling of *cool* or *trendy*. The second one comes from Japanese and is คิกขุ อาโนเนะ [kík-kòo 'ah-noe-náy] or more often just อาโนเนะ ['ah-noe-náy]. This is an innocent type of cuteness, so imagine one of those little Japanese girls in the Catholic school girl outfit; that's this type of cute. A newer way to call a girl fine or hot is ห่าน [hàhn].

- พูด ไม่ ค่อย เก่ง แต่ **หน้าตาดี**
  pôot mâi kôi gàyng dtàe NÂH-DTAH-DEE
  He's not such a good speaker, but he is **goodlooking**.

- เค้า น่ารัก แต่ ไม่ **ขึ้นกล้อง** เลย
  káo nâh-rúk dtàe mâi KÛEN-GLÂWNG leri
  She's cute but doesn't **look good in pictures** at all.

- พวก เค้า **จ๊าบ** สุด ๆ เนอะ
  pûak-káo JÁHP sòot-sòot nér
  They're totally **cute**, no?

- สไตล์ **อาโนเนะ** ก็ ชอบ มาก เลย
  sà-dtai 'AH-NOE-NÁY gâw châwp mâhl leri
  I really dig that **innocent, school-girl type of cute** style.

To call a girl *fine* or *hot* use the English word เซ็กซี่ [séhk-sêe]. If she's hot because of the way she's dressed or the way that something is put together try the word เช้ง [cháyng] or a variation of it like เช้งกะเด๊ะ [cháyng gà dáy] or เช้งวับ [cháyng wúp]. Another word I hear often used when you run into a really hot girl who dresses sexy is จูบู่ ๆ [joo-bôo joo-bôo]. You can take it a step further and say she's hot because of the surgery she had, สวยด้วยแพทย์ [sǒoi dôoi pâet], though I wouldn't recommend saying that one directly to someone's face.

- ทำไม ดู **เซ็กซี่** จัง
  tam-mai doo SÉHK-SÊE jung
  Why ya looking so **hot**?!

- หลังจาก นั้น ก็ ปรับ ตัว ให้ **เช้งวับ**
  lŭng-jàhk-núo gâw brùp-dtua-'ayng hâi CHÁYNG-WÚP
  Well, after that, I changed the way I was **put together to look really good**.

- โอ้โห...มี สาว **จูบู้ ๆ** เข้า มา ด้วย ซะ
  'ôe-hŏe mee săo JOO-BÔO JOO-BÔO kâa mah dôoi sá
  Oh man! Here are some **hot-ass** bitches coming in!

- สวย ตรงไหน เห็น แต่ **สวยด้วยแพทย์**
  sŏoi dtrohng-năi hĕhn dtàe SŎOI-DÔOI-PÂET
  How's she so hot? All I see is a **surgeon's fine work**.

Use the word หล่อ [làw] or รูปหล่อ [rôop làw] for guys. If he looks good because he's *dressed well*, girls often use the word สมาร์ท [sà-máht] or sometimes the word เท่ [tây], which means you just look *smooth, chic* or *stylish*. A newer one you might hear girls use is จิ๊บ [jíhp]. This means that a guy is *totally hot*, or that they just met a really hot guy.

- พ่อ เค้า **รูปหล่อ** นะ
  pâw káo RÔOP-LÀW ná
  Her father's really **handsome**.

- แต่งตัว ไม่ ค่อย **สมาร์ท** เท่าไร
  dtàeng-dtua mâi kôi SÀ-MÁHT tâo-rai
  Your clothes aren't so **smooth**.

- หล่อ และ **เท่** ด้วย ล่ะ
  làw láe TÂY dôoi lâ
  Handsome *and* **stylish**!

A funny way to say that someone is goodlooking enough is ไปวัดไปวาได้ [bpai wút bpai wah dâi]. You can also say ใช้ได้ [chái dâi] or if you want to mean just average looking say เฉย ๆ [chěri chěri].

- ไม่ น่ารัก หรอก ก็ พอ **ไปวัดไปวา ได้**
  mâi nâh-rúk ràwk gâw paw BPAI-WÚT-BPAI-WAH DÂI
  She's not really cute, but **good enough**.

Ugly, Plain and Rotten Faces

Now for the flipside—the not-so-goodlooking. The word น่าเกลียด [nâh glìat] is the general term you'll find for ugly in the dictionary. But I think it's a bit too rough and translates more as *ass-ugly*. If you just want to say that someone is *unattractive* or *homely*, try using ขี้เหล่ [kêe lày]. I've also seen it written as ขี้เหร่ [kêe lày] or ขี้ริ้วขี้เหร่ [kêe rúi kêe ràý]. I normally save the word น่าเกลียด [nâh glìat] for exceedingly ugly individuals or for those prone to do ugly things. A new word I've come across lately is เหี๋ยก [hìak]. This would be someone who's just completely *butt-ugly*. Another new slang word you might hear for *not handsome* is the word อบกบ ['òhp gòhp]. A sarcastic way to say someone doesn't look good is ดูไม่จืด [doo mâi jùet].

- รูป เรา เอง อย่า ดู นะ...**ขี้เหล่**
  rôop rao 'ayng yàh doo ná...KÊE-LÀY
  This is my picture. Don't look at it. I look **ugly**.

- ผู้ชาย คน นั้น ไม่ รู้ อะไร ดู...**เหี๋ยก ๆ**
  pôo-chai kohn nún mâi róo 'à-rai doo...HÌAK-HÌAK
  That guy there don't know nothing, looks **butt-ugly**, too!

- ทั้ง หน้า ทั้ง ตัว **ดูไม่จืด** เลย
  túng-nâh-túng-dtua DOO-MÂI-JÙET leri
  Wow! The face, the body, everything is just sooo irresistible!

If you want to say someone doesn't look good because they are making a sullen or rotten face then use one of the following two, หน้าบูด [nâh bòot] or หน้าบึ้ง [nâh bûeng].

- ทำไม ทำ **หน้าบูด** จัง น่ะ
  tam-mai tam NÂH-BÒOT jung nâ
  What's up with **sullen face**?

Young and Eye-Catching

If you want to call someone a *teenager* use the word วัยสะรุ่น [wai sà rôon] or วัยโจ๋ [wai jŏe] instead of just วัยรุ่น [wai rôon]. For someone or something that is eye-catching or trendy try using the word เริ่ด [rêrt]. Someone who seems young and fresh can be called ซิง [sihng] or เอาะ ['áw]. The words เฟี้ยว [féeo], เฟี้ยวฟ้าว [féeo fów] and เฮ้ว [háyo] have a similar meaning. They all describe a youthful way of looking or dressing.

- ไม่ เข้าใจ ภาษา **วัยสะรุ่น** ล่ะ
  mâi kâo-jai pah-săh WAI-SÀ-RÔON là
  I don't get **teenager**'s language.

- ไม่ ได้ ดี ไม่ ได้ เริ่ด แต่ ชั้น เป็น ตัว ของ ตัว เอง
  mâi dâi dee mâi dâi rêrt dtàe bpen dtua kǎwng dtua ayng
  I'm not good, I'm not **trendy**, but I can be myself.

- พี่สะใภ้ ยัง **ซิง** อยู่ เนอะ
  pêe-sà-pai yung SIHNG yòo nér
  Your older sister-in-law is still **pretty young**, eh?

- นี่ จะ ทำให้ **เฟี้ยวฟ้าว** กว่า เดิม
  nêe jà tam-hâi FÉEO-FÓW gwàh derm
  This'll make you look more **youthful**, more **eye-catching** than before.

Old and Unmarried

If you're not young then you're old. Here are two favorites of mine. The first one is the Thai word for *ancient* repeated twice with the second syllable of the first word, โบราณ ๆ [boe-ráhn boe-rahn]. This one can also be used with how one may act, as in *old-fashioned*. The second is the English word for *dinosaur*, ไดโนเสาร์ [dai noe sǎo]. Both of these are funnier than the normal word for old, แก่ [gàe]. I've also seen the word โอลด์ [oen] written in some periodicals as well.

- ชอบ แนว **โบราณ ๆ** ด้วย นะ
  châwp naeo BOE-RÁHN BOE-RAHN dôoi ná
  I like the **old-school** style, too.

- แก่ มาก ๆ คง เกิด ยุค **ไดโนเสาร์** ด้วย
  gàe mâk-mâk kohng gèrt yóok DAI-NOE-SǍO dôoi
  God, he's old! Probably born during the time of the **dinosaurs**.

If you want to be specific that it's an *older woman* try using สาวน้อย [sǎo nói]. If you want to go further and say that she is older and unmarried, an *old maid*, say ขึ้นคาน [kûen kahn]. The phrase ขายไม่ออก [kǎi mâi 'àwk] or คานทอง [kahn tawng] can also be used for an unmarried, *single woman*.

- เดี๋ยว กลาย เป็น **สาวน้อย** มา แล้ว
  děeo glai bpehn SǍO-NÓI mah láeo
  Watch out, you're already becoming an **old woman**.

- ไม่ เอา ผัว ก็ จะ **ขึ้นคาน** แน่นอน
  mâi 'ao pǔa gâw jà KÛEN-KAHN nâe-nawn
  If you don't get a husband here, you're gonna be like an **old maid** for sure!

- สวย ดี แล้ว ทำไม **ขายไม่ออก** เลย
  sǒoi dee láeo tam-mai **KǍI-MÂI-'ÀWK** leri
  She's pretty, so why is she **unmarried**?

Fat-Ass and Potbelly

For all the large people out there, here's a list of words to encourage you to thin up a bit. For someone who's just *chubby* I use the word ตุ้ยนุ้ย [dtôuie-nóuie] instead of the more common อวบ ['ùap]. If it's a girl you can say สบึม [sà bùem] (sometimes spelled as สบึมส์). If her chubbiness is cute and squishy, then you can use the word อึ๋ม ['ǔem]. Another cute way to refer to someone with a potbelly is พุงพลุ้ย [poong plóuie].

- ชี **ตุ้ยนุ้ย** ขึ้น รึ
  chee **DTÔUIE-NÓUIE** kûen rúe
  Has she gotten **chubbier**?

- พี่ ชอบ สาว อก **สบึมส์**
  pêe châwp sǎo 'òhk **SÀ-BÙEM**
  I like chicks with **fat** titties.

- ทำไม ผู้ชาย ไทย ชอบ จัง สาว ขาว สวย หมวย **อึ๋ม** ล่ะ
  tam-mai pôo-chai tai châwp sǎo kǎo sǒoi mǒoi '**ǓEM** lâ
  What's up with Thai dudes and being into like those **chubby**, pasty looking Chinese girls?

- ปู๊ ชั้น มี **พุงพลุ้ย**
  bpóo chún mee **POONG-PLÓUIE**
  My boyfriend has a little **potbelly**.

Although most people would rather you not call them chubby, the above words are a lot less harsh than the following words for *fat*. Instead of calling someone อ้วน ['ûan] to mean fat, try using ช้างน้ำ [cháhng nám]. For a real *fatty* or *cow* I suggest calling them a อึ่งอ่างทะเล ['ùeng 'àhng tá lae], which is a kind of sea frog, or โองตอขา ['òeng dtàw kǎh], which is like a jar with legs. A good one for a real fat-ass or ugly bitch is ผีเสื้อสมุทร [pêe sûea sà mòot], but I wouldn't use this last one unless you really want to piss a girl off.

- เค้า อ้วน มาก ดู เหมือน **ช้างน้ำ**
  káo 'ûan mâhk doo mǔean **CHÁHNG-NÁM**
  He's really fat, looks like a **walrus**.

- มี อะไร กัน กะ สาว **อึ่งอ่างทะเล** ไม่ ไหว ฟะ
  mee 'à-rai-gun gà săo 'ÙENG-'ÀHNG-TÁ-LAE mâi wăi fá
  I can't mess around with a **fat** chick!

- ใคร จะ ชอบ **ผีเสื้อสมุทร** เหมือน แก ล่ะ วะ
  krai jà châwp PĚE-SÛEA-SÀ-MÒOT mŭean gae lâ-wá
  Who the hell's gonna like a **fat, moody ass-bitch** like her!?

Head and Face

For just a normal, boring, plain type of face try the word หน้าโหล [nâh lŏe].
A popular word to describe that East Asian, Chinese type of face and eyes is
หมวย [mŏoi]. If someone rolls their eyes, a cool way to say it is กรอกตา
[gràwk dtah]. For the *nose* instead of just saying จมูก [jà mòok] change the initial *j* sound to a *dt* sound like ตะหมูก [dtà mòok]. It just sounds kind of hip and
funny. And for the head if you want to call someone *bald*, try using โป๊งเหน่ง
[bpóeng nàeng] in place of the more common หัวล้าน [hŭa láhn].

- ไม่ เห็น หล่อ เลย เค้า **หน้าโหล** ต่างหาก
  mâi hěhn làw leri káo NÂH-LŎE dtàhng-hàhk
  I don't think he's hot at all. He just has a **regular, plain face**.

- เจ๊ก ล่ะ มั้ง มี หน้าตา **หมวย** จัง เนอะ
  jéhk lâ-múng mee nâh-dtah MŎOI jung nér
  She's probably Chinese—has a real **Chinese-looking** face, no?

- ทำไม ต้อง มา **กรอกตา** ด้วย ล่ะ
  tam-mai dtâwng mah GRÀWK-DTAH dôoi lâ
  Why ya gotta **roll your** eyes?

- **ตะหมูก** ชั้น น่ารัก มะ
  DTÀ-MÒOK chún nâh-rúk má
  Is my **nose** cute?

- เหียก จัง ผู้ชาย **โป๊งเหน่ง**
  hìak jung pôo-chai BPÓENG-NÀENG
  Guys going **bald** are totally gross!

Feet and Legs

For the legs, here are two fun words for *skinny* or *boney* type of legs, ขาโต๊ะสนุ๊ก [kǎh dtóe sà-nóok] and ขาตะเกียบ [kǎh dtà-gìap], which can be translated as *snooker table legs* and *chopstick legs*.

- ผอม ก็ โอเค...แต่ ไม่ เอา สาว **ขาตะเกียบ**
  păwm gâw 'oe-kay dtàe mâi 'ao sǎo **KǍH-DTÀ-GÌAP**
  Skinny's alright, but I don't want some chick with **boney legs**.

Another word for *foot* or *feet* other than เท้า [táo] is ตีน [dteen]. Due to the sensitive nature of Thai culture when it comes to heads and feet, the word ตีน [dteen] for feet can often times sound much more rude than เท้า [táo]. Try using it instead of เท้า [táo] whenever you refer to your feet and watch your Thai friends become slowly more annoyed with you. Just don't tell them you got it from this book because they'll probably want to burn it.

- จาก หัว จรก ตีน ผม เอง ก็ หล่อ ที่ สุด ใน โลก
  jàhk hǔa jà-ròhk DTEEN pǒhm gâw làw têe sòot nai lôhk
  From head to **toe**, I'm the most handsome guy in the world!

Add the word ตีน [dteen] to the Thai word for *dog* and it means *to run fast* or *quick feet*, ตีนหมา [dteen mǎh]. Take it and add it to the Thai word for *ghost* and it mean someone who *drives fast*, ตีนผี [dteen pěe].

- เค้า วิ่ง เก่ง เหมือน ใส่ **ตีนหมา**
  káo wîhng gàyng mŭean sài DTEEN-MĂH
  He's runs **fast like the wind**.

- **ตีนผี** เหรอ ซิง ไป ไหน เนี่ย
  DTEEN-PĔE rĕr sing bpai-nǎi nîa
  Fast driver, eh? Where you racing off to so quick?

Racism, Xenophobia, Skin Color

This next topic is a sticky subject, at least for Westerners anyway—and especially Americans. Thais, however, are more straightforward in their xenophobia or outright racism. They've never really been taught (and this is especially true the further you get away from Bangkok) that racial discrimination might be considered bad. Parents will often encourage their children to be wary of foreign looking people and the Thai media propagates this as well. Generally, the yardstick is the lighter your skin the better, the darker the worse. For proof just turn on any Thai soap opera and watch all of the white-skinned beauties scamper around. Take a stroll down any one of Bangkok's backstreets and you'll quickly be forgiven for thinking that the people on Thai national television are a world—and a race—apart from the mainstream. Much of this is simply a matter of what Thai society sees as beautiful. The Japanese and Chinese also tend to say that fair skin is more beautiful, and anyone who spends enough time in the West knows how the obsession for lying out in the sun all day long to get a "tan," in other words to make one's skin darker is considered beautiful. However, I have a feeling that there are other factors involved as well.

The two biggest waves of migration into the Thai nation within the past few hundred years have been that of the Chinese and to a much lesser extent people from the Indian subcontinent. Linguistically, it's interesting to notice that the main racial slurs for Chinese- and Indian-looking people, the words เจ๊ก [jáyk] and แขก [kàek], have both fallen out of flavor for general public use, though it is still very common to hear the word แขก [kàek] on the radio or on Thai soap operas. In general it seems that as the Chinese have acquired more power and prestige in society via wealth, government and royalty the less you hear the word เจ๊ก [jáyk] used as an appropriate way to refer to someone of Chinese lineage. The word คนจีน [kohn jeen] is much more acceptable. The Indians and people of Islamic faith have had a similar experience to the Chinese regarding their adoption into Thai society, but they are nowhere near as ingrained into the system as say the Chinese are today. The word แขก [kàek], which means *guest*, is still commonly heard. A corollary can be seen in the Civil Rights struggle in America during the last century. Basically, as black Americans gained more power they were able to dictate what terms were acceptable and which ones were not for public use. The actual term itself is inconsequential compared to the right (or simply the ability) to hold sway over a nation's consciousness as to what is an appropriate term to use when referring to one's race, ethnicity or heritage. The Chinese-Thais have for the most part been able to gain this right in Thai society. The people of the Indian subcontinent, to a degree, are just starting to get there.

Taking this a step further, the general term ฝรั่ง [fà-rùng] for Occidental people is still widely used today with little regard for what Westerners might feel. Most Thais see this as a non-issue as they probably used to also see the word เจ๊ก [jáyk] and แขก [kàek] as non-issues. One could, if forced to, refer to Westerners as คนผิวสีขาว [kohn pǔi sěe kǒw] instead of ฝรั่ง [fà-rùng], and this does seem to be the trend on some news shows. But since there is no significant portion of Thai citizenry that is of European lineage or, for that matter, even foreigners that can speak Thai to argue this point intelligently, the word ฝรั่ง [fà-rùng] is unlikely to die out anytime in the near future. Most foreigners aren't really bothered by the word ฝรั่ง [fà-rùng]. If fact, it simply translates into the word for one harmless, tropical fruit—*guava*. Also, if the term does at anytime ever become abusive, a foreigner living in Thailand can simply just take themselves out of that particular situation and surround himself with people of their own ethnicity. It's not like you'll ever find a Westerner living in some small village in rural Isan for months on end who's committed and integrated into the community to such a degree that it would be difficult to remove himself. However, it's best not to kid oneself into thinking that every time a Thai uses the word ฝรั่ง [fà-rùng] they are using it as a cute, harmless way to refer to a foreigner. More often than not it's used as a slur, and a rude one at that. The following words will help you to recognize these and be able to use them as efficiently as a Thai could and often does.

To start off, here are two terms to refer to someone who is dark-skinned, ดำตับเป็ด [dam dtùp bpèht] and ดำมิดหมี [dam mìht měe]. Both terms are a little more slangy than just saying that someone has dark skin like the word คล้ำ [klám] or ผิวคล้ำ [pǔi klám]. If you want to refer to someone of mixed race then call them a *half-child* in Thai, ลูกครึ่ง [lôok krûeng].

- เป็น เด็ก ตัว **ดำมิดหมี** สอง คน นั้น ที่ มา สาย อีก แล้ว
  bpehn dèhk dtua DAM-MÌHT-MĚE sǎwng kohn nún têe mah sǎi 'èek láeo
  It's those two **dark** kids there that came late again.

- เปิด ดู ทีวี ไทย เห็น แต่ **ลูกครึ่ง** เข้า มา แสดง เท่านั้น
bpèrt doo tee-wee tai hěhn dtàe LÔOK-KRÛENG kâo mah sà-dàeng tâo-nún
Flip on the TV in Thailand and all you're gonna see are these **half-Thai half-Western** kids acting.

As stated earlier the word ฝรั่ง [fà-rùng] can have various meanings depending on the context and how it's said. It can be translated as *Westerner* or *Occidental* as easily as it can mean *foreigner*. I still believe that its original meaning was something more along the lines of *Caucasian*, *whitey* or *white-boy* and that only recently has it started to be used as a general term for anyone from the West, or even broader than this as anyone foreign from Thailand itself. A good example of this would be someone who comes from say America or England who is Black or Asian and is therefore referred to as a ฝรั่ง [fà-rùng] just as a Caucasian would. The truth is that the Thais themselves are sometimes confused on when and how to use this word. You'll have arguments with Thais on what it's supposed to refer to exactly. But then again like so many other elements of their culture, society and language I think Thais prefer this vagueness. And in case it may seem that we are overly criticizing let's not forget that in the West, especially in America, we have terms that can be just as annoying in their vagueness. A good example is the word *nigger*, which has had an interesting evolution from something that was the norm to a term that is very negative and that now today when used within some circles of the black community in America can be taken as a term of endearment or brotherhood—just don't expect to catch me using it!

- ฝรั่ง มา จาก ไหน อ๊ะ
FÀ-RÙNG mah jàhk năi 'á
Where's the **white guy** from?

Now it's important to remind ourselves that the word ฝรั่ง [fà-rùng] can be used as a racial epitaph as easily as it can be used to simply refer to a Westerner. The word ฝรั่งขี้นก [fà-rùng kêe-nóhk] translated directly means *birdshit*, but its meaning can vary. In the past ฝรั่งขี้นก [fà-rùng kêe-nóhk] meant a Thai who acted like a Westerner and was used mostly for women. The term ฝรั่งดอง [fà-rùng dawng] also has this meaning. Today you're more likely to hear the word ฝรั่งขี้นก [fà-rùng kêe-nóhk] in the context of a Westerner, most likely the backpacker type, who is miserly, dirty, stinky and overall just an unsightly mess. You can find these types all over Kao San Road in Bangkok. Sometimes I simply just hear ฝรั่งขี้นก [fà-rùng kêe-nóhk] used when a Thai can't think of any other way to demean or curse out a Westerner.

The term ฝรั่งจ๋า [fà-rùng jăh] or หรั่งจ๋า [rùng jăh] means something or someone that is overtly Western. On the other hand if something is overtly

Thai, say possibly a custom or cultural trait, you can say the word *Thai* twice in succession like this, ไทๆไทย [tái-tai]. You'll hear this one often on college campuses when a group of students are bitching about an older professor or overzealous parent.

- ภาพ นี้ ดู **หรั่งจ๋า** ไป เลย
  pâhp née doo RÙNG-JǍH bpai leri
  That movie was just **too Western**.

- แก สอน ภาษา อังกฤษ แบบ **ไทๆไทย** ไม่ รู้เรื่อง เลย
  gae sǎwn pah-sǎh 'ùng-grìht bàep TÁI-TAI mâi róo-rûeang léri
  She teaches English **way too much like a Thai**. I can't understand anything at all!

To Starve, Chow Down and then Puke

Food consumption is another part of the physical world and the Thai language has a slew of different words to describe it. If you are *dying from hunger* or *starving to death,* you can use the word ท้องแห้ง [táwng hâeng], which means *dry stomach*, or the more common ท้องร้อง [táwng ráwng]. When mealtime comes, most Thais will use one of the following three words, กิน [gihn], ทาน [tahn] or รับทาน [rúp bpà than]. But Thais have another word for eating which is extremely rude and difficult to find a matching word for it in the English language. This word is แดก [dàek] and means something along the lines of *to eat like a f—king dog* or maybe *to shovel shit into your fat, ugly face*. Basically, you're more likely to hear it used as an epithet than in everyday use. The word แดกห่า [dàek hàh] essentially has the same meaning as well. A disparaging way to describe fastfood is to use the word แดกด่วน [dàek dùan]. You might also hear the word แดก [dàek] in the phrase ตลกแดก [dtà-lòhk dàek]. This would be someone who's trying to be funny in order to get a free meal. Another funny phrase used to describe a guest who is *just waiting to eat* or waiting to see what his host will give them is คอยแดก [koi dàek].

- **ท้องแห้ง** จัง ยัง ไม่ ได้ กิน ข้าว เลย
  TÁWNG-HÂENG jung yung mâi dâi gihn-kôw leri
  Man, I'm **starving**! I haven't eaten anything yet.

- ไม่ กิน **แดกด่วน** หรอก
  mâi gihn DÀEK-DÙAN ràwk
  I don't eat that **nasty fastfood crap**.

The words โซ้ย [sóe] and สวาปาม [sà wǎh bpahm] can be used to mean *devour* or possibly *chow-down*, but they are definitely not as rude the word แดก [dàek]. And, let's say you've eaten more than you can handle, instead of saying อาเจียน ['ah jian] to mean *to vomit* or *to puke*, try using the word อ้วก ['ûak].

- โซ้ย หูฉลาม อร่อย จัง
  SÓE hǒo-chà-lǎh 'à-rôi jung
  Chowing down on some shark fin is so good!

- หนู จะ อ้วก
  nǒo jà 'ÛAK
  I'm gonna **puke**!

To Shit, Fart and Ultimately Smell Bad

After the food has been eaten there are a few ways to talk about how one may choose to discharge of it. The general word for *crap* or *shit* is ขี้ [kêe]. Like English, this word can be used to describe either the crap itself (a noun) or as the act of crapping (a verb). The word อึ ['ùe] also means *to shit*. When you *have to take a dump* you can say ปวดขี้ [bpùat kêe]. If it's so bad that you *have the runs* or *diarrhea*, use either ท้องร่วง [táwng rûang] or ท้องเดิน [táwng dern].

- เดี๋ยว ๆ จะ ขี้ ก่อน
  děeo-děeo jà KÊE gàwn
  Hold on, I'm gonna **take a dump** first.

- แวะ บ้าน ก่อน นะ ปวดขี้ จัง
  wáe bâhn gàwn ná BÙAT-KÊE jung
  Stop by the house real quit. I really **gotta drop a log**.

- เป็น ไร ฮะ ท้องร่วง รึ
  bpehn rai há TÁWNG-RÛANG rúe
  What's wrong? You **have the runs**, or something?

If it's just gas that needs to come out, instead of saying ผายลม [pǎi lohm] to mean *break wind* say ตด [dtòht] or ปล่อยแก๊ส [bplòi gáet] to mean *fart*. The air that does come out is called ลมเสีย [lohm sǐa]. Two fun ways to describe that putrid smell are เหม็นคาว [měhn kow] or maybe เป็นกะปิ [bpehn gà-bpìh]. If you're really *dirty* as well then you might hear the word ซกมก [sóhk móhk].

- ใคร **ตด** วะ
  krai DTÒHT wá
  Who the hell **farted**?

- ทำไม แก **เหม็นคาว** ล่ะ
  tam-mai gae MĚHN-KOW lâ
  Why do you stink like rotten fish?

To Piss

The word for *piss* or the act of *pissing* is ฉี่ [chèe]. A more rude word is เยี่ยว [yêeo]. I've also heard it funnily described as ชิ้งฉ่อง [chíhng chàwng]. The word ปล่อยทุกข์ [bplòi took] translated directly means *to relieve suffering* and can be used to describe either *going number one* or *going number two*. A good way of saying that you want to go number one without actually saying that you want to piss is the phrase ยิงกระต่าย [ying grà-dtai] for males and เด็ดดอกไม้ [dèht dàwk-mái] for females. If you want to be more direct than that then just say ปวดฉี่ [bpùat chèe] to mean you *need to pee*, similar to ปวดขี้ [bpùat kêe] for when you *need to poop*.

- ให้ ทุก คน **ฉี่** ก่อน เข้า รถ ละ
  hâi took kohn CHÈE gàwn kâo róht lá
  Have everyone **pee** before they get on the bus.

- เค้า ไป **ยิงกระต่าย** เหรอ
  káo bpai YIHNG-GRÀ-DTAI lěr
  He went to the bathroom?

- คง ไป **เด็ดดอกไม้** ล่ะมั้ง
  kohng bpai DÈHT-DÀWK-MÁI là-múng
  She probably went **number one**.

Eye Gook, Nose Gunk and Body Odor

A lot of words for the physical in Thai start with the word ขี้ [kêe]. The word for *eye boogers* or *eye gook* is ขี้ตา [kêe dtah]. For *nose boogers* or *snot* try using ขี้จมูก [kêe jà-mòok]. The word *ear wax* is ขี้หู [kêe hǒo] and the word for that junk that gets stuck between your teeth is ขี้ฟัน [kêe fun]. If you stink because of body odor, specifically *armpit odor*, this is called ขี้เต่า [kêe dtào]. And in general if you are dirty, instead of using the word สกปรก [sòhk gà bpròhk] try the word ซักแห้ง [súk haeng], which means you're dirty because you haven't taken a shower in quite some time.

- มี **ขี้จมูก** เยอะ เป็น ไข้ เหรอ
  mee KÊE-JÀ-MÒOK yért bpehn-kâi lěr
  You gotta lot of **snot** there. Do you have the flu?

- โอ้โห ซักแห้ง จัง ไป อาบน้ำ เด๋วนี้
  'ôe-hǒe súk-hâeng jung bpai 'àhp-nám dǎyo-née
  Man, you're dirty! Go take a shower, now!

To Have a Period

The word I hear most often to describe a women's period is ประจำดวน [bprà-jam duean], but sometimes you'll hear somebody say เป็นเม็นส์ [bpehn mehn] which is a little more direct. Most Thai women are too shy to call the pad ผ้าอนามัย [pâh 'à-nah-mai], especially if there's a male around. If they have to refer to it at all, they call it ขนมปัง [kà nǒhm bpung], which means *a slice of bread* or by the brand name *Kotex*, โกเต็ก [goe dèhk]. I've never heard the word for tampon because for whatever reason this type of applicator seems to be taboo for most Thai women.

- แวะ ที่ เซเว่น แป๊บนึง ชั้น อยาก ซื้อ **ขนมปัง** ก่อน ค่ะ
  wáe têe say-wâyn bpáep-nueng chún yàhk súe KÀ-NǑHM-BPUNG gàwn kâ
  Stop at 7-eleven real quick. I need to pick up some **pads**.

To Die

The last thing in this chapter on the physical is also the last thing you'll ever do—*die*. There are quite a few ways to say the word *die* or *death* in Thai, but I'm going to give you some of the funnier ones. Try using เด๊ด [dáyt], the Thai version of the English word for *dead*, instead of the normal ตาย [dtai]. A little more slangy than that is เด๊ดสะมอเร่ [dáyt sà maw rây], which amounts to being *as dead as a doornail*. Another good slang word for *to die* is ม่อง [mâwng] or ม่องเท่ง [mâwng tâyng]. I also sometimes hear the Chinese word ซี้ [sée] being used. Another neat one is ครึ่งผีครึ่งคน [krûeng pěe krûeng kohn], which means that you're pretty much *on your way to death* or *in a coma*. The word ไฟธาตุแตด [fai tâht dàek] translated directly means your digestive system is busted up, but also carries the connotation of death.

- หมอ นั้น **เด๊ดสะมอเร่** ไป ตั้ง นาน แล้ว ชะ
  mǎw-nún DÁYT-SÀ-MAW-RÂY bpai dtûng nahn láeo sá
  That dude's **been good and dead** for quite a while now.

- แก **ม่องเท่ง** เรียบร้อย แล้ว
  gae MÂWNG-TÂYNG rîap-rói láeo
  He's sure as hell gone and **kicked the bucket** already!

CHAPTER 4

Personal Traits & Characteristics

It's time to learn how to call someone cool—while not sounding like a dweeb. Otherwise everyone's going to think you're an idiot. This is where the chapter on Character Traits come in. The Thai word สันดาน [sǔn dahn] pretty much sums this chapter up. It means any type of trait, especially the sordid ones, which may be characteristic of any one person. Now that you have the physical down, we need to have the ability to call someone *cool* or *crass*, *lazy* or *hard-working*, *honest* or *hypocritical*.

- ไม่ เห็น แก มี **สันดาน** ดี เลย
  [mâi hěhn gae mee SǓN-DAHN dee leri]
  I don't see that guy having any good **traits** at all.

Cool, Trendy and In-Style

There are a few different ways to call someone *cool*, *trendy* or *in-style* like ซิ่ง [sîhng] and อินเทรนด์ ['ihn trehn]. You can also use the word เดิน [dern] or เดิ้น [dêrn] to say someone or something is *up-to-date*, *modern* or *stylish*. The word *international* in English has also become hip in Thai meaning someone who's abreast of all things foreign. Thais say it like อินเตอร์ ['ihn der] or they use it as a verb like โกอินเตอร์ [goe 'ihn-der]. The word เด็กแนว [dèhk naeo] means a teenager or kid that tries to follow all the new trends, especially in dress. The words เท [tây] or มะ [má] (which comes from the word *American*) can also be used to mean *cool* or *chic*. If someone is cool because he is *charming* try the phrase มีเสน่ห์ [mee sà-này]. Also, the word *style* itself has been adopted into the Thai language as สไตล์ [sà dtai].

- สไตล์ นี้ **ซิ่ง** มาก
  sà-dtai née SÎHNG mâhk
  This style is really **cool**.

- ดู **อินเทร็นด์** มาก เลย ชอบ ปะ
  doo 'IHN-TREHN mâhk leri châwp bpà
  It's really **trendy** now. Do ya like it?

- เมื่อไร ชั้น จะ **โกอินเตอร์** เหมือนกัน ล่ะ
  mûe-rai chún jà GOE-'IHN-DTER mǔean-gun là
  When am I gonna also do things internationally anyway?

- ชอบ แต่งตัว เหมือน **เด็กแนว** จัง
  châwp dtàeng-dtua mǔean DÈHK-NAEO jung
  You totally like to **dress in the most stylish stuff**.

- เรา **เท่** กว่า แก แน่นอน
  rao TÂY gwàh gae nâe-nawn
  I'm **cooler** than that guy for sure!

- เค้า **ไม่ มีเสน่ห์** เลย นะ
  káo mâi MEE-SÀ-NÀY leri ná
  He's not **charming** at all.

Being Yourself and Being Confident

In the West, part of being cool is *being confident* and *being yourself*. These concepts of individuality are starting to gain traction against the traditional culture of Thai collectivism in the way the youth act and speak nowadays. The word ฟรีสไตล์ [free sà-dtai] and the phrase เป็นตัวของตัวเอง [bpehn dtua kǎwng dtua 'ayng] clearly reflect this newfound individuality (or attitude). The first implies doing things in an original way and the second means *to be yourself* or *to be your own man*. If you are a *confident woman* in Thai society today, they may call you หญิงมั่น [yǐhng mûn]. The word for someone who is *down to Earth* or *has his head screwed on straight* is ติดดิน [dtìht dihn]. The opposite would be someone who *lives for the moment* or *just goes with the flow*, ติดลม [dtìht lohm].

- ชั้น ชอบ ผู้ชาย ที่ เป็นตัวของตัวเอง
  chún châwp pôo-chai têe BPEHN-DTUA-KǍWNG-DTUA-'AYNG
  I like guys who can **be themselves**.

- ผู้ชาย ฝรั่ง คง ยอมรับ **หญิงมั่น** ง่าย กว่า ผู้ชาย ไทย
  pôo-chai fà-rùng kohng yawm-rúp YǏHNG-MÛN ngâi gwàh pôo-chai tai
  A Western man could more easily accept a **confident woman** than a Thai could.

- บาง คน น่า จะ คิด ว่า เป็น คน **ติดดิน** ดี ยิ่ง กว่า **ติดลม**
  bahng kohn nâh-jà kíht-wâh kohn dtìht-dihn dee yîhng gwàh dtìht-lohm
  Some people probably think that being a **common man** is better than being someone who is **always living for the moment.**

Out-Of-Style, Out-Of-Date and a Redneck

The opposite of being in-style is someone who is *out-of-style* or *lame*. Try using the word เชย [cheri] or เชยแหลก [cheri làek] to express this. If it's more just a matter of not caring how you dress then use the word ปล่อยตัว [blòi dtua]. A new slang word for any guy who can't dress to meet the occasion or always looks like he's dressed for the wrong season is called ไอ้สุย ['âi sǒuie]. If someone or something they are wearing is more *out-of-date* than out-of-style then give the word ตกรุ่น [dtòhk rôon] a shot. For adults who try too hard to act like they're young or who like hanging out with teenagers, they are เด็กหนวด [dèhk nùat]. Another popular word today for anyone who dresses or acts like they come from the boonies is บ้านนอก ๆ [bâhn-nàwk bâhn-nàwk]. This basically means you're a *redneck*, a *hick* or just *way too country*.

- ทำไม ต้อง ดู **เชย** ขนาด นี้ ไป เปลี่ยน เสื้อผ้า ดี กว่า ซะ
  tam-mai dtâwng doo CHERI kà-nàht née bpai blain sûea-pâh dee gwàh sá
  Why do you have to look so **lame**? Just go change your clothes!

- ไม่ ค่อย สนใจ แต่งตัว อินเทร็นด์...**ปล่อยตัว** ง่าย กว่า
  mâi kôi sǒhn-jai dtàeng-dtua 'ihn-trehn. BPLÒI-DTUA ngâi gwàh
  I don't really care about dressing in style. Just **wearing whatever** is easier.

- **ไอ้สุย !** ไม่ รู้จัก เรียบร้อย เลย ฟะ
  'ÂI-SǑUIE mâi róo-jùk rîap-rói leri fá
  What are you wearing!? You mean you don't know what the hell formal means!?

- พี่ ตกรุ่น ละนะ ไม่ มี คอม ไม่ มี มือถือ อะไรยังเนี้ย
  pêe DÒHK-RÔON lâ-ná mâi mee kawm mâi mee mue-tǔe 'à-rai-yung-nía
  You're **behind the times**. You don't have a computer, you don't have a cell phone or like anything.

- เค้า ทำ ตัว เป็น **เด็กหนวก** ละ ชอบ ไปเด่อ กับ วัยรุ่น เท่านั้น ไง
  káo tam-dtua bpehn DÈHK-NÙAT lâ châwp bpai-dèr gùp wai-rôon tâo-nún ngai
  He totally **acts like a teenager**. He just likes to go out with teenagers.

- สะดุด บันไดเลื่อน เหรอ **บ้านนอก ๆ**
  sà-dòot bun-dai-lûean rěr BÂHN-NÂWK BÂHN-NÂWK
  You fell on the escalator? Jeez, you're a **redneck**!

Weird or Off

For those who are just a little bit *weird* try using the word เซ่อร์ [ser] or the word เบ๊อะ [bér]. Both indicate that something is just a bit off with that person.

- เค้า ทำ ตัว เซ่อร์ แบบ นี้ ไง คง ไม่ ค่อย มั่นใจ ใน ตัว เอง ละ
  káo tam-dua SER bàep-née ngai kohng mâi kôi mûn-jai nai dtua-'ayng lâ
  He's acting all **weird** like this. He's probably not that self-confident.

- ไป เยี่ยม เพื่อน **เบ๊อะ**
  bpai yîam pûean BÉR
  I gonna go visit my **weird** friend.

Awkward, Clumsy, Sloppy and Careless

Anyone who is just generally *awkward* or *clumsy* is เปิ่น [bèrn]. If they're *awkward*, *clumsy* and *sloppy* you can say the word ซี่ซั้ว [sée súa]. If they're *careless* then use the word ตาถั่ว [dtah tùa]. The phrase พูดส่งเดช [pôot sòhng dàyt] is good when someone is careless when they speak, maybe saying something they ought not to. The last word for this group is ปล่อยไก [blòi gài] and fits someone who actually *makes an ass out of himself.* Any of the word above than this is actually a good word.

- แบบว่า ชั้น **เปิ่น** ตั้งแต่ เข้า เหยียบ มหาลัย
  bàep-wâh chún BPÈRN dtûng-dtàe kâo yìap má-hǎh-lai
  Like I've been kinda **awkward** ever since I stepped into college.

- โธษ ที่ โพส ซี้ซั้ว รูป ที่ เรา มี มัน ก็ โพส ใน เว็บ ไม่ ได้
  **tôht têe póet SÉE-SÚA rôop têe rao mee mun gâw póet nai wép
  mâi dâi**
  Sorry about posting all **sloppily**. The picture that I got won't post on
  the internet.

- ชั้น ไม่ ได้ **พูดส่งเดช** จริง
  chún mâi dâi PÔOT-SÒHNG-DÀYT jihng
  I didn't say **anything careless**, really!

- เค้า **ปล่อยไก่** อีก แล้ว วะ
  káo BLÒI-GÀI 'èek láeo wá
  He **made an ass of himself** again!

To Ruin a Reputation, Break or Save Face

If someone makes such an ass of himself as to *ruin his reputation* then the word
เสียหมา [sǐa mǎh] best describes this. The word เอาปี๊บคลุมตัว ['ao bpèep
kloom dtua] is used when it gets so bad you *can't show your face in public*.
If you're just a little embarrassed and it shows on your face then try the word
หน้าแดง [nâh daeng]. The concept of *face* or *saving face* in Thailand can be
a hard one for Westerners to learn, because it simply is not granted the same
amount of importance in the West. Basically, it means being embarrassed or
doing something embarrassing, but in a Thai context it is definitely more valu-
able. Saving face or giving face can often times be more important than getting
something done right or on time. It's just a truism of Thai society that maintain-
ing a good relationship can often times be more important than completing an
agreed upon objective. A good word to use to describe when someone *breaks
face* is หักหน้า [hùk nâh]. The opposite of that—*to save face*—or repair the
situation is กู้หน้า [goo nâh].

- พูด แบบ นี้ **เสียหมา** ที่สุด
  pôot bàeb née SǏA-MǍH têe sòot
  Talking like this will totally **ruin a reputation**.

- ไป ทำ อะไร มา ไม่ เห็น ต้อง **เอาปี๊บคลุมตัว**
  bpai tam 'à-rai mah mâi hěh dtâang 'AO-BPÈE-KLOOM-DTUA
  What'd you just do? It's not like you **can't show your face in public**.

- ผม ว่า ถ้า เรา มัวแต่ มา เกรงใจ กัน กลัว ว่า เป็น การ **หักหน้า** กัน
  pŏhm wâh tâh rao mua-dtàe mah grayng-jai gun glua wâh bpehn gahn HÙK-NÂH gun
  I think if we spend all our time being overly considerate, I'm afraid that we're just going to end up **embarrassing** each other.

- หลังจากนั้น คง **กูหน้า** กัน ไม่ ได้ เลย
  lŭng-jàhk-núu kohng GOO-NÂH gun mâi dâi leri
  After that you all probably won't really be able **to save face**.

Stupid, Idiotic, Retarded and Uneducated

The next time you want to call somebody *stupid*, instead of just using the more common word โง่ [ngôe], try out งั่ง [ngûng] or เง่า [ngâo]. The word งี่เง่า [ngêe ngâo] also means *stupid*, *idiotic* or *dumb* and if you say ทำตัวงี่เง่า [tam-dtua ngêe-ngâo] or เกรียน [grian] it means *to do something stupid*, *to act a fool* or even *to start shit*. The word เซ่อ [sêr] or เซ่อซ่า [sêr sâh] also means *stupid* or *foolish*, and the word ทึ่ม [tûem] is just as fun, meaning *dumb*, *thick-headed* or *just plain stupid*. A little more colorful is the Thai word for *buffalo*, ควาย [kwai]. Thais have a thing about buffalos and if you were to simply say, "You, sir, are a buffalo," expect to see all hell break loose. I like using the word ซื่อบื้อ [sûe bûe] to call someone *clueless* or *annoyingly stupid*. It's a little more lighthearted than the words above. The word บื้อ [bûe] by itself has more of the meaning of *dense* or *slow*. A newer slang word you might also hear for stupid is เกิ๊รป [gèrp].

- ยัย **งั่ง** นี้ ไง เบื่อ มาก ล่ะ วะ
  yai-NGÛNG née ngai bùea mâhk lâ-wá
  I'm f—kin' sick of this **stupid** bitch.

- ถึงแม้ มัน จะ **งี่เง่า** ใน สายตา ของ คน ทั้งโลก แต่ มัน ไม่ **งี่เง่า** ใน สายตา ตนเอง
  tŭeng-máe mun jà NGÊE-NGÂO nai săi-dath kăwng kohn túng-lôek dtàe mun mâi NGÊE-NGÂO nai săi-dtah dtohn-'ayng
  Even though his dumb-ass looks **foolish** in the eyes of the whole world, he doesn't seem **foolish** to himself.

- ถ้า เรา ทำตัว **เกรียน** แบบ นี้ อยู่ จะ โดน เตะ แน่ ๆ
  tâh gae tam-dtua GRIAN bàeb-née yòo jà doen dtày nâe-nâe
  If you go around **startin' shit** like this, you'll get your ass kicked for sure!

- มี คน เยอะ จน งง หรือ เรา **เซ่อ** กัน แน่ เนี่ย
  mee kohn yért sá john ngohng rŭe rao sêr gun nâe nîa
  There were so many people here that we were confused. Or perhaps we were just being **idiots**?

- คิด ว่า คง มี เรา คน เดียว ล่ะมั้ง ที่ **ซื่อบื่อ** ใน เรื่อง นี้
  kíht-wâh kohng mee rao kohn deeo lâ-múng têe SÛE-BÛE nai rûeang née
  I'm probably the only one here **clueless** about this.

The word ไม่เต็มบาท [mâi dtehm bàht] means you're *not all quite there* — you're "less than a full Thai Baht coin." The words ปัญญาอ่อน [bpun yahn 'àwn] or ปัญญานิ่ม [bpun yah nîhm] is normally reserved for those who are *retarded*, but they're just as useful for calling someone stupid. Another fun way to refer to someone who is just *not so bright* or a bit *dull* is to call them ขี้เลื่อย [kêe lûei]. If that's not enough than you can use the English word *airhead* in Thai, แอร์เฮ้ด ['ae hâyt], as well. The word ตาสีตาสา [dtah sĕe dtah săh] is good to use for those *uneducated* types or *country bumpkins*. The consequence or *price of* all of this stupidity and foolishness is called เสียค่าโง่ [sĭa kâh ngôe].

- คน ๆ นี้ เค้า **ไม่เต็มบาท** ใคร ไม่ เชื่อ ก็ บ้า ล่ะวะ
  kohn kohn née káo MÂI-DTEHM-BÀHT krai mâi sûea gâw bâh lâ-wá
  This person's **not too bright**. Anyone who doesn't believe this is freakin' crazy.

- แก **ปัญญาอ่อน** รึเป่า ล่า
  gae BPUN-YAH-'ÀWN rúe-bpào lâh
  Is he **retarded** or what here?

- เค้า หัว **ขี้เลื่อย** เนอะ
  káo hŭa KÊE-LÛEI nér
  He's not so **bright**.

- เบื่อ พวก คำถาม **ตาสีตาสา** ล่ะวะ ไม่ ไหว อีก แล้ว
  bùea pûak kam-tăhm DTAH-SĔE-DTAH-SĂH lâ-wá mâi wăi 'èek láeo
  God, I'm sick of these **stupid, uneducated** questions. I can't do this crap anymore.

- ถ้า รัฐ ไม่ ทำ ก็ จะ บอก ว่า เป็น การ **เสียค่าโง** อีก
  tâh rút mâi tam gâw jà bàwk-wâh bpehn gahn **SǏA-KÂH-NGÔE èek**
  If the government doesn't do it, I just wanna say that's **the price you pay for foolishness.**

Crazy or Nuts

The most normal term I hear someone being called *crazy* or *nuts* is the word บ้า [bâh]. You'll hear this word a lot and its more common usage can mean *Yeah right!*, *What?!*, *Whatever!*, *I can't believe it!*, *No way!* In this instance the speaker is not necessarily referring to the other person as crazy but is showing disbelief or surprise. A little funnier way to say it is บ้า ๆ บอ ๆ [bâh bâh baw baw]. The words ติ๊งต๊อง [dtíhng dtáwng] (sometimes spelled as ติงต๊อง [dtihng dtáwng]) and ต๊อง [dtáwng] mean *crazy* or *silly crazy*. You'll also hear the words เซี้ยว [séeo], บ๊อง [báwng] or บ๊อง ๆ [báwng-báwng] to mean *crazy* or *insane*.

- จะ บ้า เหรอ
  jà bâh lěr
  What!? Are you freakin' crazy?!

- บ้า ๆ บอ ๆ แต่ น่ารัก นะ
  BÂH-BÂH-BAW-BAW dtàe nâh-rúk ná
  You're **nuts**, but cute!

- นักเขียน ของ เล่ม นี้ **ตึ๊งต๊อง** แน่ ๆ
  núk-kĭan kăwng lâym née DTÍHNG-DTÁWNG nâe-nâe
  The author of this book is **crazy** for sure.

- ครู **เซี๊ยว** กะ นักเรียน แสบ
  kroo SÉEO gà núk-rian sàep
  A **crazed** teacher with her wicked students.

- อันนี้ แนะนำ ว่า ต้อง ลอง เห็น **บ๊อง ๆ** แบบนี้ สนุก ไม่ เลว
  'un-née náe-nam-wâh dtâwng lawng hĕhn BÁWNG-BÁWNG bàeb-née sà-nòok mâi layo
  This I advise you just gotta try! It looks **insane** like this, but it's fun—not bad at all!

Confused and Mixed Up

Sometimes it's not stupidity or insanity but just a bit of confusion. The word for serious cases of *utter confusion* is งงเต๊ก [ngong dtâyk]. If you're *confused to death* or *puzzled to boredom* try the word เง็ง [ngehng]. The word เซ่อแดก [sêr dàek] is the type of confusion brought on by *chaos*. A good word used all the time these days is มั่ว [mûa], meaning *mixed up, messed up, chaotic* or just *all over the place*. You'll hear มั่ว [mûa] used with people, things and especially situations. A good particle to add on to the end of a phrase or sentence to indicate that you're confused about something is หว่า [wàh].

- เรา สอบ พรุ่งนี้ แล้ว ก้อ ยัง ไม่ รู้เรื่อง เหมือน กัน น่ะ **งงเต๊ก** เลย ว่า อะไร คือ อะไร ฟะ
  rao sàwp prôong-née láeo-gâw yung mâi róo-rûeng mŭean-gun nâ NGOHNG-DÂYK leri wâh 'à-rai kue 'à-rai fá
  We test tomorrow and I still don't understand anything, too. I'm **totally confused** about what the hell is what here!

- ตำรวจ **เง็ง** มา ยุ่ง กะ ชั้น ทำไม น่ะ เนี่ย
  dtam-rùat ngehng mah yôong gà chún tam-mai nâ-nîa
  A **confused-ass, bored** cop comes and bothers me, why?!

- เข้า มา เรียน ปี นึง ไม่ ได้ แต่ ละ คน แบบว่า เอ่อ **เซ่อแดก** กัน มาก ฮ่ะ
  kâo mah rian bpee nueng mâi dâi dtàe lá kohn bàep-wâh 'ĕr SÊR-DÀEK gun mâhk hâ
  We couldn't start our first year of school. Everyone was just like uhhhh… **totally confused.**

- ไอ้ มัน มั่ว กัน ไป หมด วะ
  'âi mun mûa gun bpai moth wá
  It's all **f—ked up**!

- นี่ ใคร หว่า
  nêe krai WÀH
  Uhhhh, who is this anyway?!

Boring and Lame

The general word for *boredom* is เบื่อ [bùea]. Add the prefix ซะ [sá] onto it and it sounds a little cooler, ซะเบื่อ [sá bùea]. Another good way to say that you're *bored out of your mind* or *sick of something* is เซ็ง [sehng]. If you're bored because something is *monotonous*, *not fun* or *lame* try the word กร่อย [gròi]. The word น้ำเน่า [nám nâo] can also be used to describe something as *dull* or *boring*.

- ทำงาน เจอ แต่ พวก ลูกค้า แบบ นี้ ซะเบื่อ แล้ว
  tam-ngahn jer dtàe pûak lôok-káh bàep-née SÁ-BÙEA láeo
  I'm **totally bored** of them, cause all I meet at work are these types of customers.

- งาน นี้ ไม่ เห็น สนุก เลย มัน **กร่อย** จะ ตาย
  ngahn née mâi hěhn sà-nòok leri mun gròi jà dtai
  This party's not fun at all. It's freakin' **lame**!

- ทำไม ชอบ อ่าน หนังสือ **น้ำเน่า** จัง
  tam-mai châwp 'àhn nung-sǔe nám-nâo jung
  Why do you like to read such **boring** books?

Laziness, Procrastination and Pretending to be Sick

These next few words you'll be using a lot in Thailand. The general word for *lazy* in Thai is ขี้เกียจ [kêe gìat], but its more colloquial usage implies *just not feeling like doing something* or *not wanting to do something*. The words ตัวเป็นคน [dtua bpehn kohn] also implies laziness. A good one to use with lazy government or bureaucratic officials is to call them เช้าชามเย็นชาม [cháo chahm yehn chahm]. The next time you're having problems with your visa application try this word and watch them flip out. The word for *procrastinating work* is ดองงาน [dawng ngang] and the word for *pretending to be sick* to get out of word is ป่วยการเมือง [bpòoi gahn mueang]. The word นั่งนก [nûng nóhk] is a roundabout way of calling someone lazy. It means *to sleep on your feet*. I've often heard this one used to describe security guards.

- ขี้เกียจ ไป คุย กับ แก
  KÊE-GÌAT bpai kouie gùp gae
  Ughhh, I just don't wanna talk to him now.

- ขี้เกียจ ตัวเป็นเกลียว น่ะ ทำงาน ตัวเป็นขน สนุก กว่า
  kêe-gìat dtua-bpehn-gleeo nâ tam-ngahn DTUA-BPEHN-KǑHN sà-nòok gwàh
  I don't wanna work hard, working **really slow and lazy** is more fun.

- ไม่ ต้อง เข้า ไป ใช้ ชีวิต กับ พวก **เช้าชามเย็นชาม** ล่ะ การ เป็น นักธุรกิจ ดี กว่า ข้าราชการ เยอะแยะ
  mâi dtâwng kâo bai chái chee-wíht gùp pûak CHÁO-CHAHM-YEHN-CHAHM lâ gahn-bpehn núk-tóo-rá-gìht dee gwàh kâh-râht-chá-gahn yért-yáet
  Don't go waste your life **being lazy and just waiting to pick up your paycheck**. Being a business man is a whole lot better than being a civil servant.

- อย่า มา **ดองงาน** หน่อย ได้ มั้ย ล่ะ
  yàh mah DAWNG-NGAHNG nòi dâi mái lâ
  Can you please not **procrastinate**?!

- **ป่วยการเมือง** หรือ เป็น หวัด จริง ๆ
  BPÒOI-GAHN-MUEANG rǔe bpehn-wùt jihng-jihng
  Are you **trying to get outta work** or are you really sick?

- เค้า **นั่งนก** ที่ โต๊ะ เก๋ง เนอะ
  káo NÛNG-NÓHK têe dtóht gàyng nér
  He's really good at **sleeping at his desk**, eh?

Hardworking, Work Crazed and Dead Tired

The flipside to laziness is a little hard work. An older way to say *hardworking* is ตัวเป็นเกลียว [dtua bpehn gleeo], but today that phrase can mean *inefficient*, ตัวเป็นเกลียว หัวเป็นน็อต [dtua-bpehn-gleeo hǔa-bpehn-náwt]. If you're *working constantly* or a *workaholic* then you are บ้างาน [bâh ngahn]. If you work so hard that you're *dead tired* then use the word เหงื่อตกกีบ [ngǔea dtòhk gèep]. And finally if you do find someone who *works honestly,* then the word ตงฉิน [dtohng chǐhn] is a good way to describe them.

- เค้า **บ้างาน** ล่ะ อยู่ ออฟฟิศ เสมอ
  káo BÂH-NGAHN lâ yòo 'awn-fíht sà-měr
  He's a **workaholic**, always at the office.

- เค้า ทำงาน จน **เหงื่อตกกีบ** หละ
  káo tam-ngahn john **NGÙEA-DTÒHK-GÈEP** là
  He worked till he was **dead tired**.

To Butt In, Bother, Intrude and Peek

All that hard work can go to waste if somebody butts in and annoys you. The words รบกวน [róhp guan] and ยุ่ง [yôong] are more common so give the word บังอาจ [bung 'àht] a try. It's a little bit stronger word for to *butt in* or *to bother*. The words แหย็ม [yăem], สะเออะ [sà-'èr], แจ๋น [jăen] and ทะเลอทะล่า [tá-lêr-tá-lâh] are also good ones to use for *to bother*, *to interfere* or *to intrude*. Mix them up and see which one works best with different situations. The letters ก.ข.ค. [gaw kăw kaw] stands for ก้างขวางคอ [gâhng kwăhng kaw] and means someone who *butts into* other people's business. If someone butts in by *taking a peek* at someone else's private business or activities then use the word ถ้ำมอง [tâm mawng]. I've also heard this word used to refer to *voyeurs*.

- อย่า **แหย็ม**! ชั้น ยุ่ง อยู่ อะ
  yàh **YĂEM** chún yôong yòo 'à
  Don't **bother** me! I'm busy now!

- อย่า มา **สะเออะ** เรื่อง ชาวบ้าน ถ้า ไม่ ใช่ เรื่อง ของ ตัง เอง ละ
  yàh mah **SÀ-'ÈR** rûeang chao-bâhn tâh mâi châi rûeang kăwng dtua-'ayng lá
  Don't come here and **interfere** in the community if it's not any of your business.

- ไม่ ชอบ พวก **ถ้ำมอง** เลย
  mâi châwp pûak **TÂM-MAWNG** leri
  I don't like those **voyeur** types.

To Run your Mouth, Gossip or be Speechless

If someone is bothersome because they just *talk a lot* then say that they are พูดมาก [pôot mâhk]. You'll get a reaction out of that one. The word ฝอย [fŏi] can be used for someone who is just generally *talkative* or *chatty*. To talk *nonstop* or *like a broken record* is expressed in the word ตอยหอย [dtòi hŏi]. Another good word for someone who *runs his mouth nonstop* is ชักยนต์ [chuck yohn].

- เบื่อ จัง แก **พูดมาก**
  bùea jung gae **PÔOT MÂHK**
  God, I'm sick of him. He **talks a lot**!

- ชี้ ชอบ **ฝอย** ทุก ๆ เรื่อง เลย
  chée châwp FŎI tóok-tóok rûeang leri
  She just loves **to talk a lot** about everything.

- เค้า พูด เป็น **ต่อยหอย**
  káo pôot bpehn DTÒI-HŎI
  He's just keeps on talking **like a broken record**.

If someone talks a lot because they like *to talk shit* or *gossip,* instead of using the more common ซุบซิบ [sóop síhp] try using the more slangy word เผา [pǎo]. The phrase ปากหอยปากปู [bpàhk hŏi bpàhk bpoo] is also good for this. The phrase ตีหัวเข้าบ้าน [dtee hŭa kâo bâhn] is reserved for those who talk a lot of trash but don't let others retort—*to dish it but not take it.*

- ไม่ เห็น ต้อง เอา แฟน เพื่อน มา **เผา** ซิ
  mâi-hĕhn-dtâwng 'ao faen pûean mah PǍO sí
  I don't see why ya gotta **talk crap** about your friend's girlfriend.

- ถ้า เจอ พวก **ตีหัวเข้าบ้าน** ไม่ ต้อง เริ่ม มี อะไร กัน เลย
  tâh jer pûak DTEE-HŬA-KÂO-BÂHN mâi-dtâwng rêrm mee 'à-rai gun leri
  If you do bump into those types who can **dish it but not take it,** don't even start to get involved.

To not be talkative at all, *quiet* or *reserved,* is to be เฉาปาก [chǎo bpàhk]. If you can't say anything at all because you've been rendered *speechless* then you are อึ่งกิมกี่ ['ùeng gihm gèe].

- เมื่อ ไม่ มี ใคร โต้ตอบ ก็ จะ **เฉาปาก** ไป เอง นะ
  mûea mâi mee krai dtóe-dtàwp gâw jà **CHǍO-BPÀHK** bpai
  'ayng ná
  When nobody responds I just stay **quiet** myself.

To Brag, Boast and be Pretentious

For those who like *to brag* when they talk try using the word ขี้โม้ [kêe móe].
For the *boastful* or those who like to use the word เก่ง [gàyng] a lot, meaning
skilled or *good at*, the phrase เก่งแต่ปาก [gàyng dtàe bpàhk] is always good
for cutting them down. If someone likes to act really prominent or act like
they're *too cool for school* then they are ซ่า [sâh]—also spelled as ซ่าส์. The
word หวือหวา [wǔe wǎh] means *showy* or *brazen*, and the word กระแดะ [grà
dàe] is good to use on someone who is *pretentious*. If someone is into or likes to
brag about their new stuff, you can call him or her a เห่อ [hèr] or เห่อของใหม่
[hèr kǎwng mài].

- ไม่ เห็น ต้อง **ขี้โม้** ขนาด นี้ ไง
  mâi hěhn dtâwng **KÊE-MÓE** kà-nàht née ngai
  I don't see why ya gotta be **bragging** this much.

- ชั้น ไม่ ชอบ ผู้ชาย **ซ่าส์** อ่ะ
  chún mâi châwp pôo-chai **SÂH** 'à
  I don't like guys who **act like they're too cool**.

- บาร์ นี้ **หวือหวา** เกิน ไป รึเปล่า
  bah née **WǓE-WǍH** gern bpai rúe-bplào
  This bar is too **over-the-top**.

- มี ความ **เห่อของใหม่** และ ตื่นเต้น กับ รถ นี้ ไง
  mee kwahm **HÈR-KǍWNG-MÀI** láe dtùen-dtâyn gùp róht née ngai
  I'm **really into** and excited about this car.

Arrogant, Sassy and a Smarty-pants

Bragging can lead some to being *arrogant* or *over confident*. A good word for
this is ตัวเท่าลูกหมา [dtua tâo lôok mǎh]. Someone who is *sassy* or *impudent*
is a คนผีทะเล [kohn pěe tá lae]. Anyone who dares or *has the nerve* to be any
of these things is said to have หน้าด้าน [nâh dâhn]. If you're arrogant because
you're smart—*a smarty-pants*—then you have a หัวหมอ [hǔa mǎw].

- แก มา จาก บ้านนอก บ้าน จน แล้ว ก็ **ตัวเท่าลูกหมา** แรง เยอะ สุด ๆ
  gae mah-jàhk bâhn-nâwk bâhn john láeo-gâw **DTUA-TÂO-LÔOK-MǍH** raeng yért sòot-sòot
  She comes from the country, is poor and **acts too big for her britches**.

- ไม่ ชอบ สาว **คนผีทะเล**
  mâi châwp sǎo **KOHN-PĚE-TÁ-LAY**
  I don't like **sassy** girls.

- เด็ก **หัวหมา** คิด จะ มา สอน ไร ให้ พี่ รึไง วะ
  dèhk **HǓA-MǍW** kíht jà mah sǎwn rai hâi pêe rúe-ngai wá
  That **smarty-pants** thinks he can just come in here and start teaching
  me stuff, or what?

To Sulk, Pout and be Moody

When someone can't get their way they will *sulk* or get *huffy-puffy*. The words
งอน [ngawn] or, even better, งอนตูบป่อง [ngawn dtóop bpàwng], express this
wonderfully. Anyone who does this regularly or is *moody* is called ขี้งอน [kêe
ngawn]. The word สำออย [sǎm 'ooi] means someone who will *cry* or *pout* just
to get attention.

- เค้า ไม่ รับ สาย คง **งอนตูบป่อง** ก็ ได้
  káo mâi rúp sǎi kohng **NGAWN-DTÓOP-BPÀWNG** gâw dâi
  She isn't picking up the line. She's probably **sulking**.

- ไม่ ชอบ มี แฟน **ขี้งอน**
  mâi châwp mee faen **KÊE-NGAWN**
  I don't like having a **moody** girlfriend.

A Coward and Inexperienced

A good word for *coward* or *yellow* is แหยแฝน [yǎe fàen]. If you are a *chicken*
or *chicken-hearted* then you can use the word ปอดแหก [bpàwt hàek]. A simple word for *scared* or *intimidated* is ไม่ใจ [mâi jai]. If you look really timid
as well then you are ซีด [sêet]. A good word for someone who is *surprised* is
ตาเหลือกตาปลิ้น [dtah lùeak dtah bplîhn].

- อย่า มา **ปอดแหก** แถวนี้ ฟะ
  yàh mah **BÀWT-HÀEK** tǎeo-née fá
  Don't come around here **chicken**.

- พี่ ไม่ใจ ทำไม อะ
  pêe MÂI-JAI tam-mai 'à
  Why ya so **scared**?

- ไอ้ หมอ นี้ ซีด สุด ๆ วะ
  'âi-măw-née SÊET sòot-sòot wá
  This f—kin' guy looks **weak**!

Two good ways to call someone *inexperienced* are เด็กเมื่อวานซืน [dèhk mûea-wahn suen] and ไก่อ่อน [gài 'àwn].

- เรา เคย เป็น **เด็กเมื่อวานซืน** อย่างนี้ มา ก่อน
  rao keri bpehn DÈHK-MÛEA-WAHN-SUEN yàhng-née mah gàwn
  I used to be **inexperienced** like this.

Tough, Experienced and a Leader

The opposite of someone who is weak and cowardly is someone who is *tough* and *doesn't break down*. A good word for that is เขี้ยวลากดิน [kêe lâhk dihn]. If you're an *old hand* who's *seen your share* of the world then you can use the word ชั่วโมงบิน [chûa moeng bihn]. Another way to say *experienced* is โชกโชน [chôek choen]. Have enough experience and you'll likely be the *leader* or the *head of a gang*. A newer word for this is หัวหอก [hŭa hawk]. Sometimes you'll hear the English word *boss* used to mean the leader in Thai, บอสส์ [bàwt].

- หวังว่า เรา เป็น คน **เขี้ยวลากดิน** มาก กว่า นี้ ไง ล่ะ
  wŭng-wâh rao bpehn kohn KÊEO-LÂHK-DIHN mâhk gwàh née ngai lâ
  I wish I **wouldn't give in** as easily as this.

- ถ้า อยาก เล่น หุ้น ให้ ได้ กำไร มัน จะ ต้อง มี ประสบการณ์ โชกโชน
  tâh yàhk lâyn hôon hâi dâi gam-rai mun jà dtâwng mee bprà-sòhp-gahn CHÔEK-CHOEN.
  If you wanna play the stock market to make money, you gotta have **a decent amount of experience**.

Skilled, Not So Good and Downright Crappy

Someone who is an *expert*, *skilled* or *a pro* at something is called เซียน [sian]. Someone's actual *skills* or *moves*, especially for sports, are called น้ำยา [nám yah]. Anything that's not so good is ไม่เป็นสับปะรด [mâi bpehn sùp-bpà-róht]. If somebody or something just *sucks at something* then use the word ห่วย [hòoi]. If it's a thing or an ability that *sucks* or is *half-assed* then you can also use the word สั่ว [sùa].

- จาก มือใหม่ จน ถึง **เซียน** ผม ก็ เคย เล่น บอล กับ คน หลาย คน
  jàhk mue-mài john tŭeng SIAN pŏhm gâw keri lâyn bawn gùp kohn lăi kohn
  From the newbies to the **pros**, I've played ball with a lot of people.

- เค้า มหด **น้ำยา** แล้ว
  káo moth NÁM-YAH láeo
  He's doen't have any moves left.

- ประสบการณ์ ชั้น ใน เซ็กซ์ **ห่วย** ๆ
  bprà-sòhp-gahn chún nai séhk HÒOI-HÒOI
  My experience with sex **sucks**.

- มา นั่ง วาด รูป เล่น แต่ ก็ วาด แบบ **สั่ว** ๆ
  mah nûng wâht rôop lâyn dtàe-gâw wâht bàep SÙA-SÙA
  I sat down and just drew some picture for fun, but I draw really **crappy**.

Class, Rank and Status

The concept of class, rank or status whether it be at work or in society as a whole is fairly important to Thais. Because of this there are a ton of different words and phrases to draw upon. I'm going to pick out some of the more fun ones. Some Thais will be uncomfortable with a foreigner using these terms, so it'll be up to the reader to decide how much he wants to play with the Thai psyche on this one. One way to say *rank* for institutions like the military in Thai is ตำแหน่งแห่งหน [dtam-nàeng-hàeng-hŏhn]. A shorter way to say it is ที่ตั้ง [têe dtûng]. For both the military and police, sometimes you'll also hear the phrase คนมีสี [kohn mee sĕe] to mean *someone of rank or power*. The word for *increase* in rank or *climb* the career, social, or corporate ladder is ไต่เต้า [dtài dtâo]. The word for *loose* one's rank or power is ตกกระป๋อง [dtòhk grà-bǎwng]. It depends on the sentence but the most common words used to refer to one's class or social status is either ฐานะ [tăh ná] or ชั้น [chún]. The phrase ฐานะทางสังคม [tăh ná tahng sŭng-kohm] means directly *social class*.

- อนาคต อยาก เป็น คนมีสี
  'à-nah-kóht yàhk bpehn KOHN-MEE-SĔE
  In the future I want to be a **government official**.

- เมื่อ **ฐานะทางสังคม** เปลี่ยน อำนาจ ก็ ตาม ไป ด้วย
  **mûea TĂH-NÁ-TAHNG-SŬNG-KOHM bplìan 'am-nâht gâw dtahm
  bpai dôoi**
  When your class in society changes, your power will follow.

A neat phrase to use to imply one's high status is หัวนอนปลายตีน [hŭa
nawn bplai dteen] or หัวนอนปลายเท้า [hŭa nawn bplai táo], which means
where one lays their head and feet. I like the first better because the use of the
word ตีน [dteen] at the end makes the whole phrase sharper than if you were to
use the word เท้า [táo]. This phase is used to refer to one's social background or
family lineage is. If a foreigner, especially a Westerner, were to use this phrase
most Thais wouldn't know how to react.

- แก รู้จัก มั้ย ว่า หัวนอนปลายตีน ของ เรา มา จาก **ไหน**
  **gae róo-jùk mái wâh HŬA-NAWN-BPLAI-DTEEN kăwng rao mah-
  jàhk năi**
  Do you know **who my family is**?!

The proverb ฝนตกไม่ทั่วฟ้า [fŏhn dtòhk mâi tûa fáh] encapsulates this
entire subject, meaning the rain doesn't fall evenly across the sky or *life just
isn't fair.*

High Society and the Stars

The words for *high-class, high society* or *blue-blooded* in Thai can be indicated by saying ชั้นสูง [chún sŏong], สังคมคนชั้นสูง [sŭng-kohm kohn chún-
sŏong], ตระกูลสูงส่ง [dtrà-goon sŏong-sòhng] or สูงศักดิ์ [sŏong sùk]. But,
an easier way to refer to all of this is to use the English word *high-society* in
Thai like this, ไฮโซ [hai soe]. The word ดอกฟ้า [dàwk fáh] means a *high-
class girl.* If you say ดอกฟ้าหมาวัด [dàwk fáh măh wút], it means a high-
class girl dating a low-class guy. The word for movie, music or TV *star* is ดารา
[dah rah], and the word for a *rising star* in anyone of those industries is ดาวรุ่ง
[dow rôong].

- ทำไม สวย รวยทรัพย์ และ **สูงศักดิ์**
  tam-mai sŏoi rooi-súp láe SŎONG-SÙK
  Why is she so beautiful, wealthy *and* **high-class**?

- ชี ชอบ ทำ ตัว ให้ ดู **ไฮโซ** ชะ
  chee châwp tam dtua hâi doo HAI-SOE sá
  She likes dressing and acting like she's **high-society**.

- เค้า เป็น **ดาวรุ่ง** อ่ะ หล่อ ด้วย
  káo bpehn DOW-RÔONG 'à làw dôoi
  He's a **rising star**, handsome, as well!

Low-Class and Lowbrow

The normal word for *low-class* is ชั้นต่ำ [chún dtàm] or ต้อยต่ำ [dtôi dtàm]. A really harsh way of saying of saying low-class or *trash* (like in the word *white trash*) is ขยะสังคม [kà-yà sǔng-kohm]. The word หมาวัด [mǎh wút] indicates someone of *low status*, especially in the proverb ดอกฟ้าหมาวัด [dàwk fáh mǎh wút] as mentioned before. The words กระจอก [grà jàwk] and ต๊อกต๋อย [dtáwk dtǒi] also both indicate someone who is *poor* or *low-class*. The word เจี๊ยมบอดี้ [jîam baw-dêe] is a slangy way to say เจี๊ยมตัว [jîam dtua], meaning *to know your lower status* or *to humble*. If a *poor man marries up* in a relationship then they call it ตกถังข้าวสาร [dtòhk tǔng kôw sǎhn]. The general way to say that you *look down on somebody* is ดูถูก [doo took]. Use the word ฟาดหัว [fâht hǔa] when you also have to pay or give money to that same person that you look down. The last one for this section is เบ๊ [báy] which is a fairly rude way to refer to one's *attendant* or *servant*.

- เธอ ได้ เห็น เรา **ต้อยต่ำ**
  ter dâi hěhn rao DTÔI-DTÀM
  She saw me as **low-class**.

- เค้า ก็ **ดอกฟ้าหมาวัด** จริง ๆ ไม่ เห็น เหมาะสม กัน เลย
  káo gâw DÀWK-FÁH-MǍH-WÚT jihng-jihng mâi hěhn màw-sǒm gun leri
  She's out of his league! They don't match at all.

- ไม่ เคย **ดูถูก** ใคร ซะ คน ล่ะ
  mâi keri DOO-TÒOK krai sá kohn lâ
  I've never **looked down** on anybody.

Hypocritical and Two-Faced

Unlike English the Thai language doesn't have one word that means *hypocrite*. Thai uses proverbs to get at the meaning. The two most useful ones that are closest to the English meaning of *hypocrite* are มือถือสากปากถือศีล [mǔe tǔe sàhk bàhk tǔe sǐhn] and ปากหวานก้นเปรี้ยว [bpàhk wǎhn gôhn bprêeo]. The proverb นกสองหัว [nóhk sǎwng hǔa] means *two-faced*. The phrase หน้าไหว้หลังหลอก [nâh wâi lǔng làwk] also can mean *hypocrite*—basically to say you're going to do one thing but do another when their backs are turned. Quite the opposite of all this, if you like *to tell it*

straight then it's called พูดตรง [pôot dtrohng]. Don't be surprised if a Thai gets more annoyed with you for telling it like it is than being a hypocrite.

- ขอ ให้ ปฏิบัติ ตาม ระเบียบ ให้ ได้ จริง ๆ เถอะ อย่า **หน้าไหว้หลังหลอก**
  ก็แล้วกัน
  **kăw hâi bpùt-dtìh-bùt dtah rá-bìap hâi dâi jihng-jihng tèr yàh
  NÂH-WÂI-LŬNG-LÀWK gâw-láeo-gun**
  I'd like everyone to follow the rules and regulations in earnest. Don't
  say you're going to do one thing and then do another.

- ผู้จัดการ เรา ชอบ แบบ **มือถือสากปากถือศิล**
  pôo-jùt-gahn rao châwp bàep MUE-TŬE-SÀHK BPÀHK-TŬE-SĬHN
  My manager is a **hypocrite**.

- คนไทย ส่วนมาก ไม่ ค่อย ชอบ ใคร ที่ **พูดตรง** ขนาด นี้ เท่าไร
  **kohn-tai sùan-mâhk mâi kôi châwp krai têe PÔOT-DTROHNG
  kà-nàht née tâo-rai**
  Most Thais don't really like somebody that **speaks this straight**.

To Be Fake, Forget Your Roots and Kiss Ass

The English word *fake* is now sometimes used in Thai, เฟค [fâyk], sometimes
spelled as เฟก. As well as the English meaning, it can mean to *fool yourself* or
your friends. If you go around *acting like you're really good friends* for ulterior
motives, then you can use the following two words to describe it, ตี้ซี้ [dtee sée] or
ตีสติ๊ก [dtee sà-dtíhk]. If you want to *fake a situation* or *paint a pretty picture* of an
incident, try using the word สร้างภาพ [sâhng pâhp]. Something that's *superficial*
or *simple* can be described as เผิน ๆ [pĕrn-pĕrn]. Someone who acts fake because
they forgot where they came from or *forgot their roots* is หัวลืมตีน [hŭa luem
dteen]. I've heard this one used to describe someone who got rich or village girls

who come to Bangkok and act like they grew up in the city. On the other hand, instead of saying *kiss ass* in Thai, use to *lick ass*, เลียตูด [lia dtòot]. Another word that is not quite as rough but still does the trick is เลียแขนเลียขา [lia kǎen lia kǎh].

- ทำไม ต้อง **เฟค** ด้วย ว่า มี แฟน หน้าตาดี
  tam-mai dtâwng FÂYK dôoi wâh mee faen nâh-dtah-dee
  Why ya gotta **fake** like you have a goodlooking girlfriend?

- บาง คน ไม่ ยอม คุย กับ เรา เรา ต้อง มี วิธี **ตีสติ๊ก**
  bahng kohn mâi yawm kouie gùp rao rao dtâwng mee wíh-tee DTEE-SÀ-DTíHK
  Some people just won't talk to me, so I have to have a method of **opening people up to me.**

- คำถาม นี้ ดู **เผิน ๆ**
  kam-tǎhm née doo PĚRN-PĚRN
  This question seems **superficial.**

- แก เป็น พวก **เลียตูด** ผู้จัดการ ชะ
  gae bpehn pûak LÍA-DTÒOT pôo-jùt-gahn sá
  He's one of those that **kisses** the manager's ass.

Friendly and Unfriendly

A close friend or the term *friendship* may be called ซี้ [sée]. But sometimes the meaning of this word can be unclear so it's good to say any of the following: ซี้ปึ้ก [sée bpûek], ซี้แหง [sée hǎeng], เพื่อนซี้ [pûean sée] or เพื่อนซี้ปึ้ก [pûean sée bpûek]. Sometimes you might hear Thais call their bestfriend เสี่ย [sèeo]. You'll get a laugh if you use that one. For someone unfriendly, you can describe him as ชาเย็น [chah yehn].

- อยาก เป็น **เพื่อนซี้ปึ้ก** แบบนี้ ตลอดไป
  yàhk bpehn PÛEAN-SÉE-BPÛEK bàep-née dtà-làwt bpai
  I wanna be **best friends** with you like this forever.

To Lie, Bullshit and Feign Ignorance

Instead of saying โกหก [goe hòhk] when you think someone is lying call them a เด็กเลี้ยงแกะ [dèhk líang gàe]. This basically means *the boy who cried wolf*. The word for bullshit is ตอแหล [dtaw lǎe]. Since the word ตอแหล [dtaw lǎe] can be rude, sometimes you'll hear a Thai say the English word strawberry in its place, สตรอเบอร์รี่ [sà dtraw ber rêe] to mean *bullshit*. This is similar to English when we might just say the letters *B.S.* instead of the full word *bullshit.* You might also hear the word ปากหมาน [bàhk mǎhn]. This means you're exaggerating or showing an *insincere earnestness* when you're bullshitting. This is fairly rude. Another slangy way to say *lie* is แหกตา [hàek dtah]. There are two ways to say to pretend like you don't know or *to play dumb,* ทำไก [tam gǎi] and ตีลูกเซ่อ [dtee lôok sêr].

- อย่า ทำ ตัว เป็น **เด็กเลี้ยงแกะ** หลอก คน อื่น จน ไม่ มี ใคร เชื่อ ถือ อีก แล้ว นะ
  yàh tam-dtua bpehn **DÈHK-LÍANG-GÀE** làwk kohn 'ùen john mâi mee krai chûea tǔe 'èek láeo ná
  Don't be **the boy who cried wolf**, tricking other people till no one believes you anymore.

- แก **ตอแหล** เก่ง เนอะ
  gae **DTAW-LǍE** gàyng nér
  He's a real **bullshitter**, no?

- ประชาชน โดน **แหกตา**
  brà-chah-chohn doen **HÀEK-DTAH**
  The people were **lied** to.

- อย่า มา **ตีลูกเซ่อ** แถว นี้ ซะ
  yàh mah **DTEE-LÔOK-SÊR** tǎeo-née sá
  Don't come around **playing dumb**.

Cheap, Stingy and Greedy

Someone who is *cheap* is either ขี้เหนียว [kêe nǐeo] or ขี้ตืด [kêe dtùet]. A good word for *stingy* is ทะเลเรียกพี่ [tá lay rîak pêe], another is เค็ม [kehm]. For someone who is cheap because they're always *waiting for someone else to pick up the tab*, use the word ลมทับ [lóm túp]. The word for *greedy* or *extremely selfish* is หน้าเลือก [nâh lûeak]. The word งก [ngóhk] can also be used to mean *greedy*. If someone is not greedy but *extremely envious* of another's possessions then use อิจฉาตาร้อน ['ìht chǎh dtah ráwn].

- ต้อง **ขี้ตืด** อย่า ให้ มัน ยืม ซิ
  dtâwng **KÊE-DTÙET** yàh hâi mun yuem sí
  You gotta be **cheap**. Don't let that jerk borrow anything!

- ไม่ ชอบ คน **หน้าเลือก** ขนาด นี้
  mâi châwp kohn **nÂH-LÛEAT** kà-nàht née
  I don't like people that are this **greedy**.

- คน อะไร วะ **งก** จริง ๆ
  kohn 'à-rai wá NGÓHK jihng-jihng
  What the hell kinda person is so **greedy**?

- **อิจฉาตาร้อน** อยาก จะ เป็น คน ข้าง เธอ
  'ÌHT-CHǍH-DTAH-RÁWN yàhk jà bpehn kohn kâhng-kâhng ter
  I'm **sooo jealous**. I want to be the person next to him.

Happy, Pleased, Psyched and Enthused

You often hear Thais use the English word for *happy* these days, แฮปปี้ [hâep bpêe]. The word for *pleased with* or *content with* is ชื่นสะดือ [chûen sà due]. A slangy way to say *good mood* is ลมดี [lohm dee]. Something that is really fun or relaxed is มันส์ [mun], also spelled มัน. To say the words *psyched* or *excited* use the word ดี๊ด๊า [dée dáh]. The English word *hyper* can be used in Thai to mean *enthused* or *very active*, ไฮเปอร์ [hai bper]. The words เครื่องร้อน [krûeang ráwn] and ไฟแรง [fai raeng] can also used with people to mean *enthusiastic*. The opposite *to loose enthusiasm* would be the word หมดไฟ [moth fai].

- เริ่ม **ชื่นสะดือ** ขึ้น มา บ้าง
  rêrm CHÛEN-SÀ-DUE kûen mah bâhng
  I'm getting a little more **content** with everything.

- เอา สนุก เอา **มันส์** มาก อะไร ที่ ทำ แล้ว **แฮปปี้** ก็ ทำ
  'ao sà-nòok 'ao MUN mâhk 'à-rai têe tam láeo HÂEP-BPÊE gâw tam
  I want things fun, **easy going**. Anything that I do, if makes me **happy**, I just do it.

- ทำ ตัว เหมือน **เครื่องร้อน** อะ
  tam-dtua mǔean KRÛENG-RÁWN 'à
  He's really **enthusiastic**.

- ภาวะ **หมดไฟ** ใน การ ทำงาน มัก เกิด ขึ้น เพราะ มี ความ เครียด ใน การทำงาน มาก เกิน ไป
  pah-wá MOTH-FAI nai gahn-tam-ngahn múk gèrt kûen práw mee kwahm-krîat nai gahn-tam-ngahn mâhk gern-bpai
  Losing your enthusiasm for work probably comes having to much stress at work.

Pissed Off, Disappointed, Hurt and Cruel

If you're not happy then you may be *pissed off*. A good word for *mad* or *angry* is ฉุน [chǒon] or ฉุนกึ๊ก [chǒon gúek]. For someone that is *disappointed* try using the word แห้ว [hâeo]. The new, slangy way to say that you're *hurt* or *sad* in Thai comes from the English word *hurt*, เฮิร์ต [hêrt]. Thais will often use this one for when a relationship ends. Another cool way to say *sad* is the word จ๋อย [jǒi]. The word แสบ [sàep] means someone who is *cruel*, *mean* or *wicked*. If everyone thought you were a good guy and then they saw your real, disreputable side, then you might hear the word ดีแตก [dee dtàek].

- ถ้า ใคร ทำ เป็น ว่า ไม่ สนใจ ก็ จะ **ฉุนกึ๊ก** ขึ้น มา ทันที
  tâh krai tam bpehn wâh mâi sǒhn-jai gâw jà CHON-GÚEK kûen mah tun-tee
  If anyone acts like they're not interested I'm gonna get really **pissed off** really quick.

- ไม่ กิน **แห้ว** กับ สาว คน นั้น แหละ
  mâi gihn HÂEO gùp sǎo kohn nún làe
  I won't be **disappointed** with this girl here.

- ชั้น รู้สึก **เฮิร์ต** มาก
  chún róo-sùek HÊRT mâhk
  I feel really **hurt**.

- ตัว **แสบ** จริง ๆ
  dtua SÀEP jihng-jihng
  He's really **cruel**!

Lucky and Unlucky

Something that is said to be *lucky* is เฮง [hayng] or ดวงเฮง [duang hayng]. If something is *unlucky*, then it's ซวย [sooi], ดวงซวย [duang sooi] or ซวยกะลุดม้อ [sooi gà lòot máw]. The word ดวงจู๋ [duang jǒo] can also mean *unlucky*.

- นี่ เป็น ช่วง **ดวงเฮง**
  nêe bpehn chûang DUANG-HAENG
  This has been a **lucky** time for me.

- ใคร ที่ โดน ระเบิด ตาย นี่ ต้อง บอก ว่า **ซวยกะลุดม้อ** มัน จริง ๆ
  krai têe dohn rá-bèrt dtai nêe dtâwng bàwk-wâh SOOI-GÀ-LÓOT-MÂW mun jihng-jihng
  Whoever dies in one of these bomb explosions, I just gotta say, is **very unlucky**.

CHAPTER 5
Cursing

Now that you're fluent in both the physical and mental aspect, it's time to learn how to package it all together in order to really burn someone. Learning a new language can suck because it takes a long time before one becomes as witty or sharp as the native speakers in their mother tongue.

This chapter will give you the tools to really be able to fight back in Thai. From this point on it'll be up to you whether or not you want to raise the bar in a verbal argument or smooth things out. The ability to curse in Thai will not be appreciated by your Thai friends and will be highly discouraged. But maybe, just maybe, after you learn how to talk tough in Thai, people might think twice whether or not to make you the butt of all their jokes just because you don't understand.

Mastering the วะ

The ease of usability of the four-letter curse word *f—k* in the English language for either the general purpose of cursing or manufacturing epithets way beyond its original sexual connotation is not easily reproduced in other languages. Even the Thai language does not have one single curse word that is readily adaptable and grammatically malleable as the word *f—k*. However, the Thai language does have one particular ending particle that, when utilized to the fullest, may come pretty close to the English word. This is the particle วะ [wá].

This ending particle was introduced in the chapter on Slang Basics. It's time to come back to it because it's a fundamental part of knowing how to curse in Thai. Most of the examples in this chapter will be utilizing the word วะ [wá].

Look at the two examples below. The first one is a normal question, and the second one is that same question but with this particle attached to the end.

- ไป ไหน
  bpai năi
  Where ya going?

- ไป ไหน **วะ**
  bpai năi WÁ
  Where the **hell/f—k** ya going?

This example is a little simplistic and a lot depends on the intonation of the speaker as well as to whom this question is being asked (for example, between friends or strangers on the street). Different situations can gain from using this simple yet potent ending particle. You'll get a better feel for the word as this chapter progresses because so many of the examples use the วะ [wá].

Front Words

Similar to วะ [wá] that is placed at the end of a phrase, the Thai language has two prefixes placed at the start of a word or phrase to indicate that the speaker is cursing. These are ไอ้ ['âi] and อี ['ee]. Generally, they are gender specific in the same way that guys should use the word ครับ [krúp] and girls the word คะ [kâ], but I've heard them being used across the board and because of that you'll hear the prefix ไอ้ ['âi] a lot more than you will hear อี ['ee]. Generally, the prefix ไอ้ ['âi] is used for males or other inanimate objects or situations, and the prefix อี ['ee] is reserved for females. Though, it should be noted, that part of the fun of cursing in Thai is playing with the gender roles as defined by Thai society, so please feel free to mix these up to your heart's content.

Below is an example of what exactly the prefix ไอ้ ['âi] can do to a word. The first example doesn't use it. The second one does.

- เครื่อง นี้ มัน เสีย แล้ว
  krûeang née mun sĭa láeo
  The machine's busted.

- ไอ้ เครื่อง นี้ มัน เสีย แล้ว
  '**Âl** krûeang née mun sǐa láeo
  The **damn** machine's busted.

Here ไอ้ ['âi] is used with an inanimate object and changes the meaning from just a *machine* to a *damn machine*. If you really want to make it rougher and change it to something like a *f—kin' machine*, you could utilize the วะ [wá] at the end of the phrase as well. Compare the previous examples with the following:

- ไอ้ เครื่อง นี้ มัน เสีย ล่ะ วะ
  '**Âl** krûeang née mun sǐa lâ-**WÁ**
  The **f—kin'** machine's busted!

All that happened was that we added วะ [wá] to the end of the sentence and that really took it overboard. It's also important to say that intonation plays a role. Generally, the louder and more pissed off you sound when you say something like the third example, the closer it is to having a *f—k* or *f—kin'*-type meaning.

Following is a laundry list of some of the more common words that ไอ้ ['âi] is attached to and followed by their indirect English translations. The translations, more or less carry the same weight, depending on the creativity and intensity with which the Thai sentences are uttered.

ไอ้กัน ['âi gun]	damn American / f—kin' American
ไอ้แก่ ['âi gàe]	old f—ker
ไอ้แก่หัวงู ['âi gàe hǔa ngoo]	dirty old man / dirty old f—ker
ไอ้ควาย ['âi kwai]	dumb shit /dumb f—k
ไอ้งั่ง ['âi ngûng]	dumb shit / f—kin' idiot
ไอ้ตัว ['âi dtua] / อีตัว ['ee dtua]	f—kin' guy / f—kin' slut / f—kin' bitch
ไอ้เดี้ย ['âi dtîa]	little shit
ไอ้ที่ว่า ['âi têe wâh]	goddamn comment / what he just f—kin' said
ไอ้นี้ ['âi nêe] / ไอ้นั้น ['âi nûn]	this damn one / that f—kin' one
ไอ้บ้า ['âi bâh]	f—kin' psycho / crazy f—ker
ไอ้เปรต ['âi bpràyt]	damn devil
ไอ้ยุ่น ['âi yôon]	f—kin' Jap
ไอ้เวร ['âi wayn]	goddamn bastard / f—kin' asshole
ไอ้หน้าโง่ ['âi nâh ngôe]	studid f—kin' face / dump f—ker
ไอ้หมอนั่น ['âi mǎw nûn]	that f—kin' guy
ไอ้สัตย์ ['âi sùt]	f—ker / mother f—ker / piece of shit
ไอ้หน้าหี ['âi nâh hěe]	cunt face

ไอ้หัวควย ['âi hǔa kooi]   cock head
ไอ้ห่า ['âi hàh]   piece of shit / f—ker / mother f—ker
ไอ้เหี้ย ['âi hîa]   mother f—ker / f—kin' bitch-ass

The last three are the hardest to find a direct translation to and are probably the most explicit things you could ever say in Thai. I have never heard a foreigner use any of the last three nor have I ever needed to (yet), but you will hear them in some movies or see them on the web in some chat rooms.

To Curse

A general way to say *to curse* is ด่า [dàh] but you can also say ด่าเป็นไฟ [dàh bpehn fai], which means something along the lines of *to curse like a sailor*. Another slang for cursing is เห่า [hào]. It's onomatopoeic of a dog's bark in Thai but I've also heard it refer to someone who is cursing.

- เมื่อก่อนนี้ เรา **ด่าเป็นไฟ** แต่ เดี๋ยว นี้ เบื่อ แล้ว
  mûea-gàwn-née rao DÀH-BHEN-FAI dtàe děeo née bùea láeo
  Before this I used to **curse like a sailor**, but now I'm kinda bored with it.

- ไม่ ต้อง มา **เห่า** แถว นี้ เลย
  mâi dtâwng mah HÀO tǎeo née leri
  Don't be coming around here **cursing stupid shit**!

To Talk Shit, Talk Back and Butt In

These next few words can all mean *to trash talk*, *to talk shit* or *to curse*. These are ปากหมา [bpàhk mǎh], เกรียน [grian], ทำตัวงี่เง่า [tam dtua ngêe-ngâo] and เห่า [hào]. Some have different degrees of meaning that were explained in earlier chapters.

To mean *to talk back*, be it cursing or not, use the word ย้อน [yawn].

- ความ **ปากหมา** ของ ผม คง ก่อ เรื่อง อีก แล้ว
  kwahm BPÀHL-MǍH kǎwng pǒhm kohng gàw rûeang 'èek láeo
  My **trash-talking** has probably started another problem.

- 'จารย์ เบื่อ สอน เด็ก **เกรียน** ละ วะ
  jahn bùea sǎwn dèhk GRIAN lâ-wá
  I'm goddamn sick of teaching these **foul-mouthed** kids.

- ขอโทษ ที่ **ทำตัวงี่เง่า** อีก แล้ว น่า
  kăw-tôet têe TAM-DTUA-NGÊE-NGÂO 'èek láeo nâh
  Sorry about **saying stupid shit** again.

- อย่า มา **ย้อน** ชั้น ได้ มั้ย
  yàh mah YÁWN chún dâi mái
  Can ya not **talk back** to me!

When translated into English the word เสือก [sùeak] might not seem like much but in Thai it's big deal. The word เสือก [sùeak] means *to butt in* or *to bother*. When compared to ยุ่ง [yôong] or บังอาจ [bung-'àht] from the previous chapter, the word เสือก [sùeak] carries almost the same weight as *f—k you* in English. You have to really mean it if you want to use เสือก [sùeak] though.

- อย่า มา **เสือก** แถว นี้ วะ
  yàh mah SÙEAK tăeo née wá
  Don't **f—kin'** come around in here!

To Mess With, F—k With and Piss Off

The major way to say *to mess with, to f—k with* or *to piss someone off* is to use the word กวน [guan]. Here are three exciting ways to say *to mess with*, กวนแข็ง [guan kâeng], กวนตีน [guan dteen] and กวนส้นตีน [guan sôhn dteen]. These are all pretty rude.

- จะ ไป **กวนแข็ง** คน ขอทาน ทำไม วะ
  jà bpai GUAN-KÂENG kohn-kăw-than tam-mai wá
  Why the hell ya go **mess with** a beggar?

- ไอ้สัตย์ นี้ **กวนส้นตีน** มา ตั้งแต่ เกิด
  'ai-sùt nêe GUAN-SÔHN-DTEEN mah dtûng-dtàe gèrt
  This piece of shit's been **f—kin' with people** since his bitch-ass was born.

Oh no! Oh shit!

The most common interjection you'll hear from Thais when something goes really wrong is probably the word ตาย [dtai]. Directly the word means *death* in English, but in this instance the meaning is more along the line of *Oh no!* or *Oh shit!* There are a few different ways you might hear it, but most of these contain the word ตาย [dtai]. Other four common interjections you'll hear fly out of a Thai's mouth: ต๊ายตาย [dtái dtai], ตายจริง [dtai jihng], ตายละวา [dtai lá wah] and ตายแล้ว [dtai láeo]. I remember one fairly serious car accident on the street where an older Thai lady kept saying ตายแล้ว [dtai láeo] as she stood to gawk.

- ตาย ๆ เค้า ตก เวที
  DTAI-DTAI káo dtòhk way-tee
  Oh no! He just fell off the stage!

Dammit! Shit! F—k!

The following are interjections as well but are a lot stronger. The most common one is ฉิบหาย [chìhp hǎi]. This can be translated as *dammit*, *shit* or even *f—k*. I hear Thais say this in just about everything when they stub their toe, forget their homework or be in a car wreak. It's a fairly rude word and again Thais will discourage its use.

- ฉิบหาย แว่นตา แตก ล่ะ วะ
  chìhp hǎi wâen-dtah dtàek lâ-wá
  Dammit! My freakin' glasses just broke!

The word หมั่นไส้ [mùn sâi] is a good one to yell out whenever you find yourself particularly exasperated or disgusted at a situation. The words อุวะ ['òo wá], อุบะ ['òo bá] and บะ [bá] can also be used to show disgust or anger. There are other variations for *dammit*, *shit* or *f—k* but these are good enough to get started with.

Serves You Right! Dream On!

To say *Serves you right!* or *That's what you get!* use the phrase สมน้ำหน้า [sŏhm nám nâh]. I've also heard Thais say sarcastically ช่วยไม่ได้ [chôoi mâi dâi] to mean *Serves you right!*

- เจ๊ง แล้ว เหรอ สมน้ำหน้า
  jáyng láeo lĕr SŎHM-NÁM-NÂH
  He went outta business? Good, **serves him right!**

There are two easy ways to indicate that something just can't be done. Instead of just calling something *impossible* like เป็นไปไม่ได้ [bpehn bpai mâi dâi], try saying *Dream on!* the Thai way, ฝันไปเหอะ [fŭn bpai hèr]. If you want to say *There's no way!*, try using the phrase ไม่มีทาง [mâi mee tahng].

- ฝันไปเหอะ ไม่ มี วัน เธอ รวย ขนาด นั้น นะ
  FŬN BPAI HÈR mâi mee wun ter rooi kà-nàht nún ná
  Dream on! There's never gonna be a day that you're that rich.

Screw It! Screw Him!

When you want to express your thought and *Forget it!* or *Screw it!* practically sum it up, use either ช่างเหอะ [châhng hèr] or ช่างมัน [châhng mun]. A little more slangy way would be to say ชั่งแม่ง [chûng mâeng]. To point to a person's irrelevant existence by saying *Forget him!*, add the word หัว [hŭa] to the phrase and say ช่างหัวมัน [châhng hŭa mun] or ชั่งหัวมัน [chûng hŭa mun]. You might also hear ช่างมันเป็นไร [châhng mun bpehn rai] or ช่างมันปะไร [châhng mun bpà rai] but these two are a little more old-fashioned.

- ชั่งแม่ง ไม่ สน อีก ล่ะ วะ
  CHÛNG-MÂENG mâi sŏhn 'èek lâ-wá
  Screw it! I'm not f—kin' interested anymore.

Hey! Yo! Say!

There are a few different ways to call attention to yourself in Thai. The following exclamations or yells can be perceived as rude and are normally used at the start of a phrase. It depends on the person and the intonation with which you use them, but I think that เฮ้ย [hérí] is probably the rudest way to call the attention of someone. The word เฮ้ [háy] could either be considered rude or may just be a way to get your friend's attention. On the other hand, เว้ย [wéri] and โว้ย [wóhe] are also fairly rude but are often found at the end of a phrase.

- เฮ้ย! หุบ ปาก ซะที วะ
  HÉRI hoop bpàhk sá-tee wá
  Hey! Shut the f—k up already!

- เฮ้! ไป ไหน ฮะ
  HÁY bpai nǎi há
  Hey! Where ya going?

- อะไร กัน โว้ย ไม่ เห็น ขำ อะไร เลย
  'À-RAI gun wóhe mâi hěhn kǎm 'à-rai leri
  Hey, what the hell's all this?! I don't see anything funny at all!

Get Outta Here!

The phrases *Get lost!* or *Get outta here!* in Thai carries a lot of weight. If some-one is bothering you try shouting one of the Thai versions, he may actually leave you alone. Choose from either ไปซะ [bpai sá] or ใส่หัวไป [sài hǔa bpai]. If you want to make your instructions even more explicit, you can always add วะ [wá] at the end.

- มา ยุ่ง ทำไม ล่ะ ไป ซะ
  mah yôong tam-mai lâ BPAI-SÁ
  Why are you bothering me? **Get lost!**

Fast Epithets

The rest of this chapter is made up of some quick, single or double-word com-binations. I won't give sentences for them because they are not necessary. This is the type of stuff that only needs to be yelled out once. Any attempt to add to them would probably lessen their viciousness. Again these are translated to their closest English equivalents and not on a per word basis. A lot of these words could also have ไอ้ ['âi] or อี ['ee] added to them as well for extra effect.

Bastard! / Asshole!
- ชาติหมา [châht mǎh]
- ระยำคน [rá-yam kohn]
- ระยำหมา [rá-yam mǎh]
- ไอ้เวร ['âi wayn]
- สารเลว [sǎhn layo]
- จัญไร [juhn rai]
- สัตว์นรก [sùt ná-róhk]

Hey Son! / Little Shit!
- ตัวเอ๋ [dtua 'ây]
- ลูกกระจ๊อก [lôok grà-jáwk]
- บักห่ำ [bùk hǎm]
- ห่ำน้อย [hǎm nói]

Screw You!
- สั้นตีน [sôhn dteen]

Little Bitch! (as in a sissy guy)
- ตัวเมีย [dtua mia]
- หน้าตัวเมีย [nâh dtua mia]

Bitch! / Cunt! / Crazy Bitch (in a misogynistic way)
- อีนัง ['ee nung]
- ยัยบ้า [yai bâh]
- บิทช [bìht]

Whore! / Ho! / Slut!
- อีดอก ['ee dàwk]
- แร่ด [râet]
- อีดอกทอง ['ee dàwk tawng]

F—k you!!
- เหี้ย [hîa]
- เย็ดเหี้ย [yéht hîa]
- เด็กเหี้ย [dèhk hîa]
- ไอ้เหี้ย ['âi hîa]

Mother f—ker!
- แม่ง [mâeng]
- เย็ดแม่ [yéht mâe]
- แมงมิ้ง [mâeng mueng]

CHAPTER 6
Sex

Whatever your interests (or hang-ups) may be toward this ever-present, ever-engrossing and ever-entertaining human universe, the author hopes that after this chapter you'll have the power to say just about anything on the subject that you want—and to the greatest degree possible that you want. If you do happen to find yourself blushing once or twice, no need to be shy about it, because I did. If you don't believe me take a crack at it yourself. Write down every dirty word you can think of on a sheet of paper and then walk around the office showing it to all of your colleagues. And then even better, after that try to get it published!

To Have a Crush, Hit On, Go Out On a Date and Hopefully Click

Before we start getting into the thick of it, let's begin with the simple likes. Assuming that you like the person with whom you luridly consort in private, then she/he will probably be your type. The word for *type* as in *She's my type* is สเป็ค [sà bèhk]. If you have a *crush* on someone then you can use the word แอบชอบ ['àep châwp]. Another newer word you might hear is โปร [bproe]. This means someone that you secretly like and are planning to get with. A little weirder than that, if you like to spy on them or if you are a *voyeur* then use the word แอบดู ['àep doo]. If you really do love someone then just use the word รัก [rúk]. You don't need a slang word for that one.

- ชี่ ไม่ ใช่ **สเป็ค** เรา
  chee mâi châi SÀ-BPÈHK rao
  She's not my **type**.

- อะไร กัน เนี่ย **แอบชอบ** 'จารย์ ทอม รึ
  'à-rai-gun-nîa 'ÀEP-CHÂWP jahn tawm rúe
  What's this?! You have a **crush** on Professor Tom?!

- ระวัง พวก **แอบดู** สาว ใน ห้องน้ำ นะ
  rá-rung pûak 'ÀAP-DOO săo nai hâwng-nám ná
  Be careful of **voyeurs** who watch girls in the bathroom.

After you like someone you're best bet is to start to flirt. I've started to hear the Thais in and around Bangkok use the word *flirt* from English, เล่นตา [flêrt], but you can also say the more common จีบ [jèep] or more lyrical เล่นตา [lâyn dtah] to mean *hit on*. Use the words จับไก่ [jùp gài] and ปูเสื่อ [bpoo sùea] when you mean *to hit on easy chicks* or *to go for an easy lay*. If you try to hit on or date more than one person at a time you might hear someone use this proverb, จับปลาสองมือ [jùp bpla sǎwng mue].

- เธอ ค่อนข้าง จะ ชอบ **เฟลิต** นะ
  ter kâwn-kâhng jà châwp FLÊRT ná
  She just kinda likes **to flirt**.

- **จีบ** สาว ไม่ เป็น เลย
  JÈEP sǎo mâi bpehn leri
  I'm just not good at **hitting on** chicks.

- ไป **จับไก่** หน้า เซ็นทรัล กัน ปะ
  bpai JÙP-GÀI nâh sehn-trun gun bpà
  Wanna go **hit on some easy chicks** in front of Central?

- เธอ จะ ชอบ ใคร ก็ ชอบ ไป อะ อย่า มัวแต่ **จับปลาสองมือ** อยู่ เลย
  ter jà châwp krai gâw châwp bpai hèr yàh mua-dtàe JÙP-BPLAH-SǍWNG-MUE yòo leri
  If you're gonna like someone then like them! Don't just go around trying **to go for two people at one time**.

When you want to *go out on a date, say* ออกเดท ['àwk dàyt], which is actually the Thai version of the English word *date*. The regular Thai for *going out with* or *to court* is คบ [kóhp]. The colloquial words are ควง [kuang] or ควงแฟน [kuang faen].

If your date is particularly *romantic* then just use the English word to describe it as such, โรแมนติค [roe maen dtìhk]. The correct word when you *click* with your date or *fallen for* him or her is ปิ๊ง [bpíhng]. If, on the other hand, you *don't get along,* use the phrase ไม่ถูกเส้น [mâi took sâyn].

- ไม่ เคย **ออกเดท** ชะที เลย อะ
  mâi keri 'ÀAW-DÀYT sá-tee leri 'à
  I've never **been on a date** before, not once!

- เมื่อไร ชั้น จะ **ควง** กับ คน หล่อ เหมือน กัน ล่ะ อิจฉา จัง
  mûe-rai chún jà KUANG gùp kohn làw mǔean-gun lâ 'ìht-chǎh jung
  When am I gonna **go out with** a goodlooking guy, too. I'm so jealous.

- จะ **โรแมนติค** ต้อง ใช้ จินตนาการ เพราะ สิ่งของ เล็ก ๆ น้อย ๆ สามารถ เอา มา ใช้ ได้ นะ เช่น...
  jà ROE-MAEM-DTÌHK dtâwng chái jihn-dtà-nah-gahn práw sìhng-kǎwng léhk-léhk nói-nói sǎh-mâht 'ao mah chái dâi ná châyn...
  If you're gonna be **romantic** you gotta use your imagination, because you can even use little things, like...

- เค้า **ปิ๊ง** เธอ ชัวร์
  káo BPÍHNG ter chua
  He's totally **fallen for** her.

- เค้า คง **ไม่ถูกเส้น** กัน แน่ ๆ
  káo kohng MÂI-TÒOK-SÂYN gun nâe-nâe
  They're probably not gonna **get along** for sure.

To Kiss, Grope and Try to Take Your Pants Off

Toward the end of the date if you know what you're doing you'll at least get to kiss. The Thai word for kiss is จูบ [jòop]. If you pronounce it in a high tone and with a shorter vowel then it means more like *to smack a kiss,* จุ๊บ [jóop]. If it's a Thai style kiss where you just kind of sniff at each other's checks then it's called หอมแก้ม [hǎwm gâem]. After that, the word for *to cop a feel* or *grope sexually* is แต๊ะอั๋ง [dtáe 'ǔng], but be careful with that one cause it's used more often to mean *molest.* For those of you who are quick to get laid or *can't keep their pants on,* the phrase สะดือด่วน [sà-due dùan] is a good one to use.

- ต้อง ดู ดี ๆ นะ คะ ไม่ ใช่ เพิ่ง คบ กัน แล้ว จะ **จุ๊บ** กัน แล้ว
  dtâwng doo dee-dee ná ká mâi châi pêrng kóhp gun láeo jà jòop gun láeo
  You have to really see first. You can't just can't start dating and then start **making out** immediately.

- ชอบ โดน **จุ๊บ** บ่อย จัง
  châwp doen JÓOP bòi jung
  I like to be **kissed** regularly.

- ระวัง หมอ ลามก ที่ ชอบ **แต๊ะอั๋ง** คน ไข้ สวย
  rá-wung măh lah-móhk têe châwp DTÁE-'ŬNG kohn-kâi sŏoi-sŏoi
  Watch out for those nasty doctors that like **to feel up** their prettier patients.

- ทำไม ต้อง **สะดือด่วน** ล่ะ
  tam-mai dtâwng SÀ-DUE-DÙAN lâ
  Why do we have **to rush to have** sex?

Do It and Hook Up

Like any language there's a host of different ways of talking about sex without actually having to talk about it. We'll start here since it's as good as place as any.

Similar to our English *to do it,* the Thais will often refer to the act of sex as *to have something together,* which is มีอะไรกัน [mee 'à-rai-gun]. This can be used to mean anything from just messing around to actually hooking up and doing it. Sometimes you may hear Thais making a joke about whether or not you've really *reached* one of the provinces or countries on your last trip out of Bangkok. The word ถึง [tŭeng] in Thai can be used to imply whether or not you really got laid or not.

The last word for this set is เอากัน ['ao-gun] or just เอา ['ao]. This is the harshest of the three and in some contexts can mean *to screw* or even *to f—k* in English. Though, if you look the word up in a dictionary it will probably say *to take.* Another slangy way to say *to hit it* is อึ๊บ ['úep]. This one is not as rude as เอา ['ao], but it's strong enough for a Thai national to get annoyed that a foreigner knows how to use it.

- กะ เค้า เหรอ ไม่ **มีอะไรกัน** เลย
  gà káo rěr mâi MEE 'À-RAI-GUN
  With him? No, we didn't **mess around** at all!

- ไม่ อยาก เชื่อ หนุ่มสาว สมัย นี้ กล้า **มีอะไรกัน** บน รถ กลางวัน แสก ๆ
  mâi yàhk chûea nòom-săo sà-măi-née glâh MEE 'À-RAI-GUN bohn róht glahng-wun sàek sàek
  I don't wanna believe that teenagers these days will actually dare **do it** in the car in broad daylight.

- ไป เที่ยว จังหวัด อุดร แล้ว เหรอ **ถึง** รึเปล่า
  bpai-têeo jung-wùt 'òo-dawn láeo rěr TŬENG rúe-bplào
  So you went on a trip to Udon Province? Did ya **get laid** or what?

- สงสัย ว่า เค้า เอากัน เรียบร้อย แล้ว
  sŏhng-săi wâh káo 'ao-gun rîab-rói láeo
  Look's like they've already.

- หนู อยาก **อึ๊บ** จัง
  nŏo yàhk 'ÚEP jung
  I wanna **screw**!

To Mess Around and Have a One Night Stand

To mess around in Thai is จ้าจี้ [jâm-jêe], which is sure to get a laugh or two from Thais themselves. As for ดิ่งดอง [dihng-dawng], it can mean *to mess around* or *to have sex*, though this word is an older slang and probably won't be as readably recognizable as จ้าจี้ [jâm-jêe] is to the younger crowd. The word บูม ๆ [boom-boom] can be taken to mean *to knock boots*. You're mostly likely to hear that from a girl working at a foreign bar. The word ขึ้นเตียน [kûen dtian] can mean *to have a roll in the hay*. Once I heard an older fellow refer to sex with his wife as ทำการบ้าน [tam gahn-bâhn] or *to do homework*. I wouldn't use that one if you're a student though; you'd just confuse people. A good word for *doing it in the morning* is ซ้าเช้า [sám cháo]. Watch your Thai colleagues freak out when you greet them in the morning by saying ซ้าเช้ายัง [sám cháo yung], which basically means *Have you gotten your rocks off yet this morning?* The last one for this grouping is the word for *one night stand*, which is น้ำแตกแล้วแยกทาง [nám dtàek láeo yâek tahng]. It basically translates to *cum and part*.

- ไป เล่น **จ้าจี้** กับ แฟน สนุก มาก ๆ
  bpai lâyn JÂM-JÊE gùp faen sà-nòok mâhk-mâhk
  Getting it on with my girlfriend is fun!

- ก็ ชั้น ชอบ แต่ ไม่ **ขึ้นเตียน**
  gâw chún châwp dtàe mâi **KÛEN-DTIAN**
  Well I like him, but I'm not gonna **sleep with him**.

- ให้ **น้ำแตกแล้วแยกทาง** เมื่อ เค้า ได้ ทุก อย่าง แล้ว เค้า ก็ ทิ้ง เธอ
  ไป ถ้า น้ำ ไม่ แตก เค้า ก็ ยัง ไม่ ไป นี่แหละ หัวใจ ของ ผู้ชาย
  hâi **NÁM-DTÀEK-LÁEO-YÂEK-TAHNG** mûe káo dâi took yàhng
  láeo káo gâw tíhng ter bpai tâh nám mâi dtàek káo gâw yung mâi
  bpai nêe-làet hŭa-jai kăwng pôo-chai
  Give him his **one night stand** and when he's gotten everything he wants
  already, he'll just dump you. If you don't give it to him, he won't leave
  you. So there you are—the heart of a man!

Go At It, Screw and F—k

The most politically correct way to say have sex in Thai is ร่วมเพศสัมพันธ์
[rûam pâyt sŭm-pun], but this is a rather lifeless term for something so lifegiving. If you want to say *to have sex*, then just use the word *sex* in Thai by saying
มีเซ็กซ์ [mee séhk]. It just sounds cooler and gets right to the point. You can
also use the word มั่วเซ็กซ์ [mûa séhk].

- เรา **มีเซ็กซ์** กัน อย่าง ดุเดือน
  rao **MEE SÉHK** gun yàhng dòo-duean
  We **go at it** like animals!

- ทำไม เด็ก นักเรียน กล้า ถ่าย คลิปวีดิโอ **มั่วเซ็กซ์** กัน
  tam-mai dehk núk-rian glâh tài klíhp-wee-dìh-'oe **MÛA-SÉHK** gun
  Why do these students dare tape themselves **having sex**?

From here, things start to be a bit rougher. The word ฟัน [fun] means *to f—k*
and can be used in a few different ways. In the last chapter, we'll see that the
term may be used in a nonsexual context as well similar to how *f—k* in English
can be used in many ways. The term ตีหม้อ [dtee-mâw] also can be translated
as *to f—k* or *to screw*, but this will mostly be used with prostitutes. The words
เด้า [dâo] and โด๊ะ [dóh] are both slang versions of the pretty vulgar term
กระเด้า [grà-dâo], which means *to move in and out*. I also heard the slang
word ฟาด [fâht], which means *to hit* or *to strike*, used to mean *to f—k* as well.
Probably the most vulgar Thai term that means *to f—k* is เย็ด [yéht]. Try using
this one and Thais will actively begin to dislike you. Another similar term is
เย็ดครก [yéht króhk]. Yet another incredibly vulgar way to say *to f—k cunt* is
เย็ดหี [yéht hĕe]. If you want to say *f—kable*, then just add the word น่า [nâh]
and say like this, น่าเย็ด [nâh yéht].

- คลิป นี้ มี ชาย คนเดีย **ฟัน** สาว 50 คน
  klíhp née mee chai kohn-dieo FUN săo hâh-sìhp kohn
  This clip shows one guy **f—king** fifty girls.

- แก ชอบ ไป **ดีหม้อ** พัทยา
  gae châwp bpai dtee-mâw pút-tú-yah
  He likes **to screw** Pataya **hookers**.

- เค้า กำลัง **โด๊ะ** กัน
  káo gam-lung DÓE gun
  They're **f—king**.

- พอ เรา ไม่ อยู่ มัน **ฟาด** แฟน เรา ไป เรียบร้อย ล่ะ วะ
  paw rao mâi yòo mun FÂHT faen rao bpai rîap-rói lâ-wá
  As soon as I wasn't around, that asshole went and **f—ked** my girlfriend.

- อยาก ดู นักศึกษา **เย็ด** กัน แล้ว คลิก ที่นี่
  yàhk doo núk-sùek-săh YÉHT gun láeo klíhk têe-nêe
  Want to see co-eds **f—k**? Then click here!!

- สาว นี้ ใง ก็ **น่าเย็ด**
  săo née ngai gâw NÂH-YÉHT
  This chick is so **f—kable**.

I've added two words in this group for fun. You will more likely hear these along the boarders of Laos but because there has been such an increase in the past few decades of people moving down from the Isan region to Bangkok, it is best to know these terms as well. These are สีกัน [sĕe gun] and เซิง [serng]. Basically, they both mean *to f—k* but I'll let you research on your own why these two local words are so particularly vulgar.

To Get Horny, Get Off and Climax

You'll probably hear the words เสียว [sĕeo] or มีอารมณ์ [mee 'ah-rohm] the most to mean *to get* or *to be horny*, but you'll also sometimes hear the following words as well, ร่าน [râhn] and หื่น [hùen]. In some circumstances, the word *want* can also mean that you're horny or อยาก [yàhk]. If you're really *itching for it* or *craving for it*, then use one of these two words, คัน [kun] or เงี่ยน [ngîan]. The word ปลุกอารมณ์ [bplòok 'ah-rohm] is similar to มีอารมณ์ [mee 'ah-rohm] and means *to get horny*. The word กลัดมัน [glùt mun] has been around a little bit longer, but you might still hear it once in a while. It also means *to be really horny* or *to lust for sex*. The word ตบะแตก [dtà-bà dtàek] means *to loose patience* and I doubt you'll actually ever hear anyone say this one but you might find it in some literature with a sexual connotation of just *not being able to wait for sex anymore*, so I've added it here as well.

- ลอง อ่าน ดู ดิ แล้ว จะ **เสียว** ไป เลย หละ
  lawng 'àhn doo dìh láeo jà SĚEO bpai là
  Take a look and you'll get real **horny!**

- **มีอารมณ์** บ้าง รึป่าว เวลา ที่ อยู่ กะ แฟน สองต่อสอง
  MEE-'AH-ROHM bâhng rúe-bòw way-lah têe yòo gà faen sǎwng-dtàw-sǎwng
  The time that you spend with your husband just the two of you, do you **get aroused** or not?

- ไม่ ชอบ หนัง แบบ นี้ ล่ะ มัน **หืน** ตรงไหน อะ
  mâi châwp nǔng bàep née lâ mun HÙEN dtrong-nǎi 'à
  I don't like videos like these. It doesn't **get me off** at all!

- ชั้น คิด ว่า เซ็กซ์ คือ ยา แก้ **คัน**
  chún kíht-wâh séhk kue yah gâe KUN
  I think sex is the right medicine to help **someone in heat.**

- ใคร เสียว เก่ง บ้าง มา เสียว ให้ ที **เงี่ยน** สุด ๆ แฟน ไม่ ค่อย เสียว ให้ ชะ
  krai sěeo gàyng bâhng mah sěeo hâi tee NGÎAN sòo-sòot faen mâi kôi sěeo hâi sá
  Whoever's good at getting off come here and make me **horny like crazy.** My girlfriend doesn't really do the trick for me.

If something gets you horny in the sense that it *gets you off*, then try using the word จับเส้น [jùp sâyn]. The word เล่นเสียว [lâyn sěeo] can mean either *to get off* or *to go at it*, but the word ทำเสียว [tam sěeo] pretty much means *to have sex*. The word ซู่ซ่า [sôo sâh] has various degrees of meaning but in this context may mean *in heat*, *horny*, *fervid* or even *passionate*.

- ชอบ หมอนวด **จับเส้น** ได้
  châwp mǎw-nûat JÙP-SÂYN dâi
  I like my masseuse **to get me off.**

- ผม อยาก เล่นเสียว สาว ทุก วัน
  pǒhm yàhk LÂYN-SĚEO sǎo tóok wun
  I want **to go at it with** a chick every day.

- ถ้า มี อารมณ์ **ซู่ซ่า** ก็ เข้า มา ระบาย กับ เว็บ แหล่ง นี้ ซิ
  tâj mee 'ah-rohm SÔO-SÂH gâw kâo mah rá-bai gùp wéhp làeng née sí
  If you're all **horned up** then go ahead and find your release with this website!

Now it's time to move to the climax (if we're lucky). That *point of no return* when the pleasure finally just pops is called the จุดสุดยอด [jòot sòot yâwt]. The word สำเร็จความใคร่ [săm-réht kwahm-krâi] means *to have climaxed* but this word along with จุดสุดยอด [jòot sòot yâwt] are both kind of lame. If you're going to use any word to mean that you've *cum*, then try the word เสร็จ [sèht], which just means *to finish* or *to have an orgasm*. This is the word you'll hear Thais use most of the time. A new way to say it comes directly from the English word *to finish*, but the Thais will say it like this, ฟิน [fĭhn]. A more lyrical way to say it is *to reach heaven*, or in Thai as ขึ้นสวรรค์ [kûen sà-wǔn].

- สอบถาม เรื่อง **จุดสุดยอด** ของ ผู้หญิง ว่า จะ รู้ ได้ ยังไง ว่า ชั้น ถึง จุด นั้น แล้ว เพราะ ที่ผ่านมา ไม่ เคย ถึง เลย คะ
  sàwp-tăhm rûeang jòot-sòot-yâwt kăwng pôo-yĭhng wâh jà róo dâi yung-ngai wâh chún tŭeng jòot nún láeo práw têe-pàhn-mah mâi keri tŭeng leri kâ
  I wanted to ask about a girl's **climax**, how do we know when we've reached that point, because up to now I've never reached it?

- ที่รัก **เสร็จ** ยัง
  têe-rúk SÈHT yung
  Hey baby, did ya **cum**?

- ไม่ เคย **ฝิน** ซักที เล่า
  mâi keri FǏHN súk-tee lâo
  I've never **had an orgasm**, not once!

- ชั้น มี วิธี **ขึ้นสวรรค์** มา ฝาก นะ ค่ะ ข้อ ที่ หนึ่ง คือ...
  chún mee wíh-tee KÛEN-SÀ-SǓN mah fàhk ná kâ kâw têe nùeng kue
  I've got a method that'll **make you climax** that I want to share. The first thing is...

To Poke It In, Pull It Out and Shoot Your Load

There are two main words I've heard Thais use to describe the act of *insertion*. The first is สอด [sàwt], which means *to insert*, and the second is แทง [taeng], which can be translated as *to stab*. Sometimes you might hear the word แยง [yaeng] for *to poke* as well. On the other hand, *contraction* is either เม้ม [máym] or ขมิบ [kà mìhp]. I doubt you'll ever need to have such an explicit discussion about the ol' in-and-out with your Thai colleagues. But in case you do, the phrase *in-and-out* is ชักเข้าชักออก [chúk kâo chúk 'àwk] in Thai.

- ใคร อยาก **แทง** หอย โทร หา เบอร์...
  krai yàhk TAENG hǒi toe-hǎh ber
  Anyone who's interested in **poking** some twat, please call...

- อยาก ให้ เมีย เรา ออกกำลังกาย ส่วน นั้น ฝึก การ ขมิบ ๆ เม้ม ๆ จะ ช่วย ให้ ความแข็งแรง ของ กล้ามเนื้อ กลับ คืน มา
  yàhk hâi mia rao 'àak-gam-lung-gai sùan nún fùek gahn KÀ-MÌHP-KÀ-MÌHP MÁYM-MÁYM jà chôoi hâi kwahm kǎeng-raeng kǎwng glâhm-núea glùp kuen mah
  I want my wife to exercise that area. The **contracting** and **releasing** will help bring back the strength to those muscles.

- เรา ชอบ เอา นิ้ว แยง เข้า ไป ให้ หี แฟน แล้ว **ชักเข้าชักออก** เร็ว ๆ
  rao châwp 'ao núi YAENG kâo bpai hâi hěe faen láeo CHÚK-KÂO-CHÚK-'ÀWK rayo-rayo
  I like to take my finger and **poke** it in my girlfriend's box, and then **move it in and out** real quick.

A good way to say *to pull out* or to pull out quickly so as not to come inside is ชักออก [chúk 'àwk] or ชักออกเร็ว ๆ [chúk 'àwk rayo-rayo]. If you want to *shoot your load outside*, then say หลั่งข้างนอก [lung kâhng nâwk].

Some people don't get so far and experience *premature ejaculation*, which in Thai is called ลมปากอ่าว [lôhm bpàhk 'òw]. If you don't even get the chance to come or get *blue balls*, you are อารมณ์ค้าง ['ah-rohm káhng].

But either way, after having sex and you probably don't have any energy left, Thais call this ฟ้าเหลือง [fáh lŭeang].

- ไม่ ท้อง เพราะ เคย **หลั่งข้างนอก** อะ
  mâi táwng práw keri lung-kâhng-nâwk 'à
  You're not pregnant because I **shoot my load outside**.

- ครั้ง แรก ผม ก็ **ลมปากอ่าว**
  krúng-râek pŏhm gâw LÔHM-BPÀHK-'ÒW
  Well, the first time I **prematurely ejaculated**.

- อารมณ์ค้าง ทุกที เลย ไม่ ถึงสวรรค์ หรอก
  'AH-ROHM-KÁHNG tóok-tee mâi tŭeng-sà-wŭn ràwk
  Every time I'm always **unsatisfied**. I've never climaxed.

Love Juices

There are a few different ways to call the actual fluids that escape us during these hot interactions and I'm going to give you four good ones. The word น้ำกาม, [nám gahm] is fairly common, but I think calling it น้ำรัก [nám rúk] is more fun. The word น้ำเงี่ยน [nám ngîan] can be used with guys or girls. The word ต๋อง [dtáwng] is more slangy, but I've only ever heard it used with guys. A more technical term for *sperm* is อสุจิ ['à sòo jìh], but I suggest sticking to one of the other four. If you want to say that she is *wet* or *dripping*, try either เปียก [bpìak] or เยิ้ม [yérm].

- หนู ไม่ ชอบ เลย ที่ แฟน บังคับ ให้ กลืน **น้ำรัก** ของ เค้า
  nŏo mâi châwp leri têe faen bung-kúp hâi gluen NÁM-RÚK kăwng káo
  I hate how my boyfriend makes me swallow his **cum**.

- รู้ เลย ว่า **น้ำเงี่ยน** แตก อีก แล้ว เพราะ มัน เย็น มาก ๆ
  róo leri wâh NÁM-NGÎAN dtàek 'èek láeo práw mun YÉRM mâhk-mâhk
  I already know she's **cum** because she so freakin' **wet**!

Times

Once, twice, three times...*four times*? It doesn't matter if you can do it once or ten times, the Thai language has three main words use to numerate any sexual encounter. The two more common ways to say *times* are ครั้ง [krúng] and คราว [krao]. If you want to be really rude, try the word ดอก [dàwk] to mean *number of times* you got your rocks off.

- เมื่อคืน เสร็จ สอง **ครั้ง**
  mûea-kuen sèht săwng KRÚNG
  Last night I climaxed two **times**.

- เอา กี่ **ดอก** ล่ะ วะ
  'ao gèe DÀWK lâ-wá
  How many **times** you f—k her?

All the Positions

Any of the sexual positions can be described using the word ท่า [tâh]. If you're still unsatisfied with the list I'm about to give you, then just use the word ท่า [tâh] and then describe what it is you want in Thai. It'll work most of the time. But for now let's start at the top. The easiest way to describe *being on top* is the phrase อยู่ข้างบน [yòo kâhng bohn]. If you want to say *to ride somebody*, then just say ขี่ม้า [kèe máh], which also means *to ride a horse*. But before you ride anything you need *to get up on it*. Use the words ขึ้นม้า [kûen máh] to say that. A poetic way to mean *woman on top* is หงส์เหนือมังกร or *swan*

over dragon. Straightforward terms such as ขย่ม [kà yòhm] or ขย่มต่อ [kà yòhm dtàw] mean *to ride it* or *to bounce up and down.* You may also elongate that phrase to หนุมานขย่มต่อ [hà-nóo-mahn kà-yòhm-dtàw]. If you want *to spoon* someone, then try the phrase ท่านอนตะแคง [tâh nawn dtà-kaeg]. The *69 position* is called ท่าห้าสิบเก้า [tâh hâh-sìhp-gâo]. There are two common ways to say *doggie style* or *from behind.* These are กวางเหลียวหลัง [gwahng lĕeo lŭng], which also means something like *the deer turning to look behind*, and ท่าหลัง [tâh lŭng].

- พี่ ชอบ ให้ หนู **อยู่ข้างบน** นะ ที่รัก
  pêe châwp hâi nŏo **YÒO-KÂHNG-BOHN** ná têe-rúk
  I like it when **you're on top**, baby.

- สอง มือ เธอ เกาะ ที่ ไหล่ เรา แล้ว จาก นั้น เธอ ก็ **ขย่มต่อ** เต็มที่ เลย
  sǎwng mue ter gàw têe lài rao láeo jàhk nún ter gâw **KÀ-YÒHM-DTÀW** dtehm-têe leri
  Her two hands clung on two my shoulders and from there she **rode me, bouncing up and down** like crazy!

- พี่ ชอบ **ท่านอนตะแคง** มาก ที่ สุด อะ
  pêe châwp **TÂH-NAWN-DTÀ-KAENG** mâhk-têe-sòot 'à
  I like **to spoon people** the most.

- ลอง ทำ **ท่าหลัง** ซะ แฟน คง แฮปปี้ มาก ๆ น่า
  lawng tam **TÂH-LŬNG** sá faen kohng hâep-bpêe mâhk-mâhk nâh
  Try it **from behind**. It'll probably make your boyfriend happy!

Oral

The most common word for *oral sex* in Thai is probably ใช้ปาก [chái bpàhk], which means *to use mouth.* Sometimes you might also hear the English word *oral* in its Thai version, ทำออรัล [tam 'aw-run]. A nice lyrical way to call it is ชิวหาพาเพลิน [chui-hăh pah plern], which means something like *the pleasurable tongue.* To request specifically for *fellatio*, use the word โมก [móek] or สโมก [sà móek], which means *to suck cock.* Another euphemism for *blowjob* is ร้องเพลง [ráwng playng]. On the other hand, *cunnilingus* on girls is ยกซด [yóhk sóht]. The word ลงลิ้น [long líhng] can be translated as *to eat a chick out,* and ทาสี [tah sĕe] is a good euphemism for the vulgar *to lick pussy.*

- แฟน พี่ **ใช้ปาก** เก่ง จัง เลย
  faen pêe **CHÁI-BPÀHK** gàyng jung-leri
  My girlfriend **gives** great **head.**

- ไม่ รู้ จะ ทำ ยังไง ละ อ่าย ด้วย น่า ไม่ เคย ทำออรัล
  mâi róo jà tam yung-ngai là 'âi dôoi nâh mâi keri TAM-'AW-RUN
  I don't know how to do it. I'm too shy. I've never done **oral sex** before.

- ทำไม ผู้ชาย ถึง ชอบ ให้ **สโม้ก** แล้ว ผู้หญิง ส่วนใหญ่ ชอบรึเปล่า ฮะ
  tam-mai pôo-chai tŭeng châwp hâi SÀ-MÓEK láeo pôo-yĭhng sùan-yài châwp rúe bplào há
  Why do guys like to get **blowjobs** so much and why do girls actually like to give it?

- พี่ **ยกซด** ไม่ เป็น เลย
  pêe YÓHK-SÓHK mâi bpehn leri
  I'm not any good at **eating a chick out**.

- เวลา ที่ แฟน **ลงลิ้น** ให้ เรา เรา เสียว มาก ๆ และ ก็ เสร็จด้วย น่ะ
  way-lah têe faen lohng-líhng hâi rao rao sĕeo mâhk-mâhk láe-gâw sèht dôoi nâ
  The times my boyfriend **goes down on me** I get so horny that I cum, too.

Anal

There are a few different ways to refer to anal sex in Thai, but so many of them are used for gay men or ladyboys that sometimes it's even hard to even request for it without sounding queer yourself. I've broken down the list for what's appropriate for straight guys and what's useful for the queerer of us. I've saved those last words at the end of this chapter in the section on sodomy. That leaves us with about four or five good words to indicate that you're interested in the anal. The most common is probably เข้าประตูหลัง [kâo bprà-dtoo lŭng], which translates as *to enter the backdoor*. The word เอาตูด ['ao dtòot] is also a fairly heterosexual way of saying *to have anal sex*. If you want to get more vulgar try saying เย็ดตูด [yéht dtòot] or เย็ดกน [yéht gôhn]. These both pretty much translate as *to butt f—k*. The last one for this batch sounds a little cute but because of it you might sound slightly queer if you don't say it just right, เล่นตูด [lâyn dtòot].

- ทำไม แฟน ไม่ ให้ เรา **เข้าประตูหลัง** วะ
  tam-mai faen mâi hâi rao KÂO-BPRÀ-DTOO-LŬNG wá
  Why the hell won't my girlfriend let me **do her in the butt**?

- อยาก **เล่นตูด** ชั้น ทำไม ล่ะ
  yàhk LÂYN-DTÒOT chún tam-mai lâ
  Why would you wanna **stick in my butt** anyway?

Orgies, Swinging and The Golden Shower

The most popular Thai term for orgy that you're going to hear these days comes from the English word *swinging*. Thais call it สวิง [sà wǐhng] or สวิงกิ้ง [sà wǐhng gîhng]. The word เซ็กซ์หมู [séhk mòo] also means *orgy*. If you just *invite your friend* to play along, the word ลงแขก [lohng kàek] is acceptable. On the other hand, the word เวียนเทียน [wian tian] may either mean *to gang bang* or *to gang-rape*. However, I've only ever heard the word เรียวคิว [riang kui] in its slang usage to mean *to gang-rape* or *to run a train*. If you want to be specific and mean *to double penetrate* then the word หน่อบี่ [nàw bèe] is a good choice. And finally, a golden shower is called ฉี่รดกัน [chèe róht gun].

- ชอบ **สวิง** มั้ย
  châwp SÀ-WǏHNG mái
  Do you like **orgies**?

- มี ภาพ **เซ็กซ์หมู** ปะ
  mee pâhp SÉHK-MÒO bpà
  Do ya have any pics of **group sex**?

- ไม่ ยอม **ลงแขก** อ่ะ
  mâi yawm LOHNG-KÀEK 'à
  I won't do a **gang-bang**.

- ไม่ เคย ดู หนังโป๊ **หน่อบี่** วะ
  mâi keri doo nǔng-bpóe NÀW-BÈE wá
  I've never seen a porno with **double penetration**.

To Pop Her Cherry

The main word for *losing your virginity*, guys or girls, is เสียตัว [sǐa dtua]. The phrase เสียสาว [sǐa sǎo] is used specifically for girls. The following three phrases mean *to pop one's cherry* in English. The first one is ฉีกทุเรียน [cheek tóo-rian], a direct translation of *tearing the durian fruit*. The second is เจาะไข่แดง [jàw kài daeng], which means something like *to punch the egg yolk*. The last phrase is เปิดซิง [bpèrt sihng]. You can also say เปิดบริสุทธิ์ [bpèrt bàw-ríh-sòot] to mean *to take somebody's virginity*. To sidetrack a little bit, Thais refer to sleeping with a woman who is still menstruating as *running a red light* or ฝ่าไฟแดง [fàh fai-daeg].

- สถานที่ ที่ บอก มา ก็ เป็น สถานที่ เสี่ยง ต่อ การ เสียตัว มาก
  sà-tǎhn-têe têe bàwk mah gâw bpehn sà-tǎhn-têe sìang dtàw gahn SǏA-DTUA mâhk
  The place I was talking about is a place where **losing your virginity** is a possibility.

- เรา คบ กับ ทุก คน โดย มุ่ง จะ **เจาะไข่แดง** ผู้หญิง แต่ ยัง ไม่ สำเร็จ เลย
  rao kóhp gùp tóok kohn dohe môong jà JÀW-KÀI-DAENG pôo-yǐhng dtàe yung mâi sǎm-réht ler
  I court everybody in the hope of **popping their cherry** but I've yet to be successful.

- ผม อยาก ถูก **เปิดซิง** จัง เลย ครับ
  pǒhm yàhk tòok BPÈRT-SIHNG jung leri krúp
  I really just wanna **loose my virginity**!

- ทุเรศ! ใคร จะ ชอบ ผ่าไฟแดง เล่า
  tóo-râyt krai jà châwp FÀH-FAI-DAENG lâo
  Nasty! Who wants **to do it when they're having their period**?

Helping Yourself

The most direct way to translate *masturbation* into Thai is ช่วยตัวเอง [chôoi dtua-'ayng]. You can use this with either guys or girls. Another way to say it is ทำร้ายตัวเอง [tam-rái dtua-'ayng]. For guys the most common word phase you'll hear to mean *to jerk it* or *to jerk off* is ชักว่าว [chúk wôw], which also means *to fly a kite*. The word ชักจุฬา [chúk jòo-lah] is a play on that as well. The phrase ขัดถูกกล้อง [kùt tòok glâwng] means *to polish your pipe*, and ห้ารุมหนึ่ง [hâh room nùeng] also means *to jerk off* or, translated directly, *five against one*. I've also heard ลวกเส้นก๋วยเตี๋ยว [lûak sâyn gǒuie-děeo], which means *to strain noodles*, as a euphemism for *jerking off*. An old proverb that alludes to male masturbation is ตะกายฝา ป่ายกำแพง [dtà-gai-fǎh bpài-gam-paeng], but I doubt you'll ever hear anybody say that one. For girls the main one you'll hear is ตกเบ็ด [dtòhk bèht], which means something along the lines of *to fish with a hook*. Sometimes you don't even need to spend effort to masturbate; it may even come to you in a dream. Thais also call this a *wet dream* or ฝันเปียก [fǔn bpìak].

- ทำไม ผู้ชาย ชอบ **ช่วยตัวเอง** ตลอด อ่ะ
  tam-mai pôo-chai châwp CHÔOI-DTUA-'AYNG dtà-làwt 'à
  Why do boys like **to masturbate** all the time?

- แก คง อยู่ ใน ห้องน้ำ กำลัง **ชักว่าว** อยู่ ฟะ
  gae kohng yòo nai hâwng-nám gam-lung CHÚK-WÔW yòo fá
  His stupid ass is probably in the bathroom **jerking it**!

- ทำไม ผู้หญิง ส่วนมาก ไม่ ยอมรับ ว่า ตัว เอง ชอบ **ตกเบ็ด** บ้าง ล่ะ
  **tam-mai pôo-yĭhng sùan-mâhk mâi yawm-rúp wâh dtua-'ayng
  châwp DTÒHK-BÈHT bâhng lâ**
  Why won't chicks admit to liking **to masturbate** sometimes?

- เรา **ฝันเปียก** บ่อย ๆ ตื่น มา หมอน เปียก เลย ล่ะ
  rao FŬN-BPÌAK bòi-bòi dtùen mah măwn bpìak leri lâ
  I have **wet dreams** often. Wake up and my pillow's all wet.

Your Johnson

There are many ways to refer to a *penis* in Thai as there is in English. This list won't exhaust all the possibilities but it'll get pretty damn close, more than you'll probably every need. The technical term is องคชาติ ['ohng ká châht], but I wouldn't use that unless you were at the doctor's and then you'd probably still get weird looks for calling it that. I think one of the safer ways to call it is จู๋ [jŏo]. The words เจี๊ยว [jéeo] and กระเจี๊ยว [grà jéeo] are also safe bets to refer to a *dick*. A variation on จู๋ [jŏo] like กระจู๋ [grà jŏo] or ไอ้จู๋ ['âi jŏo], or the maybe the word ไอ้เจี๊ยว ['âi jéeo] is something you'd probably want to use if you have a *small penis*. The word ไอ้หนู ['âi nŏo] is also best translated as *small dick*. One of the most vulgar term is ควย [kooi], which would probably translate best into *cock*. You'd probably get slapped for calling your peter that in front of girls. The word ห่ำ [hăm] is another good one for *penis*. You'll often hear that one in villages where everyone there seems to love to refer to adolescent boys as *little dicks* or ห่ำน้อย [hăm nói]. Other names for *johnson* is ลิงค์ [lueng] or ไอ้จ้อน ['âi jâwn]. Two of my favorite names are เจ้าโลก [jâo lôhk], which means *ruler of the word*, and นกเขา [nóhk kăo], which is like a *little bird*. You can use นกเขา [nóhk kăo] in the phrase นกเขาไม่ขัน [nóhk kăo mâi kŭn] to mean that you *can't get it up*.

- จู๋ พี่ ใหญ่ มะ
  JŎO pêe yài má
  Is **my johnson** pretty big?

- **กระเจี๊ยว** เล็ก ใหญ่ ไม่ สำคัญ มัน สำคัญ ที่ ว่า ทำ ผู้หญิงเสร็จ มั้ย
  **GRÀ-JÉEO léhk yài mâi săm-kuh mun săm-kun têe wâh tam pôo-
  yĭhng sèht mái**
  A large or a small **dick** is not important. What's important is whether you can satisfy your girl.

- ชั้น ชอบ เมื่อ **ควย** อัน ใหญ่ มุด เข้า ไป ใน รู หี ของ ตัว เองที ละ นิด...เสียว ๆ

  chún châwp mûea KOOI 'un yài moot kâo bai nai roo hěe kǎwng dtua-'ayng tee lá nít...sěeo-sěeo

  I like it when a big **cock** burrows itself inside my pussy hole little by little…so horny!!

- สาว บาง คน คง จะ กลัว **เจ้าโลก** ที่ ยาว ขนาด พี่ เนอะ

  sǎo bahng kohn kohng jà glua jâo-lôek têe yow kà-nàht pêe nér

  Some chick would probably be frightened by a **dick** as long as mine, eh?

Some fruits and vegetables can also suggest a penis. กล้วย [glôoi], the Thai word for *banana* is a good one, while กล้วยหอม [glôoi hǎwm] and กล้วยน้ำว้า [glôoi nám wáh] can also mean a *large* and *small* one. Try the word เห็ดโคน [hèht koen], which is one type of mushroom, or you can move into eggplants like the มะเขือยาว [má kǔea yow] or มะเขือเผา [má kǔea pǎo], which can mean a *long* or a *soft johnson*, respectively. Add the word โรค [rôek] to มะเขือเผา [má kǔea pǎo] and the result, โรคมะเขือเผา [rôek má kǔea pǎo], is the slang for *erectile dysfunction*. The word เดือย [duea] also refers to *dick* and is that part of a chicken's leg that juts out. Another one you might hear is มังกร [mung gawn], which just means *dragon*. The word ดอ [daw] is also a fairly rude way to say *cock* but the word ควย [kooi] probably still takes the cake for being most vulgar. You might also hear the words ท่อนล่า [tâwn lam], เจ้าหนู [jâo nǒo], ไอ้ใบ ['âi bâi], เอ็น ['ehn] and น้องชาย [náwng chai] all used to mean *dick*.

- ยิ่ง อายุ สูง ยิ่ง กลัว **โรคมะเขือเผา** ล่ะ

  yîhng 'ah-yóo sǒong yîhng glua RÔHK-MÁ-KǓEA-PǍO lâ

  The more I get older, the more I am afraid of **erectile dysfunction**.

- พอ **ท่อนล่า** เรา แข็ง เต็มที่ ก็ ชอบ ให้ แฟน ดู แล้ว จับ
  paw **TÂWN-LAM** rao kăeng dtehm-têe gâw châwp hâi faen doo láeo jùp
  When my **dick** gets hard as a rock I like to have my girlfriend see it and then grab it.

- **ไอ้ใบ้** ดีใจ แล้ว มี **เซ็กซ์** วันนี้
  'ÂI-BÂI dee-jai láeo mee séhk wun-née
  My **peter**'s happy now. Today we had sex.

Balls

There are also a few different ways to refer to your *package* but the word กระโปก [grà bpòhk] is the more common one to mean *testes*. I normally use the word ไข่ [kài] or ไข่หำ [kài hăm], which translates to *eggs*. The words ตุ้ม [dtôom], meaning *pendulum*, and พวงสวรรค์ [puang sà wŭng], meaning *heavenly bunch*, are also good ones. The classier for one of your *balls* is ลูก [lôok].

- ฉิบหาย! เมื่อกี๊ บีบ **ไข่** ล่ะ วะ เจ็บ ๆ
  chìhp-hăi mûea-gée beep **KÀI** lâ-wá jèhp-jèhp
  Son of a bitch! I just racked my **balls**! Freakin' hurts!

- พ่อ ผม มี กระโปก **ลูก** เดียว ครับผม
  pâw pŏhm mee grà-bpòhk **LÔOK** deeo krúp-pŏhm
  My father has only one **ball**.

Circumcised, Castrated or Just Impotent

The only word I've ever heard to mean whether or not your little guy is circumcised is the word ขลิบ [klìhp]. If you are ขลิบ [klìhp] then you're *circumcised*; if you are not, you're ไม่ขลิบ [mâi klìhp] and you've got something that looks like an *elephant trunk* down there. When it's hard or erect, try using the word เปิดหมวก [bpèrt mùak]. When it's soft and squiggly, try the word เหี่ยว [hèeo]. The word ตอน [dtawn] can mean *to castrate*, but if you're having problems because you're *impotent* or *have no sex drive* then just use the word ตายด้าน [dtai dâhn].

- การ **ขลิบ** จะ ช่วย ทำให้ ความ เสี่ยง ต่อ กามโรค ลดลง ใช่ มั้ย
  gahn **KLÌHP** jà chôoi tam-hâi kwahm-sìang dtàw gahm-rôek lôht-lohng châi mái
  Circumcision will help to lower the risk against STDs, right?

- ที่รัก มัน **เปิดหมวก** มา แล้ว อะ
  têe-rúk mun BPÈRT-MÙAK mah láeo 'à
  Baby, it's already **hard**!

- บางที ที่ เค้า **ตายด้าน** อาจ จะ มา จาก ความ เครียด ใน ใจ ละมั้ง
  bahng-tee têe káo DTAI-DÂHN 'àht-jà mah jàhk kwahm-krîat nai jai lâ-múng
  Sometimes when he's **got no sex drive** it probably comes from stress, I'm guessing.

Butt and Butt Hole

There are two words for *ass* that you should know. The word กัน [gôhn] is the one you can easily say in public and translates to *bottom* or *butt*. The other one is ตูด [dtòot] which means *ass*. A more colloquial word is ดาก [dàhk], but you're only likely to hear that one in the provinces. For butt hole, shit hole or ass hole, try using either รูขี้ [roo kêe] or รูกัน [roo gôhn]. Another one you might hear for *butt* is บั้นท้าย [bûn tái] which also means *the end*.

- เพลง นี้ ชื่อ "หัว ไหล่ **ตูด**" ชอบ ปะ
  playng née chûe "hǔa lài DTÒOT" châwp bpà
  This song's called "Head Shoulders **Ass**." Ya like it?

- ได้ อารมณ์ และ เสียว สุด ๆ แฟน เลีย ตรง **รูกัน** สุดยอด เลย
  dâi 'ah-rohm láe sěeo sòot-sòot faen lia dtrohng ROO-GÔHN sòot-yâwt leri
  I'll get turned on and like totally horny. My girlfriend licks my **butt hole** and it's sooo awesome!

Tits and Nips

The word you'll most often for *tits* is นม [nohm], which can also mean *milk*. Try and imagine those milky, white, squishy type of breasts you might find on a Chinese supermodel and you have the word อึ๋ม ['ǔem]. You mostly hear the word อึ๋ม ['ǔem] in the phrase ขาวสวยหมวยอึ๋ม [kǒw sǒoi mǒoi 'ǔem]. Since perceptions of beauty can differ between the East and the West, I suggest you type the phrase into a search engine on the internet for fun and see what types of pictures pop up. Then you'll understand what the phrase ขาวสวยหมวยอึ๋ม [kǒw sǒoi mǒoi 'ǔem] means better than I could ever explain it. You could also say ถัน [tǔn] to mean *breast* but I think it sounds pretty out-of-date. For *big tits* or *biggins,* just say นมใหญ่ [nohm yài]. If they're *saggy* or *National Geographic boobies* then say นมยาน [nohm yahn]. If someone is *flatchested* then they are said to have ไข่ดาว [kài dow], which also mean *eggs, sunny side up.*

- ชอบ นมใหญ่ มาก ๆ น่าจับ แล้ว น่าเล่น ล่ะ
  châwp NOHM-YÀI mâhk-mâhk nâh-jùp láeo nâh-lâyn lâ
  I love **big o' tits**. You just wanna touch them and play with them.

- เจอ ตัว จริง แล้ว เธอ เตี้ย อ้วน **นมยาน** แถม หน้า แก่ กว่า แม่ เรา
  ด้วย วะ
  jer dtua jihng láeo ter dtîa 'ûan NOHM-YAHN tǎem nâh gàe gwàh mâe rao dôoi wá
  I went to meet the real thing and she's short, fat, has **sagging tits** and she looks older than my own f—kin' mom!

- ไม่ เห็น มี **นม** เลย **ไข่ดาว** ต่างหาก หล่ะ
  mâi hěhn mee NOHM leri kài-dow dtàhng-hàhk là
  I don't see any **tits**. Looks like some **eggs done sunny-side up** instead.

For *nipples* the best word to use is หัวนม [hǔa nohm]. You might also hear people use ปทุมถัน [bpà-toom tǔn] sometimes as well. I like the word ลูกเกด [lôok gàyt], which also means *raisin.*

- เห็น ตัว จริง **ลูกเกด** แล้ว ก็ ต้อง บอก ว่า สูง สวย สง่า
  hěhn dtua-jihng LÔOK-GÀYT láeo-gâw dtâwng bàwk wâh sǒong sǒoi sà-ngàh
  I've seen her **nipples**, the real thing, and I have to say they're perky, sexy and just downright majestic.

- ส่วน **ปทมถัน** หญิง ทุก คน ชอบ ให้ ชาย ดอมดม เลีย และ สัมผัส
  ด้วย มือ หรือ ปาก
  sùan BPÀ-TOOM-TǓN yǐhng tóok kohn châwp hâi chai dawn-dohm lia láe sǔm-pùt dôoi mue rǔe bpàhk
  For the **nipples**, all women like to have their men sniff, lick and touch them using their hands or their mouth.

The Box

Here's a whole slew of words for a woman's nether regions. My favorite is จิ๋ม [jǐhm]. This is as about as safe a word as any to call a *vagina* in Thai and the one I probably use the most. Consider it the equivalent for the guy's จู๋ [jǒo]. The worst one on the list is probably the word หี [hěe] which translates best as *cunt.* The word รูหี [roo hěe] then would be the *cunt hole.* The equivalent in vulgarity for the male appendage is ควย [kooi]. The word หอย [hŏi], which really mean *shell*, I would say translates the best as *pussy*. You might also hear the words นาผืนน้อย [nah pŭen nói] or เต่า [dtào] which mean *little field* and *turtle*, respectively. I think the word หมอ [mâw] translates best into *box*, but you'll mostly only ever hear this one used for prostitutes. You can also call it a *cave* in Thai, ถ้ำ [tâm] or ถ้ำทอง [tâm tawng]. The entire area can be called โหนก [nòek] similar to the word *hump*. The words โมะ [móe] or อีโมะ ['ee móe] are mostly used for younger girls. I've also heard the word อีเฉาะ ['ee chaw] used to mean *pussy*. The word ของสงวน [kăwng sŏhng-wohn], which means *reserved property* can also be taken to mean *vagina*. Lastly, the phrases หีกะจ้อยร้อย [hĕe gà jôi rôi] and หอยกะจี๋รี่ [hŏi gà gêe rêe] both refer to a *smaller twat*.

- จิ๋ม น่ารัก จัง
  JĬHM nâh-rúk jung
  You're **twat**'s really cute.

- เรา ชอบ ให้ มี คน มา เลีย หอย บ้าง
  rao châwp hâi mee kohn mah lia **HŎI** bâhng
  I occasionally like to have my **pussy** licked by somebody.

- เค้า เปิด เข้า มา ใน กางเกงใน ชั้น เพื่อ ใช้ สอง นิ้ว แยง **นาผืนน้อย**
  จาก ข้างหลัง
  káo bpèrt kâo mah nai gahng-gayng-nai chún pûea chái săwng
  núi **NAH-PŬEN-NÓI** jàhk kâhng-lŭng
  He opened my panties from behind and slipped two fingers into my **pussy**.

- สาว โครต สวย โชว์ **โหนก** — คลิก ที่นี่
  săo kôht sŏoi choew **nòek**—klíhk têe-nêe
  Sexy girls showing their pussy—click here!

Clitoris

The word for *clitoris* in Thai is เม็ดละมุด [méht lá moot], but sometimes you'll hear a Thai use the English word *clitoris* like this, คลิตอริส [klíht dtaw ríht]. A really vulgar way to say clit is แตด [dtàet]. For the area around that, the labia, the Thai have one main word that they use, แคม [kaem].

- สำหรับ หญิง **คลิตอริส** เป็น จุด ที่ ให้ ความ เสียว ทาง เพศ ใช่มั้ย
  săm-rùp yĭhng **KLÍHT-DTAW-RÍHT** bpehn jòot têe hâi kwahm
  sĕeo tahng pâyt châi mái
  For girls the **clitoris** is the spot where girls get off, right?

- แส้น จะ เสียว ระริก ตรง เม็ด **แตด** ของ แฟน
  săen jà sĕeo rá-ríhk drohng méht DTÀET kăwng faen
  Vibrating right at my girlfriend's **clit** gets her so horned up.

To Shave or Not To Shave

The main word for *pubic hair* is หมอย [mŏi] but it's kind of rude. Two funny ways to call it are ป่าดงดิบ [bpàh dohng dìhp], which means like *rainforest*, and ขนเพชร [kŏhn pâyt], which translates into something like *diamond hair*. If someone is *shaved* or *bald* then you can use the word เกรียน [grian].

- ชอบ หอย ไม่ มี **หมอย** ล่ะ
  châwp hŏi mâi mee MŎI lâ
  I like pussy with no **pubes**.

- **ขนเพชร** ยาว มาก ควร ตัด ดี มั้ย
  KŎHN-PÂYT yow mâhk kuan dtùt dee mái
  Is it good to cut really long **pubic hair**?

- โกน ให้ **เกรียน** ดี เหอะ
  goen hâi GRIAN dee hèr
  Just shave it till it's good and **bald**!

Your Panties, Undies and Naked Ass

The next time you want to call someone naked instead of using the word เปลือย [bplueoi] try saying the phrase นุ่งน้อยห่มน้อย [nôong nói hòhm nói], which means *in the buff*. The phrase ชุดวันเกิด [chóot wun gèrt] is a good one. It translates as *birthday suit*. You might also hear the word ล่อนจ้อน [lâwn jâwn] to mean *naked* as well. If a girl is nude because she's in a strip club or a *show girl* then you can call that type of nakedness จ้ำบ๊ะ [jâm bá]. If you're in a porno, then Thais would normally use the word โป๊ [bpóe] instead.

- อยู่ บ้าน ใส่ ชุด **นุ่งน้อยห่มน้อย** ดี กว่า เนอะ
  yòo bâhn sài chóot NÔONG-NÓI-HÒHM-NÓI dee gwàh nér
  When I'm at home it's better just **to be in the buff**.

- ไม่ น่า แอบ ถ่าย เลย เค้า ไม่ ได้ มา **ล่อนจ้อน** ให้ ใคร เห็น ซะ หน่อย
  mâi nâh 'àep tài leri káo mâi dâi mah LAWN-JÂWN hâi krai hĕhn sá-nòi
  There's nothing there worth taking picture for. She didn't come out **nude** for anyone to see.

- มี ภาพ สาว ๆ เด็ด เต้น โชว์ **จ้ำบ๊ะ** ใน ผับ
  mee pâhp sǎo-sǎo dèht dtâyn choe JÂM-BÁ nai pùp
  I got some explicit **nude** pictures of girls dancing and showing off in the pub.

Someone who's not naked but wears so little that they almost might as well be is called a แต่งตัววาบหวาน [dtàeng-dtua wâhp-wǎhn]. One other showy way of dressing that has now become a word in Thai is the word บิกินี่ [bìh gìh nee], or the English *bikini*. Instead of saying กางเกงใน [gahng gayng nai] to refer to *underwear,* shorten it to ก.ก.น. [gaw gaw naw]. The common name for *undies* or *panties* though is ชั้นใน [chún nai].

- แม่ คง ไม่ ยอม ให้ ชั้น **แต่งตัววาบหวาน** ขนาด นั้น หละ
  mâe kohng mâi yawm hâi chún DTÀENG-DTUA-WÂHP-WǍHN kà-nàht nún là
  My mom probably wouldn't let me **dress that slutty**.

- เด็ก สมัย นี้ กล้า ที่ จะ ไปเที่ยว ไม่ ใส่ **ก.ก.น.** เลย
  dèhk sà-mǎi-née glâh têe jà bai-têeo mâi sài gaw-gaw-naw leri
  Kids these days actually dare go around without any **underwear**.

Porn and Toys

If everything else is not enough, here are a few ways to talk about porn and sex toys. For pornography, Thais normally use the word โป๊ [bóe] and attach it onto another word. For example, the word หนังโป๊ [nǔng bpóe] means a *porno movie*. หนังสือโป๊ [nung-sǔe bpóe] means a *porno mag*. And เว็บโป๊ [wéhp bpóe] means *internet porn*. If you ever hear the English word *clip video* being used in Thai, most of the time it's also referring to a *short pornographic video clip*, often taken with a cell phone, คลิปวีดีโด [klíhp vee-dee-'oe] or วีดีโดคลิป [vee-dee-'oe klíhp]. The English letter *X* also is used in Thai to mean porn. Here's two popular spellings for the letter *X* in Thai, เอ็กซ์ ['èhk] and เอกซ์ ['áyk]. Another popular way to talk about *sexy pics* or those type of celebrity *paparazzi pictures* is the word ภาพหวิว [pâhp wǔi].

- ทำไม เด็ก ผู้ชาย ชอบ ดู **หนังโป๊** จัง
  tam-mai dèhk pôo-chai châwp doo NǓNG-BPÓE jung
  Why do boys love to watch **porn** so much?

- มี ลิงค์ ให้ โหลด หนัง **เอ็กซ์**
  mee lihng hâi lòed nǔng-'ÁYK
  Here's a link to download some **porn**.

- เว็บไซท์ นี้ มี **ภาพหวิว** ของ สาว ๆ ดารา **โป๊**...
  wéhp-sai née mee PÂHP-WǓI kǎwng sǎo-sǎo dah-rah bpóe
  This website has **sexy pictures** of girls, celebs, **porno**…

You won't see sex toys sold on the street in Thailand because it's against the law, but you will find a lot of information on the web. The most common word I hear for sex toys is ของเทียม [kǎwng tiam], which normally refers to *dildos*. Another euphemism for *dildo* is จรวดเทียม [jà-rùat tiam], which basically means *artificial rocket*. If you hear the word ขิก [kìhk] or ปลัดขิก [bà lùt kìhk] then it's referring to any *phallic looking object* that is also used as a charm. Sometimes you'll see these being sold at a night market as a little wooden penis attached to a keychain.

- ใคร มี ขาย **ของเทียม** บ้าง ช่วย เมล์ มา ด้วย แบบว่า อยาก ได้ มั้ง
  krai mee kǎi kǎwng-tiam bâhg chôoi may mah dôoi bàep-wâh yàhk dâi mûng
  Whoever sells **sex toys** please contact by email? I think like I wanna get some.

- เค้า ว่า **ปลัดขิก** มัน โชก ดี
  káo wâh BPÀ-LÙT-KÌHK mun chôek dee
  They say that those **little penis charms** are good luck.

Girlfriend, Boyfriend, Lover and Old Flame

The most popular word for someone who is your boyfriend, girlfriend, wife or husband is the word แฟน [faen]. Old and young alike use this word more often than any other to refer to the significant other. A new word that recently sprang up is กิ๊ก [gíhk], which Thais use to describe someone who's not a boyfriend or girlfriend and yet much more than just a friend. This could mean almost anything and it almost invariably always does. I've heard Thais describe almost every type of relationship as their กิ๊ก [gíhk]. Anything from the person they might just flirt with at work, to the person down the street that they're trying to secretly sleep with, and even the mistress that they're cheating their wives with. Basically, it can mean anyone other than the outright and real girlfriend or boyfriend. Because of this vagueness, the word กิ๊ก [gíhk] has become so popular lately. Thais like that vagueness. It gives them their wiggle room and fits in perfectly with a culture that for the most part prizes vagueness over uncomfortable directness. Nowadays, in response to the word กิ๊ก [gíhk], another new term has popped up. The word ปู๋ [bpóo] is used by those who want to reassert the fact that he or she is indeed a girlfriend or boyfriend and not just a กิ๊ก [gíhk]. This is a fairly new word and not everybody uses it, but if you hear the younger kids talking about their ปู๋ [bpóo], then it's used to mean specifically their girlfriend or boyfriend—and not their กิ๊ก [gíhk].

- เบื่อ **แฟน** เรา ล่ะ วะ
  bùe **FAEN** rao lâ-wá
  I'm f—kin' sick of my **girlfriend.**

- กิ๊ก บางครั้ง ก็ ทำให้ มี ความสุข แต่ ระวัง นะ ถ้า คบ **กิ๊ก** นิสัย ไม่ ดี จะ เดือดร้อน นะ
  gíhk bahng-krúng gâw tam-hâi mee kwahm-sòok dtàe rá-wung ná tâh kóhp kíhp níh-sǎi mâi dee jà dùeat-ráwn ná
  Sometimes an **outside fling** will make you happy, but be careful. If the **fling** is with a bad person, you could end up being in trouble.

- ปู๋ ชั้น ไม่ ใช่ กิ๊ก อะ
  BPÓO chún mâi châi gíhk 'à
  He's my **boyfriend,** not a "gik."

A more standard term for the person with whom you may have an illicit affair is the word ชู้ [chóo]. This can be translated as *lover* or *mistress*. Two other words I often hear is เด็ก [déhk], which just means *kid*, or อีหนู ['ee nǒo]. I wouldn't really use these terms because someone might be confused with what you're really talking about, especially if you look foreign though it's still good to know them. The Thai language has a lot of words for *minor wife* and *major wife* as it's not uncommon for a Thai even today to take a second wife if he can financially afford it. The concept of a second or minor wife is not similar to that of the Western concept of a *mistress* or just somebody you're sleeping with. A minor wife in Thai society is basically like setting up shop all over again but on the other side of town. It's like a second family, with kids, a house, mortgage and all the rest. Because of this, a colloquial way of calling a *minor wife* is บ้านเล็ก [bâhn léhk], which also mean *small house*. A *major wife* is called บ้านใหญ่ [bâhn yài] or *large house*. A direct translation for *major wife* and *minor wife* are เมียหลวง [mia lǔang] and เมียน้อย [mia nói], respectively. Generally, that occasional fling outside of marriage and without the attachment is an affair with a ชู้ [chóo]. If your passion rekindles for someone who was an old love in the past then the appropriate phrase is ถ่านไฟเก่า [tàhn fai gào]. Lastly, the tried and true word for *baby* or *honey* is ที่รัก [têe rúk].

- เรา นะ ชอบ เป็น **ชู้** กับ แฟน ชาวบ้าน เพราะ เรา ไม่ ชอบ มีแฟน เป็น ของ ตัว เอง
  rao ná châwp bpehn **CHÓO** gùp faen chow-bâhn práw rao mâi châwp mee faen bpehn kǎwng dtua-'ayng
  I like being just the **lover** of someone's girl because I don't like having my own girlfriend.

- พอ เค้า คน นั้น มา เจอ เรา ก็ ได้ รู้ ว่า **ถ่านไฟเก่า** ลุกขึ้น มาจริง ๆ
  paw káo kohn nún mah jer rao gâw dâi róo wâh **TÀHN-FAI-GÀO** look-kûen mah jihng-jihng
  As soon as he came to meet me, I knew that the **old flames** had been rekindled.

To Cheat On and Then Dump

To talk about *having an affair* is to use the word ชู้ [chóo] in combination with another word. You can choose from คบชู้ [kóhp chóo], เป็นชู้ [bpehn chóo], มีชู้ [mee chóo] and เล่นชู้ [lâyn chóo]. The phrase คบชู้สู่ชาย [kóhp chóo sòo chai] is specifically for a *woman who cheats*. Another way to say that you've *cheated* on someone is นอกใจ [nâwk jai]. If you ever do get caught cheating on your significant other, try using this phrase นอกกายไม่เหมือนนอกใจ [nâwk gai mâi mǔean nâwk jai], which means something along the lines of *cheating with the flesh is not the same as cheating with the heart.*

- เมีย **เล่นชู้** ต้อง ระวัง ผัว
  mia **LÂYN-CHÓO** dtâwng rá-wung pǔa
  A wife who **has an affair** should be wary of her husband.

- ถ้า เป็น เรา น่ะ **คง** ไม่ กล้า ที่ จะ **นอกใจ** แฟน เรา ที่ กำลังท้อง อยู่ หรอก
  tâh bpehn rao nâ kohng mâi glâh têe jà **NÂWK-JAI** faen rao têe gam-lung táwng yòo ràwk
  If it was me I probably wouldn't dare **cheat** on my girl when she's pregnant.

Two ways to say *to dump* or *break up with* in Thai are ทิ้ง [tíhng], which is more commonly used, and ชิ่ง [chîhng].

- บอก ได้ มั้ย ทำไม จึง **ทิ้ง** ชั้น ไป ไม่ เข้าใจ
  bàwk dâi mái tam-mai jueng tíhng chún bpai mâi kâo-jai
  Can you tell me, why did you **dump** me? I don't understand.

- เค้า เพ่ง ถูก แฟน **ซิ่ง** ไป เลย
  káo pêrng tòok faen CHÎHNG bpai leri
  He was just **dumped** by his girlfriend.

Players, Perverts, Pimps and Sugar Daddies

The common word for *player* or *playboy* is เจ้าชู้ [jâo chóo]. If you're a เจ้าชู้ประตูดิน [jâo-chóo bprà-dtoo dihn], then that means you'll *sleep with anyone*. If you hear someone call you ขุนแผน [kŏon păen], then you're a *Casanova*. If it just seems like you're player or you flirt a lot, then you might be called ขี้หลี [kêe lĕe] or แซ่หลี [sâe lĕe].

- ไม่ ต้อง **เจ้าชู้** มาก นะ
  mâi dtâwng JÂO-CHÓO mâhk ná
  You don't gotta act like such a **player**.

- พวก **แซ่หลี** อ่ะ ไม่ ชอบ เลย
  pûak SÂE-LĔE 'à mâi châwp leri
  I can't stand those **guys who act like playboys**.

If you want to yell out *You're dirty!* or *Nasty!* or maybe *You're sick!!* to someone, try ทะลึ่ง [tá lûeng], ทุเรศ [tóo râyt] or ลามก [lah móhk]. If one looks like a pervert because of his *wolf eyes*, then call him หน้าหม้อ [nâh mâw]. If you get called บ้ากาม [bâh gahm] that just means you're *sex crazed*. The word กามวิตถาร [gahm wíht tăhn] pretty much means the same thing—that you're a *pervert*. If *sadism* is your thing then try the word ซาดิสม์ [sah dìht].

- ชอบ อ่าน การ์ตูน **ทะลึ่ง**
  châwp 'àhn gah-dtoon TÁ-LÛENG TÁ-LÛENG
  I like to read **dirty** comics.

- มี ผู้ชาย **หน้าหม้อ** มา ขอ เบอร์
  mee pôo-chai **NÂH-MÂW** mah kǎw ber
  The **playboy** just asked for my number.

- ผู้ชาย เป็น สัตว์ บ้ากาม แหละ
  pôo-chai bpehn sùt **BÂH-GAHM** làe
  Men are just **sex-crazed** animals.

The Thai word for a *dirty old man* refers to *old snake head* or เฒ่าหัวงู [tâo hǔa ngoo]. For older men who like younger girls the fitting proverb is วัวแก่กินหญ้าอ่อน [wua gàe gihn yâh 'àwn], which translates as *old cows eating fresh grass*. An old guy who still has strong sexual desires is called ตัณหากลับ [dtun hǎh glùp].

- ตา **เฒ่าหัวงู** เพิ่ง มา เจอ ของจริง นี่ แหละ สยอง
  dtah **TÂO-HǓA-NGOO** pêrng mah jer kǎwng-jihng nêe sà-yǎwng
  I just saw the real thing, the eyes of a **dirty old man**. It's scary!

- นี่ แหละ จึง ทำให้ เมืองไทย เรา เป็น สวรรค์ ของ ไอ้ ฝรั่ง แก่ ตัณหากลับ
  nêe-làe jueng tam-hâi mueang-tai rao bpehn sà-wǔn kǎwng 'âi-fà-rùng gàe **DTUN-HǍH-GLÙP**
  See, there you go! It makes our country of Thailand into a heaven for those old white f—kers **who can still get it up**.

The Thai word for *pimp* is แมงดา [maeng dah] and the *sex industry* or *sex trade* that he works in is called ค้าเนื้อสด [kák núea sòht]. If the guy is a *gigolo*, then he is a จิ๊กโก๋ [jíhk gǒe] or in a more a vulgar way, he's an ไอ้ตัว ['âi dtua]. The word จิ๊กโก๋ [jíhk gǒe] can also mean *gangster* or *hooligan*. Lastly, the word ป๋า [bpǎh] translates best into *sugar daddy*.

- ถ้า เอา ภาพ ไป ทำ เป็น วีซีดี ขาย ก็ แสดง ว่า หา เงิน จาก ผู้หญิง อย่าง นี้ ก็ **แมงดา** หน่ะซิ หน้าตัวเมีย จัง
  tâh 'ao pâhp bpai tam bpehn wee-see-dee kǎi gâw sà-dǎeng wâh hǎh ngern jàhk pôo-yǐhng yàhng-née gâw **MAENG-DAH** nà-síh nâh-dtua-mia jung
  If he took those pictures to make VCD and sell them, it seems to me like he's using women just to make money like a **pimp**. What a little bitch!

- ถ้า ไอ้ แก่ ไม่ รวย จะ เอา มา เป็น **ป๋า** ทำไม ละ
  tâh 'âi-gàe mâi rooi jà 'ao mah bpehn **BPǍH** tam-mai lâ
  If the old guy's not rich, why gonna have him as your **sugar daddy**?

Easy Women and Women of the Night

Any girl who goes out with a lot of guys or a *slut* is called a แรด [râet]. This is a fairly rude word. If she is an *easy girl* she may be a ไก่ [gài], but I don't hear that one used so much these days. If she sleeps with a lot of guys then you can say she goes มั่วผู้ชาย [mûa pôo-chai]. If she sleeps around to get ahead in the office, the phrase ใช้เต้าใต [chái dtâo dtài] fits her. If she just *walks really slutty* then you call that ฉาย [chǎi].

- อย่าง หญิง แต่งตัว แบบ นี้ คง ถึง เรียก ว่า แรด
  yàhng yǐhng dtàeng-dtua bàep née káo tǔeng rîak wâh RÂET
  Girls that dress this way are **sluts**.

- อย่า ไป เสียใจ เลย นี่ แค่ ผู้หญิง คน เดียว ที่ มั่วผู้ชาย นะ
  yàh bpai sǐa-jai leri nêe kâe pôo-yǐhng kohn deeo têe MÛA-PÔO-CHAI ná
  Don't be upset about it! It's just one **girl who sleeps around** a lot.

- หนู ขอ บอก เลย ว่า ไม่ ได้ ใช้เต้าใต่ อะไร ทั้ง นั้น
  nǒo kǎw bàwk leri wâh mâi dâi chái-dtâo-dtài 'à-rai túng-nún
  I just want to say that I've never used sex to get ahead or anything like that.

The politically correct way to say *prostitute* in Thai is โสเภณี [sǒe pay nee] but there are a lot of other words for it as well. You can say they *sell their body*, ขายตัว [kǎi dtua], or that they are *looking for money*, ผู้หญิงหาเงิน [pôo-yǐhng hǎh ngern] or *looking for food*, ผู้หญิงหากิน [pôo-yǐhng hǎh gihn]. If you want to be more vulgar and say something similar to *whore*, then the word กะหรี่ [gà rèe] is appropriate. The words ออหรี่ ['aw rèe] and ช็อกการี [cháwk gah ree] are variations of whore as well. Two more names referring to whore both use the word นาง [nahg]. These are นางบำเรอ [nahg bam rer] and นางฟ้าจำแจง [nahg fáh jam jaeng]. You might also hear ทำประตู [tam bprà dtoo] or คุณโส [koon sǒe] to mean *hooker* as well. The word ชั้นสูง [chún sǒong] refers to a prostitute that also keeps a day job to hide her source of income. The words อีดอก ['ee dàwk], อีดอกทอง ['ee dàwk tawng] and อีตัว ['ee dtua] all mean whore and may be used as curses [see Chapter 5]. On the other hand, the phrase ไกแก แม่ปลาช่อน [gài-gàe mâe-bplah-sâwn] refers to an *older, tricky madam* or *mama san*. The Thai word for *mama san* is มามาซัง [mah mâh sung].

- เที่ยว ผู้หญิงหาเงิน ครั้ง เดียว จะ ติด เอดส์ มั้ย
  têeo PÔO-YǏHNG-HǍH-NGERN krúng deeo jà dtìht 'àyt mái
  If I get on with a **prostitute** just once, will I catch AIDs?

- นี่ แต่งตัว ซิ ฮ่ะ ที่ เป็น แต่ง ชุด สีขาว บริสุทธิ์ ซึ่ง ดู ยังไงแล้ว มัน ไม่ เหมาะสม กับ **กะหรี่** อย่าง หล่อน เอา ซะ เลย
  nèe dtàeng-dtua síh hâ tam bpehn dtàeng-dtua chòot sěe-kǒw bàw-ríh-sòot sûeng doo yung-ngai láeo mun mâi màw-sǒhm gùp GÀ-RÈE yàhng lawn 'ao sá leri
  There see? Dressing in white as if she's a virgin, but anyway you look at it doesn't fit with a **whore** like her.

- พวก **คุณโส** เค้า เล่น ที่นี่ ทุก คืน ตั้ง แต่ 2 ทุ่ม เป็น ต้น ไป.
  pûak KOON-SǑE káo lâyn têe-nêe tóok kuen dtûng-dàe sǎwng tôom bpehn-dtôhn-bpai
  Hookers will do their thing here from eight o'clock in the evening onwards.

Baths, Brothels and Strip Clubs

A fairly popular place that Thai men go to are the อาบอบนวด ['àhp 'òhp nûat]. These are basically brothels with bathtubs. If someone frequents such an establishment, he is a ติดอ่าง [dtìht 'àhng]. A *whorehouse* is commonly called a ซ่อง [sâwng], so if you get invited to ไปเที่ยวซ่อง [bpai têeo sâwng] you know where you're being taken to. A colloquial term that means *to visit the brothel* is เที่ยวซุกซน [têeo sóok sohn]. A direct and vulgar way to say *to screw a hooker* or *to f—k a whore* is to use either of these two phrases, ตีกะหรี่ [dtee gà-rèe] or ตีหม้อ [dtee mâw]. If it's someone's first time to sleep with a prostitute, it is ขึ้นครู [kûen kroo]. Another euphemism for *whorehouse* is โรงน้ำชา [rohng nám chah], which also means *tea house*. If it is a บาร์ผี [bah pěe], it generally means that they have girls working out of the bar. A อะโกโก้ ['à goe gôe] is a *strip bar* although often times they have girls working out of there as well.

- เค้า เป็น คน **ติดอ่าง** ล่ะ
  káo bpehn kohn DTÌHT-'ÀHNG lâ
  He's **addicted to going to the bathhouse**.

- คุณพ่อ นัด เพื่อน สองสาม คน แว่บ หนี เมีย **ไปเที่ยวซ่อง** แน่นอน
  koon-pâw nút pûean sǎwng-sǎhm kohn wâep-něe mia BPAI-TÊEO-SÂWNG nâe-nawn
  Dad met up with a couple of friends to escape the little lady and **hit up a whorehouse** for sure.

- เมื่อ อายุ 18 ปี พี่ชาย พา เรา ไป **ขึ้นครู** ครั้งแรก
  mûe 'ah-yóo sìhp-bàet bpee pêe-chai pah rao bpai KÛEN-KROO
  krúng-râek
  When I was eighteen, my older brother got me **laid with a prostitute
  for the first time.**

Protection and Birth Control

Most people call a *condom* ถุงยาง [tŏong yahng] or ถุง [tŏong] for short. Sometimes you'll hear the English word for *condom* which is คอนดอม [kawn dâwm].
Other slang words for condom that you might run into are ปลอก [bplàwk], มีชัย
[míh chai], หมวกกันน็อก [mùak gun náwk] and เกราะ [gràw]. The main word
for *birth control* is ยาคุม [yah koom].

- ไม่ ได้ เอา **ถุงยาง** มา ด้วย นะ
  mâi dâi 'ao TŎONG-YAHNG mah dôoi ná
  I didn't bring a **condom** with me.

- ใส่ เกราะ ดี กว่า อ่ะ
  sài gràw dee gwàh 'à
  It's better if you use protection.

VD and STDs

If you haven't been wearing protection, you need to be aware of this next group
of words or you might just catch them. The general word for *venereal diseases*
is กามโรค [gahm rôek]. I've also heard the words โรคซุกชน [rôek sóok
some] and โอกินาวา ['oe gìh nah wah] to mean *VD*. The word เริ่ม [rêrm]
means *herpes* while the word โลน [loen] means *crabs*. If you want to say *syph-*

ilis, just use the Thai version of the English word, ซิฟิลิส [síh fíh líht]. On the other hand, โรคหนองในเทียม [rôek năwng nai tiam] refers to *chlamydia,* and หนองใน [năwng nai] means *gonorrhea.* The scariest one of the bunch is definitely HIV/AIDs. The Thais normally just say that someone is ติดเอดส์ [dtìht 'àyt] if they come up positive.

- ที่ น่า เป็น ห่วง คือ กรณี ที่ เด็ก มี ปัญหา เป็น **โรคซุกซน**
  têe nâh bpehn hùang kue gàw-ráw-nee têe dèhk mee bpun-hăh bpehn RÔEK-SÓOK-SOHN
  What's really worrisome is when kids have a problem with **STDs**.

- เมื่อ สงสัย ว่า **เป็นเอดส์** ควร จะ ไป หา หมอ ตรวจ ร่างกาย
  mûe sŏhn-săi wâh BPEHN-'ÀYD kuan jà bpai hăh măw dtrùat râhng-gai
  When you suspect you **have AIDs**, you should visit the doctor and get checked.

Sodomy

The last part of this chapter is about gays, lesbians and transvestites. There seems to be so many new slang words relevant to this group that keep popping up all the time. To fully tackle the subject, a book may need to be dedicated specifically for this subject matter. However, I'll give examples of some of the new slang words that have made their way into the vocabulary. Some English words have already been adapted into Thai like *homosexual* โฮโมเซ็กช่วล [hoe moe séhk chuan], *gay* เกย์ [gay] and *bisexual* ไบ [bai]. If you're an *in-the-closet gay,* you are either one of these two, อีแอบ ['ee 'àep] or แอบจิต ['àep jìht]. If you're an *out-of-the-closet* type then you are a สว่างจิต [sà-wàhng jìht]. If you're just *trying to hide it* then you are a สลัวจิต [sà-lŭa jìht]. If you're the *manly guy* in a gay relationship then you're the คิ่ง [kihng] or กุ๊งนาง [gôong nahng]. If you're the *girly one* then you're the ตุ๊ด [dtóot] or ตุ๊ดตู่ [dtóot dtòo]. The Thai words for *gay sex* are กินถั่วดำ [gihn tùa dam], อัดตูด ['ùt dtoot] and อัดถั่วดำ ['ùt tùa dam]. The last two may be translated as *to butt fuck* and *to pack fudge* and are both, to say the least, pretty vulgar.

- ชอบ **เกย์** ปะ
  châwp GAY bpà
  Ya like **gay men**?

- คิด ว่า แก เป็น **อีแอบ** แน่ ๆ
  kíht wâh gae bpehn 'EE-'ÀEP nâe-nâe
  I think he's an **in-the-closet** for sure.

- ทำไม ลูก พ่อ ต้อง ออก แนว ตุ๊ดตู่ ยังงี้ ล่ะ
  tam-mai lôok pâw dtâwng 'àwk naeo DTÓOT-DTÒO yung-ngée lâ
  Why does my son have to act like such an **effeminate queer?**

In a lesbian relationship, the *more butch* of the two is the ทอม [tawm] or ทอมบอย [tawm boi]. If she's the *more feminine* one, then she is the ดี้ [dêe]. You can also combine the two words and say ทอมดี้ [tawm dêe], or just say the English word *lesbian*, เลสเบี้ยน [lâyt bian]. You might hear them refer to their *vaginas* as ฉิ่งฉับ [chìhng chùp]. The word for *lesbian sex* in Thai would then be ดีฉิ่ง [dtee chìhng] or *to slap cymbals*.

- ดี้ ก็ น่ารัก แต่ ไม่ ชอบ พวก **ทอม** เลย เล่า
  dêe gâw nâh-rúk dtàe mâi châwp pûak tawm leri lâo
  Effeminate lesbians are cute, but I can't stand the **butch type** at all.

- เลสเบี้ยน ชอบ **ดีฉิ่ง** จัง
  lâyt-bian châwp DTEE-CHÌNG jung
  Lesbians love **to bump tacos.**

This last bit here is for the ladyboys, a phenomenon that you won't see on such a largescale or as widely accepted as it is in Thailand. The main word for this group is กะเทย [gà teri]. Aside from this, you don't need to know much more. However, here is a list of different names that you can refer to a *transvestite* or *fag* in Thai. All of them have their own little shades of meaning, but I'll let you do your own research on what these are:

กอ [gaw]
กะเทยควาย [gà-teri kwai]
กะเทียม [gà tiam]
ก้ามปู [gâhm bpoo]
เกย์ควีน [gay kween]
เกย์คิง [gay kihng]
ซ่อง [sawng]
ตุ๋ย [dtǒuie]
เต๋า [dtǎo]
เต๋าแตก [dtǎo dtàek]
แต๋ว [dtǎeo]
น้องเตย [náwng dteri]
นังกอ [nung gaw]
ประเทือง [bprà tueng]
ผู้ฉิ่ง [pôo chìhng]
เลดี้บอย [lay dêe boy]

เลดี้แมน [lay-dêe maen]
เศษเหล็ก [sàyt lèhk]
สาวประเภทสอง [sǎo bprà-pâyt sǎwng]
เสือใบ [sǔea bai]
หน้าหอยสังข์หลังหอยแครง [nâh hǒi sung lǔng hǒi kraeng]
เหล็กทอน [lèhk tâwn].

New words are being coined all the time for this community, so feel free to add any to the list when necessary.

- เรา ก็ เคย จูบ **กะเทย** ละ
  rao gâw keri jòop GÀ-TERI lâ
  Yeah, I've kissed a **ladyboy** before.

CHAPTER 7
Drinks & Drugs

Not everyone indulges in both drinks and drugs but many would probably attest to at least trying them once or twice and experiencing the effects firsthand. Thailand itself has one of the highest levels of alcohol consumption in the world. Whether or not you like to party much or not, the culture for it is so strong that it's a must that you have the ability to talk about this subject in Thailand.

Drunks and Druggies

There are two ways to call someone a drunk or a druggy and both of them start with the word ขี้ [kêe]. An *alcoholic* or a *drunk* is a ขี้เมา [kêe mao] and someone addicted to drugs or is a druggy is a ขี้ยา [kêe yah]. You'll probably hear the word ขี้เมา [kêe mao] a lot more often than ขี้ยา [kêe yah], if for no other reason that you'll run into more drunkards than druggies around Thailand. Being publicly drunk, especially if you're an old male, is still considered acceptable for a large portion of Thai society. This is even truer the further you are from Bangkok and start to move toward the villages.

- ไม่ ชอบ พวก **ขี้เมา**
  mâi châwp pûak KÊE-MAO
  I don't like **drunks.**

- ที่ ถนน คง ได้ เห็น ภาพ **ขี้ยา** เดิน ขอ เงิน นักท่องเที่ยว
  têe tà-nŏhn kohng dâi hĕhn pâhp KÊE-YAH dern kăw ngern núk-tâwng-têeo
  You've probably seen **druggies** walking the streets asking tourists for money.

Drunk, Drunk Already, Smashed, You've Drunk Off Your Ass!!

When someone is intoxicated, the most common term used is เมา [mao], which just means *drunk*. If someone's really *smashed* or *wasted,* then the word เมาหัวราน้ำ [mao hŭa rah nám] is appropriate. The word กริ่ม [grùem] means that you're just *half drunk* or *tipsy,* but you'll probably hear the word มึน [muen] used more often to describe someone who is *tipsy* or maybe doesn't want to admit that he is already drunk. The word เมาดิบ [mao dìhp] means that someone is *pretending* or *acting like a drunk*. The word โด๊ป [dóep] from the English word *to dope* implies that the alcoholic substance that you are using is having an effect on you but this word is used more often with drugs. Lastly, the terms ได้ที่ [dâi têe] and ดีมาแล้ว [dee mah láeo] imply that some-one is *drunk*, but these two phrases really depend on context and would prob-ably be misunderstood by a foreigner. You could use these words if you were at a party and completely wasted and when your buddy comes up to ask you how you're doing, you can only grin sheepishly and reply *I'm doing fine!* as you are *piss drunk*.

- แก คง ไป กิน เหล้า **เมาหัวราน้ำ** จน เกิด อุบัติเหตุ
  gae kohng bpai gihn lâo MAO-HǓA-RAH-NÁM john gèrt 'òo-bùt-dtì-hàyt
  He was probably **drunk off his ass** and that's why there was an accident.

- ฝน ตก ไป **กรึ่ม** เบียร์ ซิ ครับ
  fǒh dtòk bpai GRÙEM bia sí krúp
  Well it's raining, so let's go get **drunk** on beer!

- **มึน** แล้ว เหรอ
  MUEN láeo rěr
  You're already **tipsy**, eh?

- ใช่ บาง คน เมา แต่ บาง คน เค้า **เมาดิบ** ไม่ ได้ เมา จริง
  châi bahng kohn mao dtàe bahng kohn káo MAO-DÌHB mâi dâi mao jihng
  Right, some of the people are drunk but some are **just acting wasted.** They're not really drunk.

- กิน วิสกี้ มา เป็น สาม ขวด ก็ เลย **ดีมาแล้ว** น่า
  gihn wíh-sà-gêe mah bpehn sǎhm kùat gâw leri DEE-MAH-LÁEO nâh
  We've already gone through three bottles of whisky, so I think **we're doing just fine!**

To Drink, Chug, and Shoot a Shot

There may be different slang words out there that mean *to drink* but the first one that you need to know, if you don't know already, is กิน [gihn], which means *to eat*. Even though the Thais have a specific word for drinking, ดื่ม [dùem], I barely ever hear it. Unless a waitress comes up and asks you specifically *What would you like to drink?* or ดื่มอะไรดีคะ [dùem 'à-rai dee ká], you're better off just using the word กิน [gihn], as in กินเบียร์ [gihn bia] if you want to *drink beer* or กินน้ำเปล่า [gihn nám-bplào] if you want to *drink water*. Some Thais will probably tell you that it isn't correct Thai and the truth is they're right, but so what? Don't listen to them. You goal is to sound natural and colloquial, not like some proper phrasebook.

- เค้า ชอบ กิน เหล้า ทุก วัน
  káo châwp gihn lâo tóok wun
  He likes to drink alcohol everyday.

The words เฉิม [chèrm] and ตอก [dtàwk] are slang words for *drink*. In this context, they're both used to mean *to drink alcohol*. Normally, you'll hear ตอก [dtàwk] said as ตอกเหล้า [dtàwk lâo]. The words กรึ๊บ [grúep] and กรุ๊บ [gróop] are onomatopoeic names for drinking but, in this context, they often mean *to drink liquor*. The word ดวด [dùat] could be translated as *to chug* or *to shoot* a drink. The word ก๊ง [góhng] is suitable when you're sitting around *drinking with all of your friends*. When you're trying *to make your friend chug a drink* then use the word กรอกเหล้า [gràwk lâo]. The common version of *Cheers!* that I hear in Thailand is probably หมดแก้ว [mòht gâeo], which means *Bottoms up!*

- ขี้เกียจ ไป ไหน วะ **เฉิ่ม** เหล้า ดี กว่า
  kêe-gìat bpai năi wá CHÈRM lâo dee gwàh
  Hell, I don't feel like going anywhere, better just to stay here and **drink**.

- เมื่อคืน **ตอก** เหล้าขาว เข้า ไป จน เกือบ ตีสอง
  mûea-kuen DTÀWK lâo-kăo kâo bpai john gùeap dtee săwng
  Last night we were up till about two in the morn just **downing** that rice whisky.

- เสิร์ฟ ใน แก้ว เล็ก ๆ กระดก **กรึ๊บ** ทีเดียว ให้ หมด จน เมา เร็ว และ เมา แรง สุด ๆ
  ser nai gâeo léhk-léhk grà-dòhk GRÚEP tee-deeo hâi moth jà mao rayo láe mao raeng sòot-sòot
  Serve it in a little glass, pick it up and **gulp it down** in one take. You'll totally get plastered quick and hard!

- ชอบ **ดวด** วิสกี้ มาด ที่สุด
  châwp DÙAT wíh-sà-gêe mâhl-têe-sòot
  I like **to shoot** whisky the most.

- พวกเค้า มัวแต่ นั่ง **กึ๋ง** เหล้า บ้าน เพื่อน ดู วีซีดี โป๊ เท่านั้น เล่า
  pûak-káo mua-dtàe nûng GÓHNG lâo bâhn pûean doo wee-see-dee bóe tâo-nún lâo
  All they do is **sit around getting drunk** at their friend's house watching cheap porn on the VCD player.

- เรา ถูก เพื่อน จับ **กรอกเหล้า** มา เป็น กระป๋อง เบียร์ สาม ขวด นะ
  rao tòok pûean jùp GRÀWP-LÂO mah bpehn grà-bpăwng bia săhm kùat ná
  My friends **made me chug** three cans of beers.

Good and Bad Drinkers

The two names you'll most likely hear someone being called a *strong* or *good drinker* is คอแข็ง [kaw kăeng] and คอทองแดง [kaw tawng-daeng]. If you can't hold your alcohol then you are a *weak drinker or*, คออ่อน [kaw 'àwn].

- เค้า มี **คอแข็ง** มาก ๆ ไม่ เคย เห็น เมา ชะที เล่า
  káo mee KAW-KĂENG mâhk-mâhk mâi keri hěhn mao sá-tee lâo
  He can really **hold his liquor**. I've never seen him drunk, not even once!

- ตัว ใหญ่ แต่ **คออ่อน** นะ
  dtua yài dtàe KAW-'ÀWN ná
  He's a big guy but **can't hold his drink**.

Liquor, Wine, Beer and Whisky White

The general word for *alcoholic drinks* in Thai is เหล้า [lâo]. The word สุรา [sòo rah] is more formal and you'll probably only see it written on a bottle. You might hear the English word *alcohol* itself in Thai, แอลกอฮอล์ ['aen gaw haw], but it's normally used to refer to the stuff you might rub on a skin abrasion more than the stuff you want to drink. The most popular drink in the village is *rice whisky*, เหล้าขาว [lâo-kŏw], which is normally 40 degrees or 80 proof. This is because aside from straight up moonshine, this is the cheapest form of alcohol in Thailand. Most Thais in Bangkok look down on people who drink เหล้าขาว [lâo-kǎo], so don't expect to find this rice whisky served at any bar in the city. Sometimes, jokingly, when a villager does meet a foreigner he'll often refer to his drink as *whisky white*, pronounced something like วิสกี้ไวท์ [wíh-sà-gêe wai].

- **เหล้าขาว** ขวด นี้ มัน กี่ ดีกรี อะ
  LÂO-KĂO kùat née mun gèe dee-gree 'à
  What proof is this bottle of **rice whisky**?

Words like wine, beer, whisky, champagne and so on are all used in Thai now, so whenever you want to talk about a particular drink that you like just say the word in English and hope that a Thai understands you. After you've heard them pronounce the words in their own particular Thai way, just do your best to mimic them the next time. To get you started, the Thai pronunciation for *wine*, *beer* and *whisky* are ไวน์ [wai], เบียร์ [bia] and วิสกี้ [wíh-sà-gêe]. One of the most popular drinks in Thai disco or club is whisky soda, so the English word for *soda water* already in Thai is โซดา [soe dah]. Any type of alcoholic drink that inhibits your motor skills or *changes your attitude* can be referred to as น้ำเปลี่ยนนิสัย [nám bplìan ní-sǎi].

- ชั้น ไม่ ชอบ **ไวน์** เลย มัน เปรี้ยว นะ
  chún mâi châwp WAI leri mun bprêeo ná
  I don't like wine; it's sour.

- ขอ น้ำแข็ง โค้ก สอง ขวด และ **โซดา** ขวด เดียว อะ
  kǎw nám-kǎeng kóek sǎwng kùat láe SOE-DAH kùat deeo 'à
  I'll have some ice, two bottles of Coke and one bottle of **soda water**.

- พอ ได้ น้ำเปลี่ยนนิสัย เข้า ไป...เรา ก็ เริ่ม ปากหวาน
  paw dâi NÁM-BPLÌAN-NÍH-SǍI kâo bpai...rao gâw rêrm bpàhk-wǎhn
  As soon as I get some **alcohol** in me, the sweet-talking starts up.

Beer Snacks and Koozies

Any type of snack like salted peanuts or pretzels to go along with your drinking is called กับแกล้ม [gùp glâem]. Normally though Thais will drop the *L* sound so that it comes out like กับแกม [gùp gâem]. If you're at the beach you might want to ask for a *koozie* to keep your beer cool. I've heard Thais use the English word *condom* to mean a *beer koozie*, คอนด้อม [kawn-dâwn] or เบียร์คอนด้อม [bia kawn-dâwn]. If the mentioned names don't work, then call the beer koozie as ที่ใส่ขวดเบียณ [têe sài kùat bia].

- ไม่ ชอบ กับแก้ม หวาน
  mâi châwp GÙP-GÂEM wǎhn-wǎhn
  I don't like sweet **beer snacks**.

- ขอ คอนด้อม หน่อย นะ
  kǎw KAWN-DÂWM nòi ná
  I'd like a **condom for my beer** please.

Bars, Pubs, Discos and Going Out in General

The English words for *bar* and *pub* are now widely used in Bangkok, บาร์ [bah] and ผับ [pùp] but still rarely in the provinces. If you want to run into Thais drinking, then your best bet is to go to the เธค [tâyk] (also spelled เธก), the ดิสโก [dìh sà gôe] or the ดิสโก้เธค [dìh sà gôe tâyk]. These are all different ways of saying the English *disco* or *club* in Thai.

- จะ ไป เที่ยว ผับ รึเป่า อะ
  jà bpai têeo PÙP rúe-bpào 'à
  Are we going out to **the pub** or not?

- จีบ สาว ใน เธค ไม่ ต้อง ทำ อะไร มากมาย หรอก แค่ ยิ้มแย้ม ก็ ดี อยู่ แล้ว
  jeep sǎo nai TÂYK mâi dtâwng tam 'à-rai mâhk-mai ràwk kâe yíhm-yáem gâw dee yòo láeo
  Hitting on chicks in **the club**, you don't have to do too much of anything, just giving a great smile is good enough.

To say *going out* in Thai, try either ไปเดอ [bpai der] or ท่องราตรี [tâwng râht dtree]. The first one is particularly slang. If you want to go to a *party* just use the English word for it, ปาร์ตี้ [bpah dtêe] or งานปาร์ตี้ [ngahn bpah-dtêe]. You might also hear the English phrase *drink and dance* in Thai, ดริงก์แอนด์แดนซ์ [drihng 'aen daen]. Thais use it to mean just going out and having a good time. I've also heard some of the kids in Bangkok use the word ดิ้น [dîhn] to mean *to dance*.

- เมื่อคืน **ไปเดอ** ไหน มา ล่ะ แล้ว กะ ใคร อะ
  mûea-kuen BPAI-DER năi mah lâ láeo gà krai 'à
  Where'd you **go out to** last night, and with whom?

- ชุด นี้ เหมาะ กับ การ ออก **ท่องราตรี** เนอะ
  chóot née màw gùp gahn 'àawk **TÂWNG-RÂHT-DTREE** nér
  This is a good outfit for **going out**, no?

- **งานปาร์ตี้** ไม่ เห็น สนุก เลย
  NGAHN-BPAH-DTÊE mâi hĕhn sà-nòok leri
  This **party**'s not fun at all.

- เธค นี้ สุดยอด ก็ **ดิ้น** ได้ สุด ๆ
  tâyk née sòot-yâwt gâw DÎHN dâi sòot-sòot
  This **club** is sweet! You can totally **dance** here!

Bartender, Cocktail Waitress and DJ

In Bangkok you might hear Thais use the Thai translation for the English word *bartender*, บาร์เทนเดอร์ [bah tayn der]. If the bartender is a girl, then you can call her a บาร์เทนดี้ [bah tayn dêe]. If the girl serves drinks at the bar, then you can call her ผู้หญิงบาร์ [pôo yĭhng bah], or a *bar girl*. However, I wouldn't go around calling every girl that works at the bar, pub or disco a ผู้หญิงบาร์ [pôo yĭhng bah]. Some may get offended though and think that you think she works *out* of the bar as apposed to *in* the bar. Any girl dancing on stage in a disco you can pretty much call a *dancer*, แดนเซอร์ [daen ser] or a *coyote dancer*, โคโยตี้ [koe yoe dtêe]. Lastly, Thais also call the disc jockey or DJ, ดีเจ [dee jay].

- บาร์เทนเดอร์ หล่อ จัง
  BAH-TAYN-DER làw jung
  The **bartender**'s hot!

- ผู้หญิง ที่ อยู่ พัทยา ต้อง ถูก เหมา ว่า เป็น "ผู้หญิงบาร์"
  pôo-yĭhng têe yòo pút-tá-yah dtâwng tòok măo wâh bpehn PÔO-YĬHNG-BAH
  Girls in Pattaya are mostly labeled as "**bar girls**."

- อยาก จะ เป็น **แดนเซอร์** ต้อง ทำ อย่างไร บ้าง
  yàhk jà bpehn DAEN-SER dtâwng tam yàhng-rai bâhng
  What do you have to do to become a **dancer**?

Hangover

After all the drinking is said and done, the hangover sets in. Normally, if a Thai has been out drinking the night before, he'll use the phrase เมาค้าง [mao káhng] to mean that he's *got a hangover*. Today though, you'll hear Thais use variations of the English word *hangover*, แฮ้ง [háeng] or แฮงโอเวอร์ [haeng 'oe wer]. In treating hangover, the Thai word ถอน [tăwn] with a rising tone is the nearest translation for *hair of the dog*, referring to the ingestion of alcohol as treatment for hangover.

- โอ้โห **เมาค้าง** ล่า ปวดหัว มาก เลย
  'ôe-hŏe MAO-KÁHG lâh bpùat-hŭa mâhk leri
  Oh man, do I have a **hangover**! My head hurts like crazy.

To Smoke

The regular word to mean *to smoke* in Thai is สูบ [sòop] but I suggest using the word ดูด [dòot], which is more colloquial. Two ways to say *to smoke a cigarette* are ดูดบุหรี่ [dòot bòo-rèe] or ดูดยา [dòot yah]. *Tobacco*, as well as *drug* or *medicine*, is ยา [yah]. Sometimes it is even called ยากาแร็ต [yah ga réht], which is like a weird amalgamation of the Thai ยา [yah] and the English *cigarette*. The classifier for a pack of cigarette is ซอง [sawng]. If you want to smoke a *cigar*, then just use the English-based Thai word, ซิการ์ [síh gah].

- ขอ **ดูดบุหรี่** หน่อย ได้ มั้ย
  kǎw **DÒOT-BÒO-RÈE** nòi dâi mái
  Can I have **a smoke**?

- ขอ สายฝน สาม **ซอง** นะ
  kǎw sǎi-fǒhn sǎhm **SAWNG** ná
  Could you grab me three **packs** of Sai Fon cigarettes?

- ชอบ ซิการ์ มาก กว่า บุหรี่
  châwp **SÍH-GAH** mâhk gwàh bòo-rèe
  I like **cigars** more than cigarettes.

Narcotics

Thais use the same word for medicine and drugs, ยา [yah]. Illegal narcotics or *addictive drugs* are called ยาเสพติด [yah sàyp dtìht]. One of the most common drugs you'll hear Thais talk about is ยาบ้า [yah bâh], which translates as *crazy drug*. Some people say it means meth and I've heard others say that is a cheap form of speed, but my guess is that there's no guaranteeing what you'll exactly get when you buy it. The Thai name for *crystal meth* comes from the English word *ice*, ไอซ์ ['ai] or ยาไอซ์ [yah 'ai]. The Thai names of other drugs are also based on the English names, *speed* is สปีด [sà bpèet], *cocaine* is โคเคน [koe kayn], the drug *ecstasy X or E* is ยาอี [yah 'ee] or ยาเอ็กซ์ [yah 'èhk] and *special K* or *ketamine* in Thai is called ยาเค [yah kay].

- ใบไม้ "Just Say No, **ยาเสพติด!**" ไม่ ง่าย อย่าง ที่ ผู้ใหญ่ คิด นะ ครับ
  bai-mái "Just Say No, **YAH-SÀYP-DTÌHT!**" mâi ngâi yàhng têe pôo-yài kít ná krúp
  Like the sign "Just Say No To **Drugs**," it's not as easy as adults think.

- ประชาชน ทั่วไป มัก จะ ตระหนัก ถึง ปัญหา **ยาบ้า**
  bprà-chah-chohn tûa-bpai múk jà dtà-nùk tǔeng bpun-hǎh **YAH-BÂH**
  The general population has probably thought about the problem with the **yah-bah drug**.

- ไอ้ ขี้ยา มา ซื้อขาย **ยาไอซ์** ข้าง ถนน นี้ ไง ทำไม วะ
  'âi kêe-yah mah súe-kăi YAH-'AI kâhng tà-nŏhn née ngai tam-mai wá
  F—kin' druggies, why the hell do they have to buy and sell **crystal meth** on this street?

The narcotics opium (and its sister drug heroin) and marijuana have a longer history in Thailand since both are grown locally. The Thai word for *opium* is ฝิ่น [fĭhn] and the colloquial translation for *smoking opium* is เป่าปี่ [bpào bpèe]. *Heroin*, a more refined version of opium, is either the English-based เฮโรอีน [hay roe 'een] or the more slangy Thai แค๊ป [káep]. Someone who's *addicted to heroin* or any drug that comes in a small white pouch or capsule can be called ติดแค๊ป [dtìht káep]. The words โช้ก [chóhk] or สปีบ [sà bpèet] can mean *to shoot up* a drug using a needle. *Marijuana* is commonly called กัญชา [gun chah], but you may refer to it as the *peace tree* in Thai or ต้นไม้แห่งสันติภาพ [dtôhn-mái hàeng sŭn-dtìh-pâhp]. If someone *itches for a drug*, then the word เงี่ยน [ngîan] is a good way to describe the itchy feeling.

- ไม่ เคย สูบ **ฝิ่น**
  mâi keri sòop FÌHN
  I've never smoked **opium** before.

- ไป เที่ยว เชียงราย เหรอ ระวัง พวก **ติดแค๊ป**
  bpai-têeo chiang-rai rěr rá-wung pûak DTÌHT-KÁEP
  You going to Chiang Rai? Well, be careful of all those **heroin addicts**.

- ไม่ ต้อง คิด มาก นี่ สูบ มั้ย **กัญชา** นี้ ได้ ปลูก เอง นะ
  mâi dtâwng kíht mâhk nêe sòop mái GUN-CHA née dâi bplòok 'ayng ná
  Don't think too much about it. Do you smoke? This is **ganja** that I planted myself.

CHAPTER 8
Money & Vice

This last chapter will give you the slang words necessary in dealing with cash and all the wonderfully terrible things that you can do with it. And like English, the Thai Language has different names for words and other things related to money. Other related vocabulary for narcotics and prostitution have been discussed in previous chapters.

Cash, Dough and Dollars

The most common term for *money* is the word เงิน [ngern] but in colloquial speech, Thais will almost always use the word ตังค์ [dtung] or ตางค์ [dtahng] depending on whether they use a long or short vowel for its pronunciation. A little bit slangy is the word กะตังค์ [gà dtung], which is nearer to *dough* or *cash* in English.

- ไม่ มี ตังค์ เลย
  mâi mee DTUNG leri
  I ain't got no **cash**.

- แก มี กะตังค์ เยอะแยะ เล่า
  gae mee GÀ-DTUNG yér-yáe lâo
  He's loaded with **cash**!

When talking about credit cards, the English word *plastic* is the basis for the Thai เงินพลาสติก [ngern plah sà dtìhk]. The Thai word for *check*, เช็ค [chéhk], also comes from the English word. If it's a *bounced check,* then it is เช็คเด้ง [chéhk dâyng] or เค็คสปริง [ché sà-bprihng]. If you're dealing with *dollars* Thai will use either ดอล [dawn] or ดอลลาร์ [dawn lah].

- ไม่ ยอม ใช้ **เงินพลาสติก** เลย
  mâi yawm chái NGERN-PLAH-SÀ-DTÌHK ler
  I just won't use **credit.**

- ผม เคย เจอ ปัญหา **เช็คเด้ง** เพราะ ไม่ ได้ มี เงิน สด เหลือ มาก อย่าง ที่ ผม คิด เอา ไว้
  pǒhm keri jer bpun-hǎh CHÉHK-DÂYNG práw mâi dâi mee ngern-sòt lǔea-mâhk yàhng têe pǒhm kíht 'ao wái
  I've encountered problems with **bounced checks** because I didn't have as much cash on hand as I thought I did.

- เสีย กี่ **ดอล** ล่ะ
  sǐa gèe DAWN lâ
  How many **dollars** did you go through?

Loaded and Rich

If you have a whole *ton of something* like cash, you might hear the word อู้ ['ôo]. A colloquial way to say that you *have money* or you are *rich* is to have a *heavy wallet,* กระเป๋าหนัก [grà bpǎo nùk]. Another way to refer to someone who is rich is คนมี [kohn mee]. The word เงินหนา [ngern nǎh] also means that you're *loaded.* You might hear the word เสี่ย [sìa] used to indicate someone who's rich. You'll often hear this one used with old rich people, like an old industrialist or an old Chinese man.

- ชอบ ลูกค้า **กระเป๋าหนัก** หล่ะ
  châwp lôok-káh GRÀ-BPǍO-NÙK là
  I like customers **with heavy wallets.**

- ต้อง มี **เงินหนา** หรือ เส้น ข้าง ใน
  dtâwng mee ngern-nǎh rǔe sâyn kâhng-nai
  You gotta be **loaded** or know someone on the inside.

- มี **เสี่ย** ให้ การ สนับสนุน การ ก่อ ม็อบ ไล่ นายก ฯ
  mee sìa hâi gahn sà-núp-sà-nǒon gahn gàw máwp lâi nah-yók
  There was an **old rich guy** who established and paid for a mob to get
  rid of the Prime Minister.

Broke, Dirt-Poor and Borrowing Money

On the other side of the spectrum are guys with no money. If you're *broke*, then
you are ถังแตก [tǔng dtàek]. If you're completely *dead broke*, then you are
หมดตูด [moth dtòot], which also means your *ass is gone*. The words ทรัพย์จาง
[súp jahng] and โรคทรัพย์จาง [rôek súp-jahng] also mean that you're *broke*.
To have absolutely no money or be *dirt-poor* means to be กรอบ [gràwp].

- ก่อน สิ้น เดือน ทำไม **ถังแตก** ทุก ที ล่ะ
  gàwn sîhn duean tam-mai TǓNG-DTÀEK tóok tee lâ
  Why is it that I'm always **broke** before the end of the month?

- แก เสีย เงิน เดือน จน **หมดตูด** มา แล้ว
  gae sǐa ngern-duean john MOTH-DTÒOT mah láeo
  He's already gone through his entire paycheck till he's **dead broke**.

- ชั้น อยาก เที่ยว แต่ **ทรัพย์จาง**
  chún yàhk têeo dtàe SÚP-JAHNG
  I wanna go out but I'm **broke**.

If you just *can't make ends meet*, then the Thai phrase ชักหน้าไม่ถึงหลัง
[chúk nâh mâi tǔeng lǔng] is fitting. If you want to call someone a sponge for
always *bumming money,* try calling him a ดาวไต [dow tǎi] instead. If that same
guy *never returns what he borrows* or likes to use something without paying
for it, then that action is called ชักดาบ [chúch dàhp], which also means *to pull
out your sword.*

- ช่วง นี้ **ชักหน้าไม่ถึงหลัง** เท่าไร นะ
  chûang-née CHÚK-NÂH-MÂI-TǓENG-LǓNG tâo-rai ná
  These days I **can't really seem to make ends meet**.

- ใคร ว่า ตำรวจ หรือ คนมีสี จะ เป็น สุดยอด ของ **ดาวไต** ก็ ถูกต้อง
  เลย
  **krai wâh dtam-rùat rǔe kohn-mee-sěe jà bpehn sòot-yâwt kǎwng
  DOW-TǍI gâw tòok-dtâwng leri**
  Whoever said that cops or military types are the epitome of **sponging
  money** were absolutely correct.

- เค้า ชอบ **ชักดาบ** กับ ทุก คน เลย
  káo châwp chúk-dàhp gùp tóok kohn leri
  He likes **to bum money off everyone and never give it back.**

Jobless

Thais have two good colloquial expressions for someone who is jobless and broke. The first one is นั่งตบยุง [nûng dtòhp yung], which means you're *jobless* and all you do is sit around smacking the mosquitoes that land on you. The second one means you're *unemployed*, เตะฝุ่น [dtày fòon], and also translates as *to kick dust*.

- ตอน นี้ ก็ ได้ แต่ **นั่งตบยุง** เพราะ ตก งาน
  dtawn-née gâw dâi dtàe NÛNG-DTÒP-YUNG práw dtòhk-ngahn
  Right now I'm unemployed cause I lost my job.

- ไม่ เคย **เตะฝุ่น** ละ
  mâi keri DTÀY-FÒON lá
  I've never been jobless.

To Embezzle and Take a Piece for Yourself

If you are rich because you've *embezzled* or *laundered money*, that is called by Thais as ยักยอก [yúk yâwk]. But you're more likely to hear a Thai call it colloquially as งาบ [ngâhp] or โอโม ['oe moe]. If you *take a piece of the pie for yourself*, use the word เม้ม [máym] from the phrases เม้มเงิน [máym ngern] or เม้มสตางค์ [máym sà-dtàhng]. If you borrow or just take money or something and *never intend to give it back*, then you are an อม ['ohm].

- ใช้ ตอนนี้ ดี กว่า น่ะ เดี๋ย คน อื่น เอา ไป **งาบ** ซะ ก่อน
  chái dtawn-née dee gwàh nâ dĕeo kohn 'ùen 'ao bpai NGÂHP sá gàwn
  It's better if we use it now before someone else comes and just **runs off with it.**

- แก **เม้ม** สตางค์ ไป ทำ อะไร อื่น ๆ ก็ ไม่ รู้
  gae MÁYM sà-dtàhng bpai tam 'à-rai 'ùen-'ùen gâw mâi róo
  I don't know if he **took a piece for himself** to go do whatever or not!

To Steal, Snatch and Pickpocket

If you straight up *steal* some money or something else, the most common word for that is ขโมย [kà mohe]. A more slang word for it is ชิว [sui]. A fun way to say *to snatch*, *to snake* or *to jack* something is อุ๊บอิ๊บ ['óop 'íhp]. If it's just little things here and there that you're stealing, then it is called จิ๊ก [jíhk].

- พอ เข้า เว็บไซท์ ไป จะ เห็น ของ ที่ เค้า **ชิว** มา ใส่ เลย
  paw kâo wéhp-sai bpai jà hěhn kǎwng têe káo sui mah sài leri
  As soon as you look at his website you're gonna see stuff that he **stole** in it.

- **จิ๊ก** ของ เล็ก ๆ น้อย ๆ จาก ออฟฟิศ ที่ ทำงาน อยู่ ก็ ไม่ เห็น มี อะไร เลย
  JÍHK kǎwng léhk-léhk nói-nói jàhk 'aw-fíht têe tam-ngahn yòo gâw mâi hěhn me 'à-rai leri
  I don't see what's so big about snaking little things here and there from the office where I work.

The word for *pickpocket* is แซ้ง [sáeng]. If you take it a step further and sneak into someone's house *to rob* them, then you did a ตัดช่องย่องเบา [dtùt châwng yâwng bao].

- เรา ถูก **แซ้ง** ล่ะ วะ
  rao tòok SÁENG lâ-wá
  I was f—kin' **pickpocketed**.

- มัน กำลัง มอง หา ทาง เข้า บ้าน เพื่อ จะ **ตัดช่องย่องเบา** เอา ของ แน่ ๆ
  mun gam-lung mawng-hǎh tahng kâo bâhn pûea jà DTÙT-CHÂWNG-YÂWNG-BAO 'ao kǎwng nâe-nâe
  That scum is looking for a way to get into the house **to sneak in and rob** stuff for sure!

To Scam, Take Advantage of, Screw Over, F—k Over and Eventually Betray

Some people don't steal, they just scam. Most of the colloquial ways of saying *to scam* or *to deceive* in Thai start with the word ต้ม [dtôhm], which also means *to boil*. The phrases ต้มจนเปื่อย [dtôhm john bpùeoi], ต้มจนสุก [dtôhm john sòok] and ต้มตุ๋น [dtôhm dtǒon] all mean *to scam* or *to take advantage of*. The word ปอกลอก [bpàwk lâwk] can mean *to screw over*, and the word ฟัน [fun] can mean *to f—k over*, especially on the price of something. You'll also hear the word

บอกผ่าน [bàwk pàhn], which means *to screw someone over a price*. The words ดัดหลัง [dùt lŭng] and หักหลัง [hùk lŭng] both mean *to sell out* or *to betray*.

- ถึง แม้ จะ มี นัก **ต้มตุ๋น** หลอก เรา ควร มี น้ำใจ ให้ กัน
  tǔeng máe jà mee núk DTÔHM-DTǑON làwk rao kuan mee nám-jai hâi gun
  Even though there are crooks trying **to scam**, we should still show generosity toward each other.

- เค้า ถูก แฟน เก่า **ปอกลอก**
  káo tòok faen gào BPÀWK-LÂWK
  He was **screwed over** by his last girlfriend.

- สำหรับ เรื่อง ราคา คนไทย มัวแต่ **ฟัน** ชาวต่างชาติ โดย เฉพาะ ฝรั่ง ที่ มา ท่องเที่ยว
  sǎm-rúp rûeang rah-kah kohn-tai mua-dtàe FUN chow-dtàhng-châht dohe-chà-páw fà-rùng têe mah tâwng-têeo
  As far as price goes, Thais love **to f—k over** foreigners, especially Westerners.

- ทำไม ต้อง **บอกผ่าน** ล่ะ
  tam-mai dtâwng BÀWK-PÀHN lâ
  Why he's gotta **inflate the price**?

- เลว มาก ไอ้ คน ที่ **ดัดหลัง** เพื่อน
  layo mâhk 'âi kohn têe DÙT-LǓNG pûean
  That's just really despicable, people that'll **sell out** their friends.

Thief, Scoundrel and Conman

If you steal, then you may be called a thief. Instead of just using the word โจร [joen] to mean *thief*, try saying โจรห้าร้อย [joen hâh rói]. That really gets across that someone's a *scoundrel*. A thief is also a ตีนแมว [dteen maeo], which also means *cat feet*. The word for *conman* or group of conmen is สิบแปดมงกุฏ [sìhp-bpàet mohng-gòot], which also means *eighteen crowns*.

- ทำ ยังงี้ รึ เดี๋ยว กลาย เป็น ไอ้ พวก **โจรห้าร้อย** วะ
  tam yung-ngée dǎeo glai bpehn 'âi pûak JOEN-HÂH-RÓI wá
  Ya doing that? Be careful 'cause you're about to become a **scoundrel**.

- ดีแมว รู้ เข้า ไป ซิว ของ ร้าน คอม ช่วง เจ้าของร้าน กลับ บ้าน
  dteen-maeo róo kâo bpai sui kǎwng ráhn kawm chûang jâo-kǎwng-ráhn glùb bâhn
  When the owner left for home the **burglar** knew how to get into the electronics store and rob it.

- นี่ ระวัง น่ะ เป็น แก๊ง กะเทย **สิบแปดมงกุฎ**
  nêe rá-wung nâ bpehn gáeng gà-teri sìhp-bàet-mong-gòot
  Watch out! It's a gang of ladyboy **conman**.

The Mob

The Thais have incorporated the word *mafia* into their vocabulary. The mob is also called a *group of dogs*, หมาหมู่ [mǎh mòo]. The phrase พงกเสือ พวกตะเข้ [pûak sǔea pûak dtà-kây] also means the same thing.

- ตำรวจ จับ แก๊ง **มาเฟีย** ชาว อินเดีย
  dtam-rùat jùp gáeng MAH-FIA chow 'ihn-dia
  The police nabbed the Indian mafia.

- ชอบ อยู่ เป็น **หมาหมู่**
  châwp yòo bpehn MǍH-MÒO
  I like coming as a **gang**.

Crooked Cops and Jails

Thais call a crooked cop a โจรในเครื่องแบบ [joen nau krûeang bàep], which means *crook in a uniform*. If it's a *cop that gets out of line* every once in a while but could be as dirty as a โจรในเครื่องแบบ [joen nai krûeang bàep], then he is a ตำรวจนอกแถว [dtam-rùat nâwk tǎeo]. When you do get caught for doing something bad, you may be sent to คุก [kook], โรงพัก [roeng púk] or ห้องกง [hâwng gohng]. These all mean *prison* or *jail* but the last one is a slang word based on the word *Hong Kong*. If you have any connection with the cops, military, the mob or government or have filial connection with people in power, the Thais call this มีเส้น [mee sâyn].

- เรา เกลียด **โจรในเครื่องแบบ** มาก ที่ สุด
  rao glìat JOEN-NAI-KRÛEANG-BÀEP mâhk têe sòot
  I hate **dirty cops**.

- แก ถูก ไอ้ ตำรวจ ส่ง ไป **ห้องกง** ล่ะ วะ
  gae tòok 'âi dtam-rùat sòhng bpai HÂWNG-GOHNG lâ-wá
  The f—kin' cops sent him to **the slammer**.

- เค้า ได้รับ งาน ใหม่ เพราะ **มีเส้น**
  káo dâi-rúp ngahn mài práw MEE-SÂYN
  He got a new job 'cause he **knew someone on the inside**.

To Break the Rules, Counterfeit, Scam a Free Ride, Kidnap and Find a Scapegoat

If you do *break the rules* or go against the grain, Thais have a phrase for it, ชกใต้เข็มขัด [chóhk dtâi kěhm kùt], which also means *to hit below the belt*. If *counterfeiting* is your game, you are doing ย้อมแมว [yám maeo], which also means *to dye a cat*. Anything that is a counterfeit or fake is called เก [gǎy]. If you're able *to scam a ticket for half price*, Thais call it ตีตั๋วเด็ก [dtee dtua dèhk] and if you're able *to get a free ride* all together, this is called เต้า [dtâo]. A slangy way to say *to kidnap* is อุ้ม ['ôom] and if you ever need a *scapegoat* for any of these crimes, they're called แพะรับบาป [páe rúp bàhp].

- ระวัง ร้าน **ย้อมแมว** ขาย น่ะ ไม่ เอา ของ เก๊ ละ
  rá-wung ráhn YÁWM-MAEO kǎi nâ mâi 'ao kǎwng GǍY LÁ
  Watch out for this shop selling **counterfeits**. I don't want anything **fake**.

- เป็น สมาชิก ก็ เลย **ตีตั๋วเด็ก** ได้ ง่าย
  bpehn sà-mǎh-chíhk gâw leri DTEE-DTǓA-DÈHK dâi ngâi
  I'm a member so it's easy for me **to get a ticket at half price**.

- **เต้า** รถ บัส มา เหรอ
  DTÂO róht bùs mah rěr
  So ya **snagged a free ride** on the bus here?

- เรื่อง นี้ เค้า เป็น **แพะรับบาป** ล่ะ มั้ง
  rûeng née káo bpehn PÁE-RÚP-BÀHP lâ-múng
  In this case she's a **scapegoat**, I think.

Going Out of Business, the Stock Market and Financial Crisis

When a company *leases*, changes hands or liquidates, you'll often hear Thais use the word เซ้ง [sáyng]. Another Chinese word that's made it into the Thai vocabulary to mean *to go out of business* is เจ๊ง [jáyng]. The big one hit Thailand in the summer of 1997. Called the Asian Financial Crisis, it started with the devaluation of the Thai baht. Some Thais refer to this event as ต้มยำกุ้ง [dtôhm yam gôong] or ต้มยำกุ้งดีซีส [dtôhm yam gôong dee-sêet], named after the spicy Thai soup, *tom yam gung*. On the other hand, a more colloquial way to call the *stock market* is ตลาดหุ้น [dtà-làht hôon].

- ต้องการ **เซ้ง** ร้าน ขาย เสื้อผ้า หน้า ม.เกษตร ราคา ถูก มี ลูกค้า ประจำ สนใจ สอบถาม รายละเอียด ได้ ที่...
  dtâwng-gahn SÁYNG ráhn kǎi sûea-pâh nâh maw gà-sàyt rah-kah tòok mee lôok-káh bprà-jam sǒhn-jai sàwp-tǎhm rai-lá-'iat dâi têe...
  Clothes for **sale**! In front of Kasetsart University! Good Price! Steady customers! For further details interested parties contact here at…

- บริษัท นั้น **เจ๊ง** ไป แล้ว
  baw-ríh-sùt nún JÁYNG bpai láeo
  That company already **went out of business**.

- สาเหตุ ที่ ทำ ให้ เกิด **ต้มยำกุ้งดีซีส** นั้น มี ด้วย กัน หลาย ประการ
  sǎh-hàyt têe tam-hâi gèrt DTÔHM-YAM-GÔONG-DEE-SÊET nún mee dôoi-dun lǎi bprà-gahn
  There are many causes for the start of the **Asian Financial Crisis**.

To Argue Over an Issue and Fight

A correct way to say *to have an argument* with someone is เถียง [tǐang] or the more slangy ซัด [sóht]. If the argument reaches the point of *physical fighting*, Thais will often use ชกมวย [cóhk mooi], which also means *to box*. Two more lyrical versions for the word *to fight* are ตะริดติ๊ดชิ่ง [dtà ríht dtíht chûeng] and ตี้ตาต่าตี้ [dtée dtah dtàh dtée].

- **เถียง** กะ แฟน เหรอ
  TǏANG gà faen rěr
  Were ya **arguing** with your girlfriend?

- บางที วันเสาร์ ก็ ตอก เหล้าขาว กับ เพื่อน ไป ก่อ เรื่อง **ตะริดติ๊ดชิ่ง** ข้างนอก
  bahng-tee wun-sǎo gâw dtàwk lâo-kǒw gùp pûean bpai gàw rûeang DTÀ-RÍHT-DTÍHT-SÛENG kâhng-nâwk
  Sometimes on Saturdays I'll get wasted with the boys, go start some shit, **get into fights** outside.

To Beat, Punch, Hit, Scratch and Claw

When you start using words like เฉิ่ม [chèrm], then the fighting is getting rougher. The word means *to beat* or *to punch*. The word ตุน [dtún] also means *to hit* or *to beat*, but I don't hear that one used very often. The word ฟ้อนเล็บ [fáwn léhp] means *to scratch* or *to claw*. I've only ever heard that one used to describe a girl's fight.

- แก พูด มาก เดี๋ยว จะ **เฉิ่ม** ปาก แก ฟะ
  gae pôot mâhk dĕeo jà CHÈRM bpàhk gae fá
  You f—kin' talk a lot. Watch out, I'm going to **beat** your face in.

- ชอบ ดู สาว **ฟ้อนเล็บ** กัน อย่าง แรง
  châwp doo săo FÁWN-LÉHP gun yàhng raeng
  I love to watch chicks **scratch and claw** at each other.

To F—k Up, Terrorize and Knock Out

Use the word โซ่ย [sôhe] to say that you really just destroyed somebody or that you *f—ked him up*. It also means *to beat to death*. The phrase รุมกินโต๊ะ [room gihn dtóe] means to terrorize as a posse or *to beat up as a gang*. Sometimes you'll hear the English word for *knock* as in *to knock out* used in Thai as well, น็อก [náwk]. Lastly, the word ตื๊บ [dtûep] means *to crush*.

- **โซ่ย** มัน ซะ!
  SÔHE mun sá
  F—k him up!

- เค้า โดน **น็อก** เลย
  káo doen NÁWK leri
  He was totally **knocked out**.

To Gamble and Cheat

The most common word for *gamble* in Thai is พนัน [pá nun] and one of the most common games you'll see being played in villages is ไฮโล [hai loe], which is a type of *dice game* similar to craps. If they play the *state lottery*, the colloquial way to say it is หวย [hǒoi], but sometimes you'll hear Thais use the Thai version of the English word *lottery*, ลอตเตอรี่ [lâwt der rêe]. If you hear the word เล่นไพ่ [lâyn pâi] then that means people are *gambling with cards*. They could also just be playing cards but I've never met a Thai who knew how to use a card deck for anything other than to gamble. The word ญาติมิตร [yâht míht] can also mean *to play cards*. If you cheat at any of these games, you are ลักไก [lúk gài].

- เล่น การ พนัน **ไฮโล** กัน อยู่ มี นัก **พนัน** จำนวน มาก เมื่อ ตำรวจ จับ
  lâyn gahn pá-nun HAI-LOE gun yòo mee núk-pá-nun jam-nuan mâhk mûea dtam-rùat jùp
  A large number of **gamblers** were playing **Thai craps** when the police caught them.

- ทำไม ชอบ ซื้อ **หวย** จัง
  tam-mai châwp súe HǑOI jung
  Why do you like **to play the lottery** so much?

- เล่นไพ่ ไม่ เป็น อะ
  LÂYN-PÂI mâi bpehn 'à
  I don't **play cards** very well.

Cards and Poker

The *cards* themselves are called ไพ่ [pâi] and the game of *poker* is called ไพ่ป๊อก [pâi bpáwk]. *Clubs* are called ดอกจิก [dàhk jìhk]. *Spades* are โพดำ [poe dam] and *diamonds* and *hearts* are หลามตัด [lǎhm dtùt] and หัวใจ [hǔa jai], respectively. If you're having a *good hand* or *good luck*, then Thais call it มือขึ้น [mue kûen]. If it's a *bad hand* or *bad luck*, then it's called มือตก [mue dtòhk]. Thais have a proverb for this luck, ตาดีก็ได้ ตาร้ายก็เสีย [dtah-dee-gâw-dâi dtah-rái-gâw-sǐa], which basically means *You win some, you lose some!*

- ไม่ ชอบ เล่น **ไพ่ป๊อก**
  mâi châwp lâyn PÂI-BPÀWK
  I don't like to play **poker**.

- เมื่อไร จะ มี มือขึ้น ล่ะ
  mûe-rai jà mee MUE-KÛEN lâ
  When am I ever gone have some **good luck**?

English – Thai Word List

A

a lot of *adj./adv.* ตุน [dtun], ติ๊ม [dtuem], อึน ['uen], เยอะ (เยอะ ๆ) [yér], เยอะแยะ [yér yáe], สุดตีน [sòot dtèen], อื๊อจือเหลียง ['ûe jue lǐang], อื๊อซ่า ['ûe sâh], แฮ [hae]

ability *n.* น้ำยา [nám yah]

about *adv.* ซะ [sá], ซัก [súk]

about to *adv.* กะลัง [gà lung]

absent-minded *adj.* ซึมกะทือ [suem gà tue]

absolutely beautiful *adj.* เช้งกะเด๊ะ [cháyng gà dáy]

A/C (air conditioning) *n.* แอร์ ['ae]

to accidentally do something that belies your gayness *v.* เต๋าแตก [dtǎo dtàek]

to act a fool *v.* งี่เง่า [ngêe ngâo], ทำตัวงี่เง่า [tam dtua ngêe ngâo]

to act like a player (playboy) *v.* ขี้หลี [kêe lěe]

to act like you're best friends *v.* ตีสติ๊ก [dtee sà dtíhk]

to act out *v.* แอ๊ค ['áek]

to add everything (som-tam) *v.* แซ่บ [sâep]

addicted only to *v.* มั่วแต่ [mua dtàe]

adult not acting his age *n.* เด็กหนวด [dèhk nùa]

adulterer *n.* ชู้ [chóo]

to advertise *v.* ตีปี๊บ [dtee bpéep]

again *adv.* อีก ['ìk]

Again?! *phr.* เอาอีกแล้ว ['ao 'èek láeo]

to agree *v.* โอคา ['oe kay]

Ah? *interj.* อ๊ะ ['á], โอ๊ะ ['óh]

Ah!/Ahhh! *interj.* อา ['ah], เอ ['ay], ฮะ [há], ว๊าย (ว๊าย) [wái]

Ahhh, come on. *part.* เหอะน่า [hèr nâh], เถอะน่า ['èr nâh]

aimlessly *adv.* โต๋เต๋ [dtǒe dtǎy]

air-head *n.* แอร์เฮ้ด ['ae hâyt]

air hostess *n.* นางฟ้า [nahng fáh]

Alas! *interj.* โธ่ [tôe]

album *n.* อัลบั้ม ['un bûn]

alcohol *n.* เหล้า [lâo], แอลกอฮอล์ ['aen gaw haw]

all *adj.* ติ๊ม [dtuem]

all messed up *adj./v.* มั่ว [mûa]

already *adv.* ละ [lâ], ซะแล้ว [sá láeo]

already *part.* ซะที [sá tee]

Alright! *part.* นะ [nâ], น่า [nâh]

Alright! *interj.* เออ ['er]

Alright already! *interj.* อ้า ['âh]

Alright already, I got it! *interj.* เออน่ะ (เออน่า) ['er nâ]

Alright then! *phr.* ดีละ [dee lá], เอาละ ['ao lá]

also (shows surprise) *adv.* ซะด้วย [sá dôoi]

American *adj.* มะกัน (ม'กัน) [ma gun]

amphetamine *n.* ยาบ้า [yah bâh]

anal sex *v.* เข้าประตูหลัง [kâo bprà dtoo lǔng]

and *prep.* กะ [gà]

Andaman coast of Thailand *n.* ทะเลหน้านอก [tá lay nâh nâwk]

to annoy *v.* ติ๊ม [dtuem], บังอาจ [bung 'àht]

annoying kid **n.** หำน้อย [hăm nói]

Arab (derogatory) **n.** แขก [kàek]

arbitrarily **adv.** ตื้อ ๆ [dûe dûe]

to argue over an issue **v.** ซด [sóht]

around here **adv.** แถวนี้ [tăeo née]

to arouse sexually **v.** ปลุกอารมณ์ [bplòok 'ah rohm]

arrogant but really small shit **adj.** ตัวเท่าลูกหมา [dtua tâo look mǎh]

as **conj.** กอ [gâw]

as little as **adv.** ซัก [súk], ซะ [sá]

Asian Financial Crisis of 1997 that started in Thailand **n.** ต้มยำกุ้งดีซีส [dtôhm yam gôong dee dêet], ต้มยำกุ้ง [dtôhm yam gôong]

to ask (rudely) what class someone comes from **phr.** ตักน้ำใส่กะโหลกชะโงกดูเงา [dtùk nám sài gà lòek chá ngôek doo ngao]

ass **n.** ตูด [dtòot], ดาก [dàhk]

Asshole! **interj.** ชาติหมา [châht mǎh]

at all **adv.** เลย [léri], เลย [leri]

at any rate... **adv.** ยังไงก็ตาม [yung ngai gâw dtahm]

at ease about **v.** เชื่อดี [chûea dee]

at what time? **adv.** เมื่อไร [mûe rai]

attendant **n.** เบ [báy]

attention grabbing **adj.** เอ้ว [háyo]

to avoid your work/duties **v.** โดด [dòet], โดดร่ม [dòet rôhm]

awesome **adj.** เจ๋ง [jǎyng], เจ๋งเป้ง [jǎyng bpâyng], เด็ดดวง [dèht duang], เด็ดสะระตี่ [dèht sà rá dtèe]

awkward **adj.** เชย [choei], ซกมก [sóhk móhk]

awesome **adj.** เด้ย [dtêri], เช็ด [chéht]

B

baby **n.** ที่รัก [têe rúk]

to back up **v.** ซัพพอร์ต [súb páwt]

background (class) **n.** หัวนอนปลายตีน [hǔa nawn bplai dteen],

หัวนอนปลายเท้า [hǔa nawn bplai táo]

backpacker **n.** ฝรั่งขี้นก [fà rùng kêe nóhk]

to backtrack on forward progress **v.** ถอยหลังเข้าคลอง [tǒi lǔng kâo klawng]

bad (sucks) **adv.** ห่วย [hòoi], ห่วยแตก [hòoi dtàek]

bad blood **n.** ซีฟิลิส [síh fíh líht]

bad tempered **adv.** งอนตุ๊บป่อง [ngawn dtóop bpàwng]

to badger **v.** ตื้ม [dtúem]

Bah! **interj.** ถุยส์ (ถุย) [tǒuie]

bald (as in pubic hair) **adj.** เกรียน [grian]

bald (as in your own ugly head) **adj.** โป๊งเหน่ง [bpóeng nàyng]

balls **n.** ไข่ [kài], ไข่ห่า [kài hǎm], เจี๊ยว [jéeo], ตุ่ม [dtôom], ห่า [hǎm]

ball(s) **cl.** ลูก [look]

bar **n.** บาร์ [bah], ผับ [pùb]

bar girl **n.** ผู้หญิงบาร์ [pôo yǐng bah]

bar that a girl works out of **n.** บาร์ผี [bah pěe]

barbecue, BBQ **n.** บาร์บีคิว [bah bee kiu]

to bark like a dog **v.** เห่า [hào]

bartender **n.** บาร์เทนเดอร์ [bah tayn der]

bartender (girl) **n.** บาร์เทนดี้ [bah tayn dêe]

Bastard! **interj.** ชาติหมา [châht mǎh], ไอ้เวร ['âi wayn]

(to) be against change **v.** ถอยหลังเข้าคลอง [tǒi lǔng kâo klawng]

(to) be all horned up **v.** เสียว [sěeo]

(to) be in (cool) **adj.** อินเตอร์ ['in dter]

(to) be interested in **v.** สน [sǒhn]

(to) be into your new toys **v.** เห่อของใหม่ [hèr kǎwng mài]

(to) be involved together **v.** มีอะไรกัน [mee 'a rai gun]

(to) be okay *v.* โอคา ['oe kay]

(to) be on the job search (after loosing your job) *v.* เตะฝุ่น [dtày fòon]

(to) be on top *v.* อยู่ข้างบน [yòo kâhng bohn]

(to) be one way only *v.* เอาแต่ ['ao dtàe]

(to) be sloshed *v.* เมาดิบ [mao dìhp]

(to) be sure of *v.* เชื่อดี [chûea dee]

(to) be unbathed *v.* ซักแห้ง [súk hâeng]

(to) be yourself *v.* เป็นตัวของตัวเอง [bpehn dtua kǎwng dtua ayng]

(to) beat *v.* เฉิ่ม [chèrm]

(to) beat to death *v.* โซย [sôhe]

beautiful (because of make-up or dress) *adj.* เช้งวับ [cháyng wúp], เช้ง [cháyng]

(to) become an old maid *v.* ขึ้นคาน [kûen kahn]

beer koozie *n.* คอนด้อม [kawn dâwm]

beer snacks *n.* กับแก้ม [gùp gâem]

behind the times *adj.* ตกรุ่น [dtòhk rôon]

best *adj.* เต๊ย [dtêri]

best friends *v.* เพื่อนซี้ [pûean sée], เพื่อนซี้ปึ๊ก [pûean sée bpûek], ซี้แหง [sée hǎeng]

the best piece *n.* ชิ้นปลามัน [chíhn bplah mun]

to betray *v.* คัดหลัง [dùt lǔng]

big-boned *adj.* อวบ ['ùap]

bikini *n.* บิกินี่ [bìh gìh nee]

(a) bird in the hand is worth two in the bush *phr.* กำขี้ดีกว่ากำตด [gam kêe dee gwàh dtòht]

birth control pills *n.* ยาคุม [yah koom]

birthday suit *n.* ชุดวันเกิด [chóot wun gèrt]

bisexual/bi *adj.* ไบ [bai]

bitch *n.* ยัย [yai], ยัยคน [yai kohn], บิทช [bìht chá], นัง [nung]

(to) bitch at an old person *v.* ถอนหงอก [tǎwn ngàwk]

a blast! *adj.* ซี้ดปาก [séet bpàhk]

blog *n.* บล็อก [blàwk]

blood brothers *v.* ซี้แหง [sée hǎeng], เพื่อนซี้ปึ๊ก [pûean sée bpûek], เพื่อนซี้ [pûean sée]

blue balls *n.* อารมณ์ค้าง ['ah rohm káhng]

boastful *adj.* ขี้โม้ [kêe móh]

body *cl.* ตัว [dtua]

boo-hoo *op.* โฮ [hoe]

bored outta your mind *v.* เซ็ง [sehng]

to borrow and not give back *v.* อม ['ohm]

to B.O.S. *v.* กินสตรอร์เบอร์รี่ [gin sa dtraw ber ree], ตอแหล [dtaw lǎe]

boss *n.* บอสส์ [báwt]

to bother *v.* แหย่ม [yàem]

bounced check *n.* เช็คเด้ง [chéhk dâyng]

bowling *n.* ทอยแก่ [toi gàen], โบว์ลิ่ง [boe lîhng]

box *n.* นาผืนน้อย [nah pǔen nói], หี [hěe], อีเฉาะ ['ee chaw], อีโมะ ['ee móe]

to box *v.* ตุ๊น [dtúo]

the boy who cried wolf *n.* เด็กเลี้ยงแกะ [dèhk líang gàe]

boyfriend *n.* แฟน [faen]

to brag *v.* ฝอย [fǒi]

bragging *adj.* เก่งแต่ปาก [gàyng dtàe bpàhk]

brand-new *adj.* ถอดด้าม [tàwt dâhm]

brat *n.* ลูกกระจ๊อก [lôok grà jáwk]

brazen *adv.* หวือหวา [wǔe wǎh]

(to) break (as in hit the breaks on your car) *v.* เบรก [bràyk]

(to) break off relations *v.* ตัดเชือก [dtùt chûeak], ตัดเป็นตัดตาย [dtùt bpehn dtùt dtai], ตัดหางปล่อยวัด [dtùt hǎhng bplòi wút]

breasts *n.* นม [nohm]

breeze (easy) *adj.* สบายมาก [sà bai mâk]

bribery *adv./n.* ใต้โต๊ะ [dtâi dtóh]

bride price *n.* ค่าสินสอด
[kâh sǐhn sàwt]

(to) bring people's attention to something *v.* ตีปี๊บ [dtee bpéep]

(to) bring sand to the beach
(as in to waste effort/time) *phr*
เอามะพร้าวห้าวไปขายสวน

(to) bring up an issue in order to move
forward *v.* ชูธง [choo tohng]

(to) bring up an old subject *v.* ฉายซ้ำ
[chǎi sám]

broke *v.* ถังแตก [tǔng dtàek],
ทรับย์จาง [súp jahng],
โรคทรัพย์จาง [rôek súp jahng]

brownnose *v.* เลียตูด [lia dtòot],
เลียแขนเลียขา [lia kǎen lia kǎh]

brutal *adj.* แสบ [sàep]

buck (USD) *n.* ดอล [dawn],
ดอลลาร์ [dawn lah]

(to) bullshit *v.* ตอแหล [dtaw lǎe],
กินสตรอร์เบอร์รี่ [gin sa dtraw ber
ree], แหกตา [hàek dtah]

bummed *adj.* จอย [jǒi]

(to) bump tacos *v.* ตีจิ๋ม [dtee chìng]

(to) burn the midnight oil *adv./v.* โต้รุ่ง
[dtóe rôong], อดตาหลับขับตานอน
['òht dtah lùp kùp dtah nawn]

bush (pubic hair) *n.* หมอย [mǒi]

bush (vagina) *n.* นาผืนน้อย [nah
pǔen nói], อีเฉาว ['ee chaw]

busily *adv.* ตัวเป็นเกลียว [dtua bpehn
gleeo]

but *conj.* ตะว่า [dtà wâh],
ทว่า [tá wâh]

but only *adv.* ชะ [sá], ชัก [súk]

but only a bit *adv.* ชักนิด [súk nít]

but only once *adv.* ชะที [sá tee],
ชักที [súk tee]

butch gay guy *n.* คิง [kihng]

butch lesbian *n.* ทอม [tawm]

butt *n.* ตูด [dtòot]

to butt f—k *v.* อัดตูด ['ùt dtòot],
เอาตูด ['ao dtòot]

to butt f—k (male on male) *v.*
อัดถั่วดำ ['ùt tùa dam]

to butt in *v.* บังอาจ [bung 'àht],
ทะเท่อทะล่า [tá-lêr tá-lâh]

to buy a ticket for half price *v.*
ตีตั๋วเด็ก [dtee dtǔa dèhk]

C

to call a spade a spade *phr.*
ขวานผ่าซาก [kwǎhn pàh sâhk]

can't find the right words to say *v.*
ตันคอหอย [dtun kaw hǒi]

can't get it up *v.* นกเขาไม่ขัน
[nók kǎo mâi kun]

to care *v.* สน [sǒhn]

to care about *v.* แคร์ [kae]

careless *adj.* ชี้ชั้ว [sée súa], เซ่อซ่า
[sêr sâh]

carelessly *adv.* ส่งเดช [sòhng dàyt]

cash *n.* กะตังค์ [gà dtung], สะตังค์ [sà
dtung], ตังค์ [dtung], ตางค์ [dtang]

celebrity *n.* ดารา [dah rah]

cell phone *n.* มือถือ [mue tǔe]

to censor *v.* เซ็นเซอร์ [sehn sêr]

certain *v.* ชัวร์ [chua]

certainly *adv.* แน่ [nâe], แหงแซะ
[ngǎe sáe], แหง [ngǎe], แหง๋น ๆ
[ngǎen ngǎen]

champagne *n.* แชมเปญ [chaem
bpayn]

change *n.* กะตังค์ [gà dtung]

to change hands *v.* เซ้ง [sáyng]

to change often *v.* ชักเข้าชักออก
[chúk kâo chúk 'àhk]

to change your citizenship *v.* โอนชาติ
['oen chat]

chaotic *adj.* เซ่อแดก [sêr dàek]

charge card *n.* เงินพลาสติก [ngern
plah sà dtìk]

charming *adj.* มีเสน่ห์ [mee sà này]

to chase the dragon *v.* เป่าปี่ [bpào bpèe]

to chastise nonstop *v.* ด่าเป็นไฟ [dàh bpehn fai]

chauffeur *n.* โชเฟอร์ [choh fer]

cheap (sucks) *adv.* ห่วย [hòoi], ห่วยแตก [hòoi dtàek]

a cheat *n.* ขี้โกง [kêe gohng]

(to) cheat on somebody *v.* นอกใจ [nâwk jai]

(to) cheat on your husband *v.* คบชู้ [kóhp chóo], คบชู้สู่ชาย [kóhp chóo sòo chai]

(to) cheat on your wife *v.* เป็นชู้ [bpehn chóo]

(to) cheat out of *v.* ตุ๋น [dtŏon]

(to) cheat someone out of something *v.* ต้ม [dtôhm], ต้มจนเปื่อย [dtôhm johm bpùeoi]

to check *v.* เช็ก (เช็ค) [chéhk]

to cheer on *v.* เชียร์ [chia], เชลียร์ [chá lia]

to cheat on your husband *v.* มีชู้ [mee chóo]

chic *adj.* เท่ [tâh]

chick *n.* สาว [săo], นัง [nung]

chicken (coward) *n.* หน้าตัวเมีย [nâh dtua mia]

Chinese person (derogatory) *n.* เจ๊ก [jáyk]

chlamydia *n.* โรคหนองในเทียม [rôek năwng nai tiam], หนองในเทียม [năwng nai tiam]

to chow down *v.* โซ้ย [sóoe]

Christ! *interj.* ฉิบหาย [chìhp hăi]

chubby *adj.* อวบ ['ùap]

chubby (for women) *adj.* สบึม (สบึมส์) [sà buem]

to chug *v.* ดวด [dùat]

cigar *n.* ซิการ์ [síh gah]

cigarettes *n.* ยา [yah], ยากาแร็ต [yah gah ráeht]

circumcised *v.* ขลิบ [kà lìhp]

the clam (chlamydia) *n.* หนองในเทียม [năwng nai tiam]

the clap (gonorrhea) *n.* โรคหนองใน [rôek năwng nai], หนองใน [năwng nai]

class and lineage *n.* หัวนอนปลายตีน [hŭa nawn bplai dteen], หัวนอนปลายเท้า [hŭa nawn bplai táo]

claw *v.* ฟ้อนเล็บ [fáwn léhp]

to click (using a mouse) *v.* คลิ้ก (คลิ๊ค) [klíhk]

clear *adj.* ถนัดถนี่ [tà nùt tà neè]

to climb the career/social/corporate ladder *v.* ไต่เต้า [dtài dtâo]

climax *n.* จุดสุดยอด [jòot soot yâwt]

to climax quickly *v.* ฟิน [fihn]

clit *n.* แตด [klít dtaw rít], คลิตอริส [klít dtaw rít], เม็ดละมุด [mét lá moot]

clitoris *n.* คลิตอริส [klít dtaw rít], เม็ดละมุด [mét lá moot]

club *n.* คลับ [klúp], ดิสโก้ [dìht sà gôe], ดิสโก้เธค [dìht sà gôe tâyk], เธค (เทก) [tâyk]

clubs (playing cards) *n.* ดอกจิก [dàwk jìhk], ไพดอกจิก [pâi dáwk jìht]

clueless (esp. about girls) *adj.* ซื่อบื้อ [sûe bûe]

clumsy *adj.* ซกมก [sóhk móhk]

cocaine *n.* โคเคน [koe kayn], ยาโคเคน [yah koe kayn]

cocktail waitress *n.* บาร์เทนดี้ [bah tayn dêe]

coke *n.* โคเคน [koe kayn]

to collect too much taxes *v.* ถอนขนห่าน [tăwn kŏhn hàhn]

college *n.* มหาลัย [má hăh lai]

come ahhhn now *part.* นะ [ná]

to come on as a good buddy *v.* ตีสนิท [dtee sà dtíhk]

to commit adultery (for men) *v.* เป็นชู้ [bpehn chóo]

to commit adultery (for women) *v.* เล่นชู้ [lâyn chóo]

compatible *adj.* ดวงสมพงศ์ [duang sŏhm pohng]

to complain *v.* ว่า [wâh]

complete boredom *v.* ซะเบื่อ [sá bùea]

complete shit *adj.* ระย่า [rá yum]

completely *adv.* เต็มเปา [dtehm bpao], เต็มร้อย [dtehm rói], เต็มรัก [dtehm rúk], ซะ [sá]

computer *n.* คอม [kawm]

condom *n.* ถุงยาง [tŏong yahng], คอนด้อม [kawn dâwm], ปลอก [bplàwk]

concentrating only on *v.* มัวแต่ [mua dtàe]

concert *n.* คอนเสิร์ต [kawn sert]

concubine *n.* นางบำเรอ [nahng bam rer]

confused *adj.* เซ่อแดก [sêr dàek]

confused to death *adj.* เง่ง [ngehng]

conservative perspective *n./adj.* ฝ่ายขวา [fài kwăh], เอียงขวา ['iang kwăh], หัวโบราณ [hŭa boe rahn]

(to) console one's self *v.* ปลอบตัวเอง [bplàwp dtua ayng]

(to) contract/compress the vagina *v.* เม้ม [máym], ขมิบ [kà mìhp]

conveniently *adv.* ฉลุย [chà lŏuie]

cool *adj.* จ๊าบ [jáhp], เจ๋ง [jăyng], แจ๋ว [jăeo], เจ๋งเป้ง [jăyng bpâyng], เด้น [dêrn], เท่ [tâh], มะ [má], เริด (เริ่ด) [rêrt]

cooter *n.* เต่า [dtào], หอย [hŏi]

cop who breaks the rules *n.* ตำรวจนอกแถว [dtam rùat nâwk tăeo]

Correct? *adv.* ใช่มั้ย (ใช่มั้ย) [châi mái]

could ya *part.* นะ [ná], นา [nah], หน่อยซิ [nòi síh]

country (hick) *adj.* บ้านนอก ๆ [bâhn náwk bâhn nâwk]

course *n.* คอร์ส [káwt]

cow (fat) *n.* โอ่งต่อขา ['òeng dtàw kăh], อิ่งอ่างทะเล ['ùeng àhng tá lay]

coward *n.* หน้าตัวเมีย [nâh dtua mia]

cowardly *adj.* แหยแฝน [yăe fàen]

crabs *n.* โลน [loen]

crack head *n.* ขี้ยา [kêe yah]

to cram for a test *v.* ติว [dtiu]

crap *n.* ขี้ [kêe]

(to) crap *v.* อึ ['ùe], ขี้ [kêe]

crap load *adj./adv.* เยอะ (เยอะ ๆ) [yér], เยอะแยะ [yér yáe]

crappy *adj.* ส่ว [sùa]

craps (Thai version) *n.* ไฮโล [hai loe]

crazy *adj.* บ้า [bâh], บ้า ๆ บอ ๆ [bâh bâh baw baw], บ๋อง [báwng], ดิ๋งต๋อง (ดิงต๋อง) [dtĭhng dtăwng], เซี้ยว [séeo], ต๋อง [dtăwng], ไม่เต็มบาท [mâi dtehm bàht]

crazy f—k *n.* ไอ้บ้า ['âi bâh]

credit card *n.* เงินพลาสติก [ngern plah sà dtĭk]

creepy facial expression *n.* หน้าหม้อ [nâh mâw]

(to) criticize *v.* ว่า [wâh]

(to) criticize *phr.* ถ้ามือไม่พายอย่าเอาเท้าราน้ำ [tâh mue mâi pai yàh 'ao táo rah nám]

(to) croak (die) *v.* ซี้ [sée]

crooked *adj.* ขี้โกง [kêe gohng]

crooked cop *n.* ตำรวจนอกแถว [dtam rùat nâwk tăeo]

crummy *adj.* ส่ว [sùa]

crush *n.* กิ๊ก [geek]

(to) crush *v.* ตื๊บ [dtûep]

(to) cry *v.* เป่าปี่ [bpàa bpèe]

culprit *n.* ตัวเอ๋ [dtua 'ây]

cum *n.* น้ำกาม [nám gahm], น้ำเงี่ยน [nám ngîan], น้ารัก [nám rúk], ต๋อง [dtáwng], สำเร็จความใคร่ [săm réht kwahm krâi], เสร็จ [sèht]

to cum *v.* ถึง [tŭeng]

to cum already *v.* ฟิน [fihn]

(to) cum outside *v.* หลั่งข้างนอก [lùng kâhng nâwk]

cunnilingus *n.* ยกซด [yóhk sóht], ปากช่องคลอง [bpàhk châwng klawng], ลงลิ้น [lohng lín]

cunt *n.* อีโมะ ['ee móe], อีเฉาะ ['ee chaw], หม้อ [mâw], หอย [hǒi], หี [hěe], จิ๋ม [jǐm], นาผืนน้อย [nah pǔen nói]

to curse *v.* เห่า [hào]

to curse quickly *v.* ด่าเป็นไฟ [dah bpehn fai]

cute *adj.* จ๊าบ [jáhp]

cute (in an innocent way) *adj.* คิกขุ [kíhk kòo], คิกขุ อาโนเนะ [kíhk kòo 'ah noe náy]

cruel *adj.* แสบ [sàep]

crummy *adv.* ห่วย [hòoi], ห่วยแตก [hòoi dtàek]

crystal meth *n.* ยาไอศ์ [yah 'ai], ไอศ์ (ไอส์) ['ai]

D

daft *adj.* งั่ง [ngûng]

damn *part.* ไอ ['âi], อี ['ee], ฟะ [fá], วะ (ว) [wá], หา [hàh]

Damn! ฉิบหาย [chihp hǎi], บ๊ะ [bá]

Damn American(s) *interj.* ไอ้กัน ['âi gun]

Damn Jap! (derogatory) *interj.* ไอ้ยุ่น ['âi yôon]

Damn you! *interj.* ไอ้ห่า ['âi hàh]

Dammit! *interj.* บ๊ะ [bá], ฉิบหาย [chìhp hǎi], วะ [wá], ไอ้ห่า ['âi hàh]

to dance to really hard *v.* ดิ้น [dîhn]

daredevil *adj.* เพี้ยว [féeo]

dark *adj.* ดำมิดหมี่ [dam míht měe]

dark-skinned women *n.* ดำตับเป็ด [dam dtùp bpèht]

dead *v.* เด๊ด [déht]

dead as a doornail *v.* เด๊ดสะมอเร่ [déht sà maw rây]

dead tired *adj.* เหงื่อตกกีบ [ngùea dtòhk gèep]

dear *part.* เอย ['éri]

(to) debauch *v.* มั่วเซ็กซ์ [mûa séhk]

debutant *n.* ดอกฟ้า [dàwk fáh]

deceitful *adj.* ขี้โกง [kêe gohng]

(to) decide absolutely *v.* ฟันธง [fun tohng]

deep (profound) *adj.* ถึงกึ๋น [tǔeng gǔen]

definitely *adv.* เลย [leri], เล้ย [léri], แน่ [nâe], ชัวร์ป๊าบ [chua bpáhp], แหง [ngǎe], แหงแซะ [ngǎe sáe], แหง๋น ๆ [ngǎen ngǎen]

(to) delay *v.* ดึงเกม [dueng gaym]

delicious *adj.* แซ่บ [sâep]

to demote *v.* เด้ง [dâyng]

dense (stupid) *adj.* บื้อ [bûe]

(to) deny your roots *v.* หัวลืมตีน [hǔa luem dteen]

(to) depend on yourself *v.* พึ่งพาตัวเอง [pûeng pah dtua 'ayng]

deranged *adj.* บ้า ๆ บอ ๆ [bâh bâh baw baw]

(to) desert *v.* ชิ่ง [chîng]

disappoint... แห้ว [hâeo]

designer *n.* ดีไซเนอร์ [dee sai ner]

diamonds (playing cards) *n.* ข้าวหลามตัด [kôw lǎhm dtùt], ไพ่ข้าวหลามตัด [pâi kôw lǎhm dtùt]

dice *n.* เต๋า [dtǎo]

dice game in Thailand *n.* ไฮโล [hai loe]

dick *n.* ควย [kooi], ดอ [daw], จู๋ [jǒo], เจ้าโลก [jâo lôek], เจ้าหนู [jâo nǒo], ไอ้ใบ้ ['âi bâi], กระเจี๊ยว [grà jíeo], นกเขา [nók kǎo], ท่อนล่า [tâwn lam], เอ็น ['ehn]

dictionary *n.* ดิก (ดิ๊ก) [dihk], ดิกชันนารี (ดิคชันนารี่) [dìhk chun nah rêe]

to die *v.* ซี้ [sée], ม่อง [mâwng], ม่องเท่ง [mâwng têyng], ไฟธาตุแตก [fai tâht dàek]

diet *n.* ไดเอ็ต [dai 'èht]

different (odd) *adj.* เซอร์ [ser]

digits (for phone number) *n.*
เบอร์ [ber]

dike *n.* ทอม [tawm],
ทอมบอย [tawm boi]

dildo *n.* ของเทียม [kǎwng tiam],
จรวดเทียม [jà rùat tiam]

dipshit *n.* เง่า [ngâo], โง่เง่า [ngôe
ngâo], ไอ้งั่ง [ngûng], ไอ้หน้าโง่ ['âi
nâh ngôe], เซ่อ [sêr], เซ่อซ่า [sêr sâh]

dirty *adj.* ทะลึ่ง [tá lûeng], ทุเรศ [tú
râyt], ลามก [lah móhk]

Dirty! *interj.* ท้วยส์ [tóoi]

dirty magazine *n.* หนังสือโป๊ [nǔng
sǔe bóe]

dirty old man *n.* เฒ่าหัวงู [dtâo hǔa
ngoo], ไอ้แก่หัวงู ['âi gàe hǔa ngoo]

disappointed *adj.* จอย [jǒi]

disco *n.* เธค (เทก) [tâyk],
ดิสโก้ [dìht sà gôe]

discothèque *n.* ดิสโก้ [dìht sà gôe],
ดิสโก้เธค [dìht sà gôe tâyk], เธค
(เทก) [tâyk], คลับ [klúp]

(to) disgust *v.* หมั่นไส้ [mùn sâi]

to dish it but not take it *v.*
ดีหัวเข้าบ้าน [dtee hǔa kâo bâhn]

disk jockey *n.* ดีเจ [dee jay]

(to) dismiss *v.* เด้ง [dâyng]

disorderly *adj.* เฟอะฟะ [fér fá]

(to) disrespect your elders *v.*
ถอนหงอก [tǎwn ngàwk]

DJ *n.* ดีเจ [dee jay]

(to) do a chick on her period *v.*
ผ่าไฟแดง [fàh fai daeng]

(to) do as others around you do *v.*
เข้าเมืองตาหลิ่ว [kâo mueang dtah lìu]

(to) do it *v.* เอา ['ao], เอากัน ['ao gun],
จ้ำจี้ [jâm jêe], ดิงดอง [dihng dawng],
มีอะไรกัน [mee 'a rai gun]

(to) do it before you get out of bed for
the day *v.* ซ้ำเช้า [sám cháo]

to do oral on a guy *v.* โม้ก [móek]

to do oral sex *v.* ทำออรัล [tam 'aw run]

to do something internationally *v.*
โกอินเตอร์ [goh 'in dter]

to do something stupid or offensive *v.*
เกรียน [grian]

doggy style *n.* กวางเหลียวหลัง
[gwahng lěeo lǔng],
ท่าหลัง [tâh lǔng]

dollar *n.* ดอลลาร์ [dawn lah],
ดอล [dawn]

don't need to... *adv.* ไม่เห็นต้อง
[mâi hěhn dtâwng]

Don't start! อย่าเพิ่ง [yàh pêrng]

to double-cross *v.* ตัดหลัง [dùt lǔng]

dough *n.* กะตังค์ [gà dtung]

to down in one gulp *v.* ดวด [dùat]

dowry *n.* ค่าสินสอด [kâh sǐhn sàwt]

drag queen *n.* กะเทย (กระเทย)
[gà teri]

Drat! บ๊ะ [bá], อุบ๊ะ ['òo bá]

Dream on! ฝันไปเถอะ [fǔn bpai tèr]

to dress like a slut *v.* แต่งตัววาบหวาน
[dtàeng dua wâhp wǎhn]

to drink *v.* เฉ่ม [chèrm], ถอง [tǎwng]

to drink alcohol *v.* ตอกเหล้า
[dtàwk lâo]

to drink alcohol in the morning to rid a
hangover *v.* ถอน [tǎwn]

to drink and dance *v.*
ดริงก์แอนด์แดนซ์ [drihg 'aen daen]

drip (gonorrhea) *n.*
โรคหนองใน [rôek nǎwng nai],
หนองใน [nǎwng nai]

droopy tits *n.* นมยาน [nohm yahn]

(to) drop (your girlfriend) *v.* ชิ่ง [chîng]

drug addict *n.* ขี้ยา [kêe yah]

druggie *n.* ขี้ยา [kêe yah]

drunk *v.* เมา [mao]

drunk (drunkard) *n.* ขี้เมา [kêe mao]

drunk already *adj.* ดีมาแล้ว [dee mah
láeo], ได้ที่ [dâi têe]

dude *n.* หมอ [mǎw]

dumb *adj.* โง่ [ngôe], ทึ่ม [tûem]

dumb ass *adj.* เซ่อ [sêr], ซกมก [sóhk móhk], เซ่อซ่า [sêr sâh]

dumb ass guy *n.* ไอ้บ้า ['âi bâh]

dumbstruck *v.* อึ้งกิมกี่ ['ùeng gim gèe]

(to) dump *v.* ชิ่ง [chîng]

dweeb *adj.* เชยแหลก [choe làek]

E

(to) eat and wait for someone else to pick up the tab *v.* ล้มทับ [lóhm túp]

(to) eat out a chick *v.* ลงลิ้น [lohng lín]

easily *adv.* ฉลุย [chà lǒuie]

East coast of Thailand *n.* ทะเลหน้าใน [tá lay nâh nai]

easy to handle *adj.* สบายมาก [sà bai mâk]

easy women *n.* ไก่ [gài]

easygoing *adj.* มันส์ (มัน) [mun]

to eat *v.* ถอง [tǎwng]

to eat a chick out *v.* ยกซด [yóhk sóht]

to eat like a dog *v.* แดก [dàek]

to eat like a f—kin' dog *interj.* แดกห่า [dàek hàh]

to eat like a gluttonous fat-body *v.* แดก [dàek]

to eat quickly *v.* โซ้ย [sóoe]

ecstasy/X/E (ephedrine) *n.* ยาอี [yah 'ee], อี ['ee]

Eee! ว้าย (ว๊า) [wái]

effeminate gay guy *n.* ตุ๊ด [dtóot], เต๋า [dtǎo], แต๋ว [dtóot], อีแอบ ['ee'àep]

Eh! ไง [ngai], แฮะ [háe], โอ๊ะ ['óh], เนอะ [nér], นะ [ná]

either way *adv.* ยังไง [yung ngai yung ngai]

elephant trunk (penis) *v.* ไม่ขลิบ [mâi kà lìhp]

to embezzle *v.* โอโม ['oe moe], งาบ [ngâhp]

endlessly *adv.* ตะบัน [dtà bpun], ตะบี้ตะบัน [dtà bêe dtà bpun]

to enjoy *v.* เอ็นจอย ['ehn joi]

enough but not great (to know) *adv.* งู ๆ ปลา ๆ [ngoo ngoo bplah bplah]

entrance examination *n.* เอ็น (เอน) ['ehn]

to envy *v.* อิจฉาตาร้อน ['iht chǎh dtah ráwn]

to escape *adv.* ชะแว้บ [chá wáep], ซะแวบ [sá wáep]

even just a bit *adv.* ซักนิด [súk nít]

even so *adv.* ยังไงก็ดี [yung ngai gâw dee]

ever again *adv.* ซะ [sá]

every one of *adj.* ตะละ [dtà lá]

everyone for themselves *adv.* ตัวใครตัวมัน [dtua krai dtua mun]

exactly *adj.* แหละ [làe]

exactly this/that one *adj.* ไง [ngai]

excellent *adj.* เด็ดสะระดี่ [dèht sà rá dtèe], เด็ดดวง [dèht duang], เช็ด [chéht]

excuse *n.* ข้ออ้าง [kâw âhng]

exhausted *adj.* เดี้ยง [dîang]

experienced *n.* ชั่วโมงบิน [chûa mo-eng bin], โชกโชน [chôhk chohn]

expert *n./adj.* เซียน [sian]

expressions *n.* น้ำคำ [nám kam]

exquisite *adj.* เนี้ยบ [níap]

excessively *adv.* เหลือกิน [lǔea gin], เหลือแดก [lǔea dàek]

extremely *adv.* โคตร [kôht], เดี๊ยะ [día], เต็มเปา [dtehm bpao], เต็มรัก [dtehm rúk], เหลือกิน [lǔea gin], เหลือเกิน [lǔea gern], เหลือแดก [lǔea dàek]

eye-catching *adj.* เฉี่ยว [chèeo], เฟี้ยว [féeo], เริด (เริ่ด) [rêrt], เฮ้ว [háyo]

F

factory worker (female) *n.* ฉันทนา [chǔn tá nah]

fag *n.* เหล็กท่อน [lèhk tâwn], ถั่วดำ
[tùa dam], เศษเหล็ก [sàyt lèhk]

(to) fail *v.* แห้ว [hâeo]

fair-skinned *adj.* แดงร่มใบ
[dtaeng rôhm bai]

fake *adj.* เฟค (เฟก) [fáyk]

(to) fake *v.* สร้างภาพ [sâhng pâhp]

familiar *adj.* เป็นกันเอง
[bpehn gun 'ayng]

famous *adj.* มีชื่อเสียง [mee chûe sĭang]

fan (of a movie star, music group, etc.)
n. แฟน [faen]

fan of something *n.* สาวก [săh wóhk]

fan club *n.* แฟนคลับ [faen klúp]

fart *n.* ลมเสีย [lohm sĭa]

to fart *v.* ตด [dtòht], ปล่อยแก๊ส
[bplòi gáet]

fascist tendency *adj.* เอียงขวา
['iang kwăh]

fashionable *adj.* อินเทรนด์ ['in trehn]

fashionable person *n.* เด็กแนว
[dèhk naeo]

fast *adj.* ซิ่ง [sîhng], เฟี้ยว [féeo]

fast driver *n.* ตีนผี [dteen pĕe]

fast-food *n.* แดกด่วน [dàek dùan]

fat *adj./adv.* ตุ้มต๊ะตุ้มต๊ะ [dtôom dtá
dtôom dtá]

fat (for women) *adj.*
สะบึม (สะบึมส์) [sà buem],
อึ่งอ่างทะเล ['ùeng àhng tá lay]

fatty *n.* อึ่งอ่างทะเล ['ùeng àhng tá
lay], โอ่งต่อขา ['òeng dtàw kăh]

faux pax *v.* ปล่อยไก่ [bplòi gài]

favorite get-up/clothes *n.* ตัวเก่ง
[dtua gàyng]

fed up *v.* ซะเบื่อ [sá bùea]

to feel bad *v.* เอิร์ด [hért]

to feel the urge to *v.* ต่อม [dtàwm]

feet *n.* ตีน [dteen]

to feign ignorance *v.* ทำไก๋ [tam găi]

fellatio *n.* ชิวหาพาเพลิน [chiu hăh
pah plern], ออรัลเซ็กซ์ ['aw run séhk]

fervid *adj.* ซู่ซ่า [sôo sâh]

to fight *v.* ตะริดติ๊ดชึ่ง [dtà ríht dtíht
sùeng], ตื๊น [dtún], ฟ้อนเล็บ
[fáwn léhp]

to fight as a posse *v.* รุมกินโต๊ะ [room
gin dtóe]

to fight on *v.* ตี๊ตาต่าตี๊ [dtée dtah
dtàh dtée]

to fight over a subject *v.* ซด [sóht]

filthy rich *adj.* กระเป๋าหนัก
[grà băo nùk]

final paycheck (comes with pink slip)
n. ซองขาว [sawng kŏw]

(to) finally realize *v.* ถึงบางอ้อ [tŭeng
bahn 'âw]

fine *adj.* เซ็กซี่ [séhk sêe]

Fine! เออ ['er]

Fine then! ดีแล้ว [dee láeo],
ดีละ [dee lá]

(to) finger yourself *v.* ตกเบ็ด [dtòhk bèht]

(to) fire *v.* เด้ง [dâyng]

first-year college student *n.* เฟรชชี่
[frâyt chêe]

fits well *adj.* ฟิต [fíht]

(to) flake off *adv.* ชะแว้บ [chá wáep],
ชะแว้บ [sá wáep]

flavorless *adj.* กินข้าวแกงจืด
[gin kôa gàeng jùet]

(to) flip-flop *v.* ชักเข้าชักออก [chúk
kâo chúk 'àhk], ซิกแซ็ก [síhk sâek]

(to) flirt with *v.* จีบ [jeep],
เฟลิต (เฟลิท) [flért]

(to) flirt (with the eyes) *v.*
เล่นตา [lâyn dtah],
เล่นหูเล่นตา [lâyn hŏo lâyn dta]

(to) do anal *v.* เล่นดูด [lâyn dtòot]

fool *n.* ไอ้งั่ง [ngûng], เงา [ngâo],
โง่เง่า [ngôe ngâo]

(to) fool *v.* แหกตา [hàek dtah],
ตุ๋น [dtŏon]

foolish *adj.* เซ่อซ่า [sêr sâh],
งั่ง [ngûng], โง่ [ngôe]

foot *n.* ตีน [dteen]

for a long time *adv.* ชะนาน [sá nan], เหงือกแห้ง [ngùeak hâeng]

for fun/pleasure *adv.* เล่น [lâyn]

for like forever *adv.* เหงือกแห้ง [ngùeak hâeng]

for sure *adv.* ชัวร์ป๊าบ [chua bpáhp], แน่ [nâe], แหง็น ๆ [ngăen ngăen], แหง [ngăe], แหงแชะ [ngăe sáe]

forever *adv.* ชะ [sá]

Forget about it! ปลงซะ [bpohng sá]

Forget him! ช่างหัวมัน [chùng hŭa mun], ช่างหัวมัน [châhng hŭa mun]

Forget it! ช่างแมง [chùng màeng], ช่างหัวมัน [châhng hŭa mun], ช่างมัน [châhng mun], ช่างมันปะไร [châhng mun bpa rai], ช่างมันเป็นไร [châhng mun bpehn rai]

to forget where you come from *v.* หัวลืมตีน [hŭa luem dteen]

forward (sluttish) *adj.* ทะลึ่ง [tá lûeng]

frail *adj.* มะเขือเผา [má kŭea păo]

frank and beans *n.* เจี๊ยว [jéeo]

freakin' *part.* ฟะ [fá], วะ (ว๊ะ) [wá], ไอ้ ['âi], อี ['ee]

freakin' *adv.* โคตร [kôht], ชิบหาย [chíhp hăi]

Freakin' retard! โง่เง่าเต่าตุ่น [ngôe ngâo dtào dtòon]

free style *n.* ฟรีสไตล์ [free sà dtai]

fresh (new) *adj.* ถอดด้าม [tàwt dâhm]

fresh (sexual) *adj.* ทะลึ่ง [tá lûeng]

freshman *n.* เฟรชชี่ [frâyt chêe]

friendly manner *n.* กันเอง [gun 'ayng]

F—k! เหี้ย [hîa], แมง [mâeng], ฉิบหาย [chíhp hăi], วะ [wá]

to f—k *v.* เด้า [dâo], โด๊ะ [dóe], กระเด้า [grà dâo], ตีม่อ [dtee mâw], ฟัน [fun], ฟาด [fàht]

to f—k a whore *v.* ตีม่อ [dtee mâw]

f—k-buddy *n.* กิ๊ก [geek]

to f—k someone up *v.* โซ่ย [sôhe]

to f—k over *v.* ฟัน [fun]

to f—k with *v.* กวนตีน [guan dteen], กวนส้มตี [guan sôhm dteen]

F—k you! ไอ้เหี้ย ['âi hîa]

f—kin' *adj./adv.* โคตร [kôht], ระย่ำ [rá yum]

f—kin' *part.* วะ (ว๊ะ) [wá], ฟะ [fá], อี ['ee], ไอ้ ['âi]

f—kin' American(s) *adj.* ไอ้กัน ['âi gun]

f—kin' animal *n.* ไอ้สัตย์ ['âi sùt]

F—kin' bastard! ระย่ำหมา [rá yum măh], ระย่ำคน [rá yum kohn], ไอ้สัตย์ ['âi sùt]

F—kin' dipshit! โง่เง่าเต่าตุ่น [ngôe ngâo dtào dtòon]

full-bodied but cute *adj.* อิ่ม ['ŭem]

full of energy *adj.* ไฮเปอร์ [hai bper]

full of it *adj.* กินสตรอร์เบอร์รี่ [gin sa dtraw ber ree]

the full ten yards *adv.* เต็มร้อย [dtehm rói], เต็มรัก [dtehm rúk]

fun *adj.* มันส์ (มัน) [mun]

to fuss *v.* ดูดี๋ [dŏo dĕe]

G

(to) gang-bang *v.* เวียนเทียน [wian tian]

(to) gang-rape *v.* เรียงคิว [riang kiu]

(to) gank (steal) *v.* ชิว [siu], อุบอิบ ['óop 'íp]

gay *n.* เกย์ [gay], ถั่วดำ [tùa dam], ประเทือง [bpà tueang], เศษเหล็ก [sàyt lèhk], เหล็กท่อน [lèhk tâwn]

gay who hasn't come out yet *n.* แอบจิต ['àep jit]

Gee! แฮะ [háe]

(to) get a free lunch on others *v.* ลมทับ [lóhm túp]

(to) get a lift *v.* เต่า [dtào]

(to) get along well *v.* ดวงสมพงศ์ [duang sŏhm pohng]

(to) get horny *v.* จับเส้น [jùp sâyn]

(to) get it (understand) *v.*
เก็ท (เก็ต) [géht]

(to) get it on *v.* จ้าจี้ [jâm jêe],
เอากัน ['ao gun]

(to) get laid *v.* ถึง [tǔeng]. ฟาด [fâht]

(to) get off *v.* เล่นเสียว [lâyn sěeo],
จับเส้น [jùp sâyn]

(to) get on this *v.* ขึ้นม้า [kûen máh]

Get outta here! *phr.* ไปซะ [bpai sá]

(to) get ready *v.* ชง [chohng]

(to) get registered *v.* ดีทะเบียน
[dtee tá bian]

(to) get what you deserve *v.*
สมน้ำหน้า [sǒhm nám nâh]

(to) get with a hooker *v.* ตีมือ
[dtee mâw]

(to) get worked up about something *v.*
ฮือฮา [hue hah]

(to) get your morning wood off *v.*
ช้ำเช้า [sám cháo]

gigolo *n.* แมงดา [maeng dah],
ไอ้ตัว ['âi dtua]

girl *n.* สาว [sǎo], นัง [nung]

girl on top *n./v.* ขี่ม้า [kèe máh],
หงส์เหนือมังกร [hǒhng nǔea mung
gawn], หนุมมานขย่มตอ
[hà nǒo mahn kà yòhm dtaw]

girl who dresses and acts like a Westerner *n.* ฝรั่งขึ้นก [fà rùng kêe nóhk]

girl who's out of your league *n.*
ดอกฟ้ากับหมาวัด [dàwk fáh gùp
mǎh wút]

girlfriend *n.* แฟน [faen]

girl's cherry *n.* ไข่แดง [kài daeng]

girlie bar *n.* บาร์ผี [bah pěe]

(to) give a blowjob (BJ) *v.*
ใช้ปาก [chái bàhk], โม๊ก [móek]

(to) give a Thai-style kiss *v.* หอมแก้ม
[hǎwm gâem]

(to) give head *v.* ท่าออรัล [tam 'aw
run], ใช้ปาก [chái bàhk],
โม๊ก [móek]

(to) give it a go *v.* เซิ้บ ๆ [sérp sérp]

(to) give money (reluctantly) to someone you look down on *v.*
ฟาดหัว [fâht hǔa]

to give moral support *v.* เชลียร์ [chá lia]

Go! ไปซะ [bpai sá]

Go ahead! เอาซิ ['ao sí]

(to) go fashionable *v.* โกอินเตอร์
[goh 'in dter]

Go for it! ลุยเลย [louie leri]

Go f—k yourself! ไอ้เหี้ย ['ài hîa]

go-go bar *n.* อะโกโก ['à goe gôe]

(to) go number one (men) *v.*
ยิงกระต่าย [ying gra dtài]

(to) go number one (women) *v.*
เก็บดอกไม้ [gèp dàwk mái]

(to) go number two *v.* อึ ['ùe]

(to) go on a date *v.* ออกเดท
(ออกเดต) ['àwk dayt]

(to) go out and party *v.*
ดริงก์แอนด์แดนซ์ [drihg 'aen daen]

(to) go without sleep *phr.*
อดตาหลับขับตานอน
['òht dtah lùp kùp dtah nawn]

golden shower *v.* ฉี่รดกัน
[chèe róht gun]

gonna (going to) *adv.* กะลัง [gà lung]

gonorrhea *n.* โรคหนองใน [rôek
nǎwng nai], หนองใน [nǎwng nai]

gooey stuff (chlamydia) *n.*
หนองในเทียม [nǎwng nai tiam]

good enough *adj.* ตุ๋ย [dtóuie]

good enough *adv.* เอาดี ['ao dee]

good-for-nothing kid *n.* ลูกกระจ๊อก
[lôok grà jáwk]

goodlooking *adj.* หน้าตาดี
[nâh dtah dee]

goodlooking (for guys) *adj.* รูปหล่อ
[rôop làw]

good mood *v.* ลมดี [lohm dee]

(to) goof off *adv.* ชะแว้บ [chá wáep],
ชะแว้บ [sá wáep]

gorgeous *adj.* เซ้งกะเด๊ะ
[cháyng gà dáy]

Got it! *interj.* เออ ['er],
เออซิวะ ['er sí wá]

(The) grass is always greener on the
other side. *phr.* รักพี่เสียดายน้อง
[rúk pêe sǐa dai náwng]

grave (thinking) *adj.* ซึมกะทือ
[suem gà tue]

great *adj.* เนี๊ยบ [níap]

Great! *interj.* เออ ['er]

green with envy *v.* อิจฉาตาร้อย
['ìht chǎh dtah ráwn]

group sex *n.* เซ็กซ์หมู่ [séhk mòo]

groupie *n.* แฟน [faen], สาวก
[sǎh wóhk]

(to) groove to a fast beat *v.* ดิ้น [dîhn]

(to) guess *v.* มั่วซั่ว [mûa sûa]

Gulf of Thailand coast *n.*
ทะเลหน้าใน [tá lay nâh nai]

guy *n.* หมอ [mǎw]

guy who acts like a chick *n.* ตุ๊ด [dtóot]

guy who is always borrowing cash *n.*
ดาวใก [dow tǎi]

guy who lives off a girl *n.* แมงดา
[maeng dah]

guy who marries up *n.* ตกถังข้าวสาร
[dtòhk tǔng kôw sǎhn]

guy who will go with any girl *n.*
เจ้าชู้ประตูดิน [jâo chóo bprà
dtoo din]

H

Ha! *part.* ฮะ [há]

Ha-hah! *interj.* ฮะฮ้า [há háh],
ฮะไฮ้ [há hái]

ha/ha-ha *op.* ฮ่ะ [hâ], ฮ่ะ ๆ [hâ hâ],
ฮา (ฮา ๆ) [hah], ฮ่า ๆ [hâh hâh]

hair of the dog *v.* ถอน [tǎwn]

half-assed *adj.* สั่ว [sùa]

half Thai-half whatever *n.* ลูกครึ่ง
[look krûeng]

half-witted *adj.* ปัญญานิ่ม
[bpun yah nîhm]

handsome *adj.* รูปหล่อ [rôop làw],
หล่อ [làw], หน้าตาดี [nâh dtah dee]

handy *n.* มือถือ [mue tǔe]

hangover *n.* แฮงโอเวอร์
[haeng 'oe wêr]

happy *adj.* แฮปปี้ [háep bpêe]

hard knock life *n.* ชีวิตบัดซบ
[chee with bùt sóhp]

to harm as a mob *v.* รุมกินโต๊ะ
[room gin dtóe]

harsh *adj.* แสบ [sàep]

(to) have a broken heart *v.*
อกหัก ['òhk hùk]

(to) have a crush on somebody *v.*
แอบชอบ ['àep châwp]

(to) have a girl ride you *v.*
หนุมมานขยมตอ [hà nǒo mahn kà
yòhm dtaw]

(to) have a hangover *v.* แฮ้ง [háeng],
เมาค้าง [mao káhng]

(to) have a little roll in the hay
morning time *v.* ซ้ำเช้า [sám cháo]

(to) have a loose tongue *v.* พูดส่งเดช
[pôot sòhng dàyt]

(to) have a lot of dough *adj.* มีกะตังค์
[mee gà dtung]

(to) have a lover (women) *v.*
คบชู้ [kóhp chóo], มีชู้ [mee chóo],
คบชู้สู่ชาย [kóhp chóo sòo chai]

(to) have a threesome *v.* ลงแขก
[lohng kàek]

(to) have a wet dream *v.* ฝันเปียก
[fǔn bpìak]

(to) have an orgasm *v.*
สำเร็จความใคร่ [sǎm réht kwahm
krâi], เสร็จ [sèht]

(to) have an orgy *v.* ลงแขก [lohng
kàek], เวียนเทียน [wian tian]

(to) have anal butt-sex *v.* เล่นตูด [lâyn
dtòot], อัดตูด ['ùt dtòot]

(to) have anal sex (specifically male on male) *v.* อัดถั่วดำ ['ùt tùa dam]

to have done something together *v.* มีอะไรกัน [mee 'a rai gun]

to have game *adj.* มีเสน่ห์ [mee sà này]

to have gay sex (male) *v.* ตุ๋ย [dtŏuie]

to have sex *v.* มั่วเซ็กซ์ [mûa séhk], มีเซ็กซ์ [mee séhk], เอา ['ao], เอากัน ['ao gun], เล่นเสียว [lâyn sĕeo], อึ๊บ ['úep], ติงตอง [dihng dawng]

to have sex with many men *v.* มั่วผู้ชาย [mûa pôo chai]

to have sexual desire *v.* มีอารมณ์ [mee 'ah rohm]

to have studied in the West *n./adj.* หัวนอก [hŭa nâwk]

to have the girl get on top *v.* ขึ้นม้า [kûen máh]

to have the power to get what you want *phr.* ชี้นกเป็นนก ชี้ไม้เป็นไม้ [chée nóhk bpehn nóhk chée mái bpehn mái]

to have to piss bad *v.* ปวดฉี่ [bpùat chèe]

to have to shit bad *v.* ปวดขี้ [bpùat kêe]

to have zero contact *v.* ตัดเป็นตัดตาย [dtùt bpehn dtùt dtai]

Hay-hahh! *op.* เฮฮา [hay hah], เฮ้ว [háyo]

he (him) *pron.* เค้า [káo], แก [gae], เธอ [ter], มัน [mun]

he-he *op.* อิ ๆ [híh híh]

healthy *adj.* ฟิต [fíht]

hearts (cards) *n.* หัวใจ [hŭa jai], ไพ่หัวใจ [pâi hŭa jai]

Heh! แฮะ [háe]

helicopter *n.* แมงปอ [maeng bpaw], เฮลิคอปเตอร์ [hay líh kâwp dter]

Hell! *interj.* ฉิบหาย [chìhp hǎi], วะ [wá]

to help out *v.* ซัพพอร์ต [súb páwt]

Here! *n.* นี่แน่ [nêe nâe]

Here, take it! *interj.* เอา ['ao]

hermaphrodite *n.* กะเทย (กระเทย) [gà teri]

heroin *n.* แค๊ป [káep]

herpes (simplex) *n.* เริม [rerm], โรคเริม [rôek rerm]

Hey!/Hi! *interj.* เฮ้ [háy], เฮ้ย (เฮ้ย) [héri], ไฮ้ [hái], ไง [ngai], แน่ะ [nâe]

hick *adj.* บ้านนอก ๆ [bâhn náwk bâhn nâwk]

hickish *adj.* เชย [choei]

high-class girl *n.* ดอกฟ้า [dàwk fáh]

high society *adj.* ไฮโซ [hai soe]

high-society debutante *n.* ดอกฟ้า [dàwk fáh]

Hindu believer *n.* แขก [kàek]

hip *adj.* ซิ่ง [sîhng]

hippy *n.* ฮิปปี้ [híb bpêe]

to hit *v.* ตื๊น [dtúo], เฉ่ม [chèrm], ฟ้อนเล็บ [fáwn léhp]

to hit it (masturbate) *v.* ชักว่าว [chúk wôw]

to hit it in the booty *v.* เข้าประตูหลัง [kâo bprà dtoo lŭng]

to hit on *v.* จีบ [jeep]

to hit on another person's spouse *v.* ตีท้ายครัว [dtee tái krua]

to hit on easy chicks *v.* จับไก่ [jùp gài]

to hit up the whorehouse *v.* ไปเที่ยวซ่อง [bpai têeo sâwng]

to hit your balls *v.* บีบไข่ [bèep kài]

Hm! *interj.* อึ [húe]

Hmmmm? *interj.* เอ่ [' ǎy]

ho *n.* แรด (แรด) [râet]

Hold on! อย่าเพิ่ง [yàh pêrng]

homely *adj.* ขี้เหล่ (ขี้เหร่) [kêe lày], ขี้ริ้วขี้เหร่ [kêe ríu kêe rày]

homosexual *n.* โฮโมเซ็กซ์ชวล [ho mo séhk chuan], กะเทย (กระเทย) [gà teri], เกย์ [gay]

honestly *adj.* ซีเครียด [see krîat]

Honestly... *adv.* เอาจริงเอาจัง ['ao jihng 'ao jung]

honey *n.* ที่รัก [têe rúk], หวานใจ [wǎhn jai]

honey *part.* เอ๋ย ['éri]

honey *pron.* เธอ [ter]

(to) hoo-hah *v.* ฮือฮา [hue hah]

hooked on *v.* มัวแต่ [mua dtàe]

hooker *n.* อีตัว ['ee dtua]

horny *v.* เสียว [sěeo], มีอารมณ์ [mee 'ah rohm]

Horse's ass! *interj.* โง่เง่าเต่าตุ่น [ngôe ngâo dtào dtòon]

hot (beautiful because of makeup or dress) *adj.* เช้งวับ [cháyng wúp], เช้ง [cháyng]

hot (goodlooking) *adj.* เซ็กซี่ [séhk sêe], เช้งกะเดะ [cháyng gà dáy]

hot (handsome for guys) *adj.* หล่อ [làw]

hot topic *n.* ช็อตเด็ด [cháwt dèht]

How? ยังไง [yung ngai], ไง [ngai], ไร [rai]

How could/can it? ได้ไง [dâi gnai], ได้ยังไง [dâi yung gnai]

How's it going? เป็นไง [bpehn ngai], ว่าไง [wâh ngai]

however *adv.* ยังไงก็ดี [yung ngai gâw dee], ยังไงก็ตาม [yung ngai gâw dtahm]

huffy-puffy *adj.* ขี้งอน [kêe ngawn], งอน [ngawn], งอนตุ๊บป่อง [ngawn dtóop bpàwng]

Huh? *interj.* อ๊ะ ['á], โอ๊ะ ['óh], ว้า [wáh]

to humble *v./adj.* ถ่อมตัว [tà lòhm dtua]

hung-over *v.* เมาค้าง [mao káhng], แฮ้ง [háeng]

hungry *phr.* ท้องร้อง [táwng ráwng], ท้องแห้ง [táwng hâeng]

to hurt (feelings) *v.* เฮิร์ต [hért]

husband *n.* แฟน [faen]

hyper/hyperactive *adj.* ไฮเปอร์ [hai bper]

hypocrite/hypocritical *n/adj.* มือถือสากปากถือศีล [mue tǔe sàhk bàhk tǔe sǐhn]

I

I (me) *pron.* ชั้น [chún], เรา [rao], เดี๊ยน [dían], อะอั๊น ['à 'ûn], กู [goo]

I'm okay! ส.บ.ม. [sǎw baw maw]

I'm okay; don't worry! ส.บ.ม.ย.ห. [sǎw baw maw yaw hǎw]

I don't see why ya gotta... *adv.* ไม่เห็นต้อง [mâi hěhn dtâwng]

I get it now! ออ ['áw]

I guess... *part.* มั้ง [múng], ละมั้ง [lâ múng]

I swear! เชื่อหัวไอ้เรื่อง [chûea hǔa 'âi rueang]

ice cream *n.* ไอติม ['ai dtim]

ideological leader *n.* หัวหอก [hǔa hawk]

idiot *n.* เง่า [ngâo], ควาย [kwai], โง่เง่า [ngôe ngâo], ปัญญาอ่อน [bpun yah àwn], ไอ้งั่ง [ngûng], ไอ้หน้าโง่ ['âi nâh ngôe]

Ieee! *interj.* ว้าย (ว๊าย) [wái]

if not like that... *phr.* ไม่ยังงั้น [mâi yung ngúng]

If the boss doesn't move, neither will the employees. หัวไม่ส่ายหางไม่กระดิก [hǔa mâi sài hǎng mâi grà dìhk]

If you're not gonna help then get outta the way! ถ้ามือไม่พายอย่าเอาเท้าราน้ำ [tâh mue mâi pai yàh 'ao táo rah nám]

ill-fated *adj.* ดวงจู [duang jǒo]

illegal payment *adv./n.* ใต้โต๊ะ [dtâi dtóh]

illiterate person *n.* ตาสีตาสา [dtah sěe dtah sǎh]

imp *n.* ลูกกระจ๊อก [lôok grà jáwk]

imperative commands *part.* ซะ [sá]

in a mess *adj./v.* มั่ว [mûa]

in a while *adv.* ชะนาน [sá nan]

in ages *adv.* ชะนาน [sá nan]

In all honesty… *adv.* เอาจริงเอาจัง ['ao jihng 'ao jung]

in bad style *adj.* เชย [choei]

in like forever *adv.* ชะนาน [sá nan]

in heat *adj.* ซู่ซ่า [sôo sâh]

in style *adj.* มะ [má]

in-the-closet gay *n.* แอบจิต ['àep jìt]

in trend *adj.* เดิ้น [dêrn], ซิ่ง [sîhng]

in what way? *adv.* ยังไง [yung ngai], ไง [ngai]

inexperienced little shit *n.* เด็กเมื่อวานซืน [dèhk mûea wahn suen]

indeed *adv.* เชียว [cheeo]

independent *v.* พึ่งพาตัวเอง [pûeng pah dtua 'ayng]

Indian *n.* แขก [kàek]

indifferent *adj.* ชิล [chin]

informal *adj.* เป็นกันเอง [bpehn gun 'ayng]

insane *adj.* บ๋อง [báwng], บ้า [bâh]

interesting point *n.* ช็อตเด็ด [cháwt dèht]

(to) interfere *v.* แหยม [yǎem]

international *adj.* อินเตอร์ ['in dter]

internet *n.* อินเตอร์เน็ท ['in dter neht]

Is that so? งั้นเหรอ [ngún rěr]

Islamic believer *n.* แขก [kàek]

Isn't it so? ใช่มั้ย (ใช่มั๊ย) [châi mái]

it *pron.* มัน [mun]

It's obvious! *part.* ซิ [síh], ซิ่ [sîh], นะซิ [ná síh]

to itch for a drug or sex *v.* เงี่ย [ngîan]

it's-all-good type of attitude *adj.* ชิล [chin]

J

Japanese person (derogatory) *n.* ยุ่น [yôon]

jerk that starts shit *n.* งี่เง่า [ngêe ngâo]

to jerk off *v.* ชักว่าว [chúk wôw], ชักจุฬา [chúk jòo lah], ขัดถูกลอง [kùt tǒo glâwng], ตะกายฝา ป่ายกำแพง [dtà gai fǎh bpài gam paeng], ลากเส้นก๋วยเตี๋ยว [lûak sâyn gǒoi děeo]

jet-black *adj.* ดำมิดหมี [dam míht měe]

jetlag *v.* ปรับเวลาไม่ทัน [bprùp way lah mâi tun]

Jew *adj.* เค็ม [kehm]

jobless *adj.* นั่งตบยุง [nûng dtòhp young]

johnson *n.* นกเขา [nók kǎo]

jubilant *v.* ดี๊ด๊า [dée dáh]

to jump for joy *v.* กระดี๊กระด๊า [grà dée grà dáh]

just *adv.* ซะ [sá], ซัก [súk], แหละ [làe]

just a bit *adv.* ซักกะติ๊ด [súk gà dtíht], ซักนิด [súk nít]

just a sec *adv.* แป๊บนึง [bpáep nueng], แป๊บเดียว [bpáep deeo]

just a sec ago *adv.* เมื่อกี้ [mûe gée]

just now *adv.* ตะกี้ (ตะกี้) [dtà gée], เมื่อกี้ [mûe gée]

just once *adv.* ชะที [sá tee], ซักที [súk tee]

just this *part.* นี่ [nêe]

(to) just wanna do one thing *v.* เอาแต่ ['ao dtàe]

K

(to) keep a piece of the pie for yourself *v.* เมมส์ตางค์ [máym sà dtàhng]

to keep on rocking/trucking *v.* เตะปี๊บดัง [dtày bpée dung]

(to) keep your gay male partner placated *v.* ซ้อง [sawng]

ketamine *n.* ยาเค [yah kay], เค [kay]

kid who doesn't know anything *n.*
เด็กเมื่อวานซืน [dèhk mûea
wahn suen]

Kick ass! แจ๋ว [jăeo]

(to) kidnap *v.* อุ้ม ['ôom]

(to) kill *v.* โซ้ย [sôhe]

(to) kill a hangover by drinking in the
morning *v.* ถอน [tăwn]

kind *cl./n.* ยัง [yung]

(to) kiss *v.* จูบ [jòop], จุ๊บ [jóop]

(to) kiss ass *v.* เลียตูด [lia dtòot],
เลียแขนเลียขา [lia kăen lia kăh]

(to) know little and be able to do even
less *v.* ถ่อไม่ถึงน้ำ ค้าไม่ถึงดิน
[tàw mâi tŭeng nám kám mâi
tŭeng dihn]

(to) know what's what *v.* รู้ภาษา
[róo pah săh]

L

labia *n.* แคม [kaem]

lady-boy *n.* กะเทย (กระเทย) [gà teri],
ประเทือง [bpà tueang],
หน้าหอยสังข์หลังหอยแครง [nâh
hŏi sŭng lŭng hŏi kraeng]

lady-friend *n.* กิ๊ก [geek]

laid back *adj.* ชิล [chin], เป็นกันเอง
[bpehn gun 'ayng]

laugh today, cry tomorrow *phr.*
ชั่วเจ็ดทีดีเจ็ดหน [chûa jèht tee dee
jèht hŏhn]

(to) launder money *v.* งาบ [ngâhp]

lawyer *n.* ทนาย [tá nai]

lazy *adj.* เช้าชามเย็นชาม [cháo
chahm yehn chahm], ตัวเป็นขน
[dtua bpehn kŏhn]

lazily *adv.* โต๋เต๋ [dtŏe dtăy]

leader of a gang *n.* หัวหอก
[hŭa hawk]

(to) leave your position *v.*
ถอดหัวโขน [tàwt hŭa kŏhn]

leisurely *adv.* โต๋เต๋ [dtŏe dtăy]

(the) left (left thinking) *n./adj.*
ฝ่ายซ้าย [fài sái], เอียงซ้าย ['iang sái]

lesbian (the butch one) *n.* ทอม [tawm]

lesbian (the more feminine of the two)
n. ดี้ [dêe]

lesbo/lesbian *n.* เลสเบียน (เลสเบี้ยน)
[lâyt bian]

less abrupt *part.* ชะหน่อย [sá nòi]

to let it all out *v.* ระบาย [rá bai]

to let it be *v.* ช่างมัน [châhng mun],
ช่างมันปะไร [châhng mun bpa rai],
ช่างมันเป็นไร [châhng mun bpehn rai],
ช่างหัวมัน [châhng hŭa mun]

Let it go! ปลงซะ [bpohng sá]

to let one rip *v.* ปล่อยแก๊ส [bplòi gáet]

to let things pile up *phr.*
ดินพอกหางหมู [dihn pâw hăhng
mŏo]

let's *part.* เหอะ [hèr], เหอะน่า
[hèr nâh], เฮอะ [hér], เถอะ [tèr],
เถอะน่า ['èr nâh]

lewd *adj.* ลามก [lah móhk]

liar *n.* เด็กเลี้ยงแกะ [dèhk líang gàe]

a liberal/liberal perspective *n./adj.*
ฝ่ายซ้าย [fài sái], เอียงซ้าย ['iang sái]

to lie *v.* ตอแหล [dtaw lăe],
กินสตรอร์เบอร์รี่ [gin sa dtraw ber
ree], แหกตา [hàek dtah]

to lie with no shame whatsoever *v.*
ตอแหลกระแตวับ [dtaw lăe grà
dtae wúp]

life is not all beer and skittles *phr.*
ชั่วเจ็ดทีดีเจ็ดหน [chûa jèht tee dee
jèht hŏhn]

like... *conj.* แบบว่า (แบ่บว่า) [bàep wâh]

like a broken record *adv.* ตอยหอย
[dtòi hŏi] like a

like a fat cow *adj./adv.* ตุ้มต๊ะตุ้มต๊ะ
[dtôom dtá dtôom dtá]

like a loser *adj.* เชย [choei],
เชยแหลก [choe làek]

like a synch *adv.* ฉลุย [chà lŏuie]

like a teenager *adj.* เอ๊าะ ['áw]

like a work horse *phr.* ตัวเป็นเกลียว
หัวเป็นน็อต [dtua bpehn gleeo hŭa
bpehn náwt], ตัวเป็นเกลียว [dtua
bpehn gleeo]

to like somebody in secret *v.*
แอบชอบ ['àep châwp]

like that *adj.* งั้น [ngún], ยังงั้น [yung
ngúng], ยังโงน [yung ngóen]

Like that! นั่นแหละ [nûn làe]

like this *adj.* ยังงี้ [yung ngée]

likes to visit the massage parlor/broth-
el often *adj.* ติดอ่าง [dtìht 'àhng]

limp dick *n.* ทำเหี่ยว [hăm hèeo],
นกเขาไม่ขัน [nók kăo mâi kun]

lineage and class *n.* หัวนอนปลายตีน
[hŭa nawn bplai dteen],
หัวนอนปลายเท้า [hŭa nawn
bplai táo]

to liquidate *v.* เซ้ง [sáyng]

liquor *n.* เหล้า [lâo], แอลกอฮอล์
['aen gaw haw]

to list *v.* ลิสต์ [lít]

listless *adj.* ซึมกะทือ [suem gà tue]

a little (to know) *adv.* งู ๆ ปลา ๆ
[ngoo ngoo bplah bplah]

little bitch of a dude *n.* หน้าตัวเมีย
[nâh dtua mia]

little brat *n.* ห่าน้อย [hăm nói]

the little guy (penis) *n.* เจ้าหนู
[jâo nŏo]

little shit (kid) *n.* ลูกกระจอก [lôok
grà jáwk], ห่าน้อย [hăm nói]

a load of *adj.* อืน ['uen]

loaded (rich) *adj.* กระเป๋าหนัก [grà
băo nùk], มีกะตังค์ [mee gà dtung]

to look after *v.* เท็กแคร์ [téhk kae]

look before you leap *phr.*
ดูตามม้าตาเรือ [doo dtah máh
doo ruea]

to look for an easy lay *v.*
จับไก่ [jùp gài], ปูเสื่อ [bpoo sùea]

to look for trouble *v.* หาเหาใส่หัว
[hăh hăo sài hŭa]

to look intoxicated *v.* เมาดิบ [mao dìhp]

to look the other way *phr.*
เอาหูไปนาเอาตาไปไร่ ['ao hŏo
bpai nah 'ao dtah bpai râi]

loony *adj.* บ้า ๆ บอ ๆ
[bâh bâh baw baw]

to loose before you win *v.* ตกม้าตาย
[dtòhk máh dtai]

to loose your virginity (female) *v.*
เสียตัว [sĭa dtua], เสียเนื้อเสียตัว
[sĭa núea sĭa dtua],
เสียสาว [sĭa săo]

a lot of *adj.* เยอะ (เยอะ ๆ) [yér],
เยอะแยะ [yér yáe], ตึม [dtuem],
ตัน [dtun], สุดตีน [sòot dtèen], อืน
['uen], อื้อจือเหลียง ['ûe jue lĭang],
อื้อซ่า ['ûe sâh], แฮ [hae]

love at first sight *n.* รักแรกพบ
[rúk râek póhp]

lover *n.* ชู้ [chóo]

low *adj.* ระย่ำ [rá yum]

(to) lube up *v.* หล่อลื่น [làw lûen]

M

made up (as in make-up or dress) *adj.*
เซ้งวับ [cháyng wúp], เซ้ง [cháyng]

major/main wife *n.* บ้านใหญ่
[bâhn yài]

to make a final decision *v.* ฟันธง
[fun tohng]

to make a list *v.* ลิสต์ [lít]

to make a problem *v.* หาเหาใส่หัว
[hăh hăo sài hŭa]

to make an ass of yourself *v.* ปล่อยไก่
[bplòi gài]

to make an effort to go *v.* ถ่อ [tàw]

to make horny *v.* เล่นเสียว [lâyn sĕeo]

to make late *v.* ดึงเกม [dueng gaym]

to make lesbian love *v.* ตีฉิ่ง
[dtee chìng]

to make love *v.* อึ๊บ ['úep], มีเซ็กซ์ [mee séhk]

to make queer motions unintentionally *v.* เต๋าแตก [dtǎo dtàek], แต๋วแตก [dtóot dtàek]

to make sense *v.* เวิร์ก (เวิร์ค) [wérk]

to make someone drunk *v.* กรอกเหล้า [gràwk lâo]

to make someone chug their drink *v.* กรอกเหล้า [gràwk lâo]

to make sure *v.* เช็ก (เช็ค) [chéhk]

to make yourself likeable *v.* ตีสติ๊ก [dtee sà dtíhk]

man *n.* หมอ [mǎw]

Man… *interj.* โธ่ [tôe]

man whore *n.* ไอ้ตัว ['âi dtua]

many *adj.* ตึม [dtuem], อืน ['uen], เยอะ (เยอะ ๆ) [yér], เยอะแยะ [yér yáe], อื้อจือเหลียง ['ûe jue lǐang], อื้อซ่า ['ûe sâh]

massage parlor and bath *n.* อาบอบนวด ['àhp 'ôhp nûat]

to masturbate *v.* ช่วยตัวเอง [chôoi dtua 'ayng], ทำร้ายตังเอง [tam rái dtua ayng], ชักว่าว [chúk wôw]

to masturbate (guys) *v.* ตะกายฝา ป่ายกำแพง [dtà gai fǎh bpài gam paeng], ชักว่าว [chúk wôw], ลวกเส้นก๋วยเตี๋ยว [lûak sâyn gǒoi děeo]

to masturbate (for women) *v.* ตกเบ็ด [dtòhk bèht]

maxi pad *n.* ขนมปัง [kà nǒhm bung]

maybe *part.* มั้ง [múng], ละมั้ง [lâ múng]

mechanic *n.* ช่างฟิต [chàhng fít]

merely *adv.* ชัก [súk], ชะ [sá]

merely a little *adv.* ชักนิด [súk nít]

merely one time *adv.* ชักที [súk tee], ชะที [sá tee]

(to) mess around *v.* มีอะไรกัน [mee 'a rai gun], จ้าจี้ [jâm jêe]

messed up *adj./v.* มั่ว [mûa]

(to) mess with *v.* กวนตีน [guan dteen], กวนแข้ง [guan kâeng], แหยม [yǎem]

meth (methamphetamine) *n.* ยาไอซ์ [yah 'ai], ไอซ์ (ไอส์) ['ai]

to mind your own business *idiom.* เอาหูไปนาเอาตาไปไร่ ['ao hǒo bpai nah 'ao dtah bpai râi]

minor wife *n.* บ้านเล็ก [bâhn léhk], อีหนู ['ee nǒo]

to miss someone *v.* คิดถึง [kíht tǔeng]

to miss (fail) *v.* แหว [hâeo]

to miss your plane *v.* ตกเครื่อง [dtòhk krûeang]

to miss your ride/bus *v.* ตกรถ [dtòhk róht]

mistress *n.* ชู้ [chóo], อีหนู ['ee nǒo], บ้านเล็ก [bâhn léhk]

mixed person (ethnically) *n.* ลูกครึ่ง [look krûeng]

mixed up *adj.* เซ่อแดก [sêr dàek], มั่ว [mûa]

modern *adj.* ชิ่ง [sîhng], เดิ้น [dêrn], อินเตอร์ ['in dter]

modest *v./adj.* ถล่มตัว [tà lòhm dtua]

money *n.* ตังค์ [dtung], ตางค์ [dtang], กะตังค์ [gà dtung]

money spent on different traditions of a society *n.* ภาษีสังคม [pah sěe sung kohm]

moody *adj.* ขี้งอน [kêe ngawn]

more *adj.* อิก ['ìk]

More?! เอาอีกแล้ว ['ao 'èek láeo]

more than is needed *adv.* เว่อร์ [wêr], โอเวอร์ ['oe wêr]

moron(ic) *n./adj.* ปัญญาอ่อน [bpun yah àwn], ปัญญานิ่ม [bpun yah nîhm]

the most *adj./adv.* กว่าเพื่อน [gwàh pûean], เดี๊ยะ [día], เช็ด [chéht], แฮ [hae]

most likey *part.* มั้ง [múng], ละมั้ง [lâ múng]

Mother f—ker! แม่ง [mâeng], ไอ้เหี้ย ['âi hîa], เหี้ย [hîa]

to motivate yourself *v.* คันตัวเอง [dun dtua 'ayng]

to move ahead *v.* พาส (พาสส์) [páht]

to move in and out (sex) *v.* เด้า [dâo], กระเด้า [grà dâo]

to move to a strong beat *v.* ดิ้น [dîhn]

moves *n.* น้ำยา [nám yah]

movie star *n.* ดารา [dah rah]

much *adj.* จ๋าบ [jáhp], ตึ่ม [dtuem], อื้อจือเหลี่ยง ['ûe jue lïang], อื้อซ่า ['ûe sâh]

my girl/love *pron.* เธอ [ter]

N

to nag *v.* ดูดี่ [dŏo dĕe], ติ๊ม [dtúem]

naked *adj.* ลอนจอน [lawn jâwn], โป๊ [bpóe]

nasty *adj.* ทุเรศ [tú râyt], ลามก [lah móhk]

Nasty! ท้วยส์ [tóoi]

National Geographic boobies *n.* นมยาน [nohm yahn]

naturally *adv.* ชัวร์ป๊าบ [chua bpáhp]

to naturalize (citizenship) *v.* โอนชาติ ['oen chat]

naughty (sexual) *adj.* ทะลึ่ง [tá lûeng]

nevertheless *adv.* ยังไงก็ดี [yung ngai gâw dee]

new *adj.* ถอดด้าม [tàwt dâhm]

new celebrity *n.* ดาวรุ่ง [dow rôong]

No? เนอะ [nér], นะ [ná]

No, I mean... เอ้ย ['éri]

no problem *adj.* สบายโก๋ [sà bai gŏe]

No way?! จริงเหรอ [jing rĕr]

non-stop *adv.* ต่อยหอย [dtòi hŏi]

nose *n.* ตะหมูก [dtà mòok]

Not a chance! ไม่มีทาง [mâi mee tahng]

not at all *part.* หรอก [ràwk]

not bad *adj.* ไม่เลว [mâi layo]

to not be able to compete *v.* ตกม้าตาย [dtòhk máh dtai]

to not be able to do anything right *v.* ถ่อไม่ถึงน้ำ ค้ำไม่ถึงดิน [tàw mâi tŭeng nám kám mâi tŭeng dihn]

to not get a hard-on *v.* นกเขาไม่คัน [nók kăo mâi kun]

to not give a damn what happens to him/it *v.* ช่างหัวมัน [châhng hŭa mun]

to not give others the chance to retort *v.* ตีหัวเข้าบ้าน [dtee hŭa kâo bâhn]

to not have any money *v.* ทรับย์จาง [súp jahng]

not really/not like that *part.* หรอก [ràwk]

not so bright *adj.* ไม่เต็มบาท [mâi dtehm bàht]

to not take a shower *v.* ซักแห้ง [súk hâeng]

Not so loud! จุ๊ (จุ๊ ๆ) [jóo]

not so smooth *adj.* ซื่อบื้อ [sûe bûe]

not willing to put effort into your work *adj.* เช้าชามเย็นชาม [cháo chahm yehn chahm]

Not yet! อย่าเพิ่ง [yàh pêrng]

not yourself *adj.* เฟค (เฟก) [fáyk]

noticeable *adj.* เฮ้ว [háyo]

now *part.* ชะที [sá tee]

Now I understand! อ้อ [' ăw]

nude *adj.* โป๊ [bpóe]

nuts *adj.* ต๊อง [dtáwng], เซี้ยว [séeo], ติ๊งต๊อง (ติงต๊อง) [dtíhng dtáwng], บ้า ๆ บอ ๆ [bâh bâh baw baw], บ้า [bâh], บ๊อง [báwng], ไม่เต็มบาท [mâi dtehm bàht]

nutsack *n.* ไข่ [kài], ไข่ห่ำ [kài hăm], ตุ้ม [dtôom], ห่ำ [hăm]

O

obese *adj./adv.* ตุ้มต๊ะตุ้มต๊ะ
  [dtôom dtá dtôom dtá]

occasion *n.* ที่ [tee]

odd *adj.* เซ่อร์ [ser]

of course *part.* ซิ [síh], ซิ่ [sîh], ซี
  [see], ซี่ [sêe], นะซิ [ná síh]

off (doesn't seem right) *adj.* ดูไม่จืด
  [doo mâi jùet]

off (weird) *adj.* เซ่อร์ [ser]

office *n.* ออฟฟิศ ['aw fít]

Oh! *interj.* โอ ['oe], โอ้ ['ôe], อ้าว
  ['ôw], อุย ['óuie], อุยตาย ['óuie dtai],
  อุบ ['óop]

Oh... *interj.* โธ่ [tôe]

Oh f—k! *interj.* ตายละวา [dtai lá wah]

Oh no! *interj.* ตายจริง [dtai jing], ตาย
  (ต๊าย) [dtai], โอ๊ยตาย ['óhe dtai]

Oh, now I get it! อ๋อ ['ăw]

Oh shit! ตาย (ต๊าย) [dtai], ตายจริง
  [dtai jing], ต๊ายตาย [dtái dtai],
  ตายละวา [dtai lá wah], ตายแล้ว
  [dtai láeo], โอ๊ยตาย ['óhe dtai],
  ซี้เลี้ยว [sée léeo]

Oh wow! โอ้โห ['ôe hŏe], โอ้โฮ ['ôe
  hoe], โอ้โอ้เฮ้ะ ['ôe hoe háy]

Oh yeah? จริงเหลอ [jing lěr]

Ok! ok... อ้า ['âh]

Ok! *interj.* เออ ['er], เออซีวะ ['er sí wá]

Ok! *phr.* เอาละ ['ao lá]

Ok now! *part.* น่า [nâh], น่ะ [nâ]

okay (as in good) *adj.* ตุ๋ย [dtóuie]

old and without a husband *adj.*
  ขึ้นคาน [kûen kahn]

an old hand *n.* ชั่วโมงบิน [chûa
  moeng bin]

old maid *n.* สาวขึ้นคาน [săo kûen kahn]

old man/old timer *n.* ไอ้แก่ ['âi gàe]

Old men like young girls.
  วัวแก่กินหญ้าอ่อน
  [wua gàe gin yâh 'àwn]

old perv *n.* ไอ้แก่หำ้ง ['âi gàe hŭa ngoo]

old uneducated person *n.* ตาสีตาสา
  [dtah sĕe dtah săh]

older person who hangs out with
  teenagers *n.* เด็กหนวด [dèhk nùa]

on the dole *adj.* นั่งตบยุง
  [nûng dtòhp young]

on the surface *adv.* เผิน [pěr]

on your own *adv.* ตัวใครตัวมัน
  [dtua krai dtua mun]

one *adj.* นึง [nueg]

one night stand *phr.*
  น้ำแตกแล้วแยกทาง [nám dàek
  láeo yâek tahng]

the one to blame *n.* ตัวเอ้ [dtua 'ây]

100% *adv.* เต็มร้อย [dtehm rói]

only *adv.* ลูกเดียว [lôok deeo],
  ชะ [sá], ซัก [súk]

only a little bit *adv.* ซักกะติ๊ด
  [súk gà dtíht]

only this and/or that *part.* นี่ [nêe]

Oo-hoo! อู้ฮู ['ôo hoo]

or not *adv.* รึไม่ [rúe mâi]

or not at all *adv.* รึเป่า [rúe bpào],
  รึป่าว [rúe bpòw]

or something... *adv.* อะไรยังเนี้ย
  ['a rai yung nía]

Or what? รึไง [rúe ngai]

or whatever... *adv.* อะไรยังเนี้ย
  ['a rai yung nía]

oral sex *n.* ออรัลเซ็กซ์ ['aw run séhk],
  ชิวหาพาเพลิน [chiu hăh pah plern]

orgasm *n.* จุดสุดยอด [jòot soot yâwt]

to orgasm *v.* เสร็จ [sèht],
  สำเร็จความใคร
  [săm réht kwahm krâi]

orgy *n.* เซ็กซ์หมู่ [séhk mòo]

Ouch! *interj.* อุย ['ouie], อุ้ย ['óuie],
  อูย ['ouie], อุยหน่า ['ouie nàh],
  โอย ['ohe], โอ๊ย ['óhe]

out of date *adj.* เฉิ่ม [chèrm], เชย
  [choei], เชยแหลก [choe làek],
  ตกรุ่น [dtòhk rôon]

out of it (mind) *adj.* ซึมกะทือ
[suem gà tue]

out of sight out of mind *phr.*
ไกลตาไกลใจ [glai dtah glai jai]

out of style *adj.* เฉิ่ม [chèrm]

out of touch with what's going on *adj.*
ซื่อบื้อ [sûe bûe]

over *adv.* โอเวอร์ ['oe wêr], เว่อร์ [wêr]

over the top *adv.* หวิอหวา [wǔe wǎh]

over there *adj.* งู้น [ngôon], นู้น [nôon]

overconfident for such insignificance
adj. ตัวเท่าลูกหมา
[dtua tâo look mǎh]

overtly queer man *n.* แต๋ว [dtóot], เต๋า
[dtǎo]

P

to pack fudge *v.* ตุ๋ย [dtǔie]

pack of cigs *cl.* ซอง [sawng]

package *n.* ไขห่ำ [kài hǎm], เจี๊ยว [jéeo]

Pah! *interj.* ถุยส์ (ถุย) [tǔie]

pain in the ass *v./adj.* บังอาจ
[bung 'àht]

panicky *adj.* เจ๊กตื่นไฟ [jáyk dtùen fai]

panties *n.* ชั้นใน [chún nai]

part of a whole *adv.* ชะ [sá]

to party *v.* ดริงก์แอนด์แดนซ์
[drihg 'aen daen]

party bus *n.* ฉิ่งฉับทัวร์
[chìhng chùp tua]

to pass *v.* พาส (พาสส์) [páht]

to pass gas *v.* ปล่อยแก๊ส [bplòi gáet]

passionate *adj.* ซู่ซ่า [sôo sâh]

to pay for a young girl up front to
have at a later time *v.* ตกเขียว
[dtòhk kěeo]

to peck a kiss *v.* จุ๊บ [jóop]

to pee *v.* ฉี่ [chèe]

to pee (men) *v.* ยิงกระต่าย
[ying gra dtài]

to pee (want to really bad) *v.* ปาดฉี่
[bpùat chèe]

to pee (women) *v.* เก็บดอกไม้
[gèp dàwk mái]

to pee on each other *v.* ฉี่รดกัน
[chèe róht gun]

to peek at *v.* แอบดี ['àep dee]

peevish *adj.* ขี้งอน [kêe ngawn],
งอนตุ๊บป่อง [ngawn dtóop bpàwng]

penis *n.* จู๋ [jǒo], ควย [kooi], กระเจี๊ยว
[grà jíeo], เจ้าโลก [jâo lôek], ดอ
[daw], ท่อนล่า [tâwn lam], นกเขา
[nók kǎo], เอ๊น ['ehn], ไอ้ใบ้ ['âi bâi]

penniless *adj.* โรคทรัพย์จาง
[rôek súp jahng]

penny-pinching *adj.* เค็ม [kehm],
ขี้เหนียว [kehm]

perfect *adj.* เพอร์เฟกต์ [per fák],
เนี๊ยบ [níap]

person *cl.* ตัว [dtua]

person with white skin *n.* ฝรั่ง [fà rùng]

perspiration *n.* เหื่อ [hùea]

pervert (perv) *n.* บ้ากาม [bâh gahm],
กามวิตถาร [gahm wíht tǎhn]

to pester *v.* ดึ๊ม [dtúem]

peter *n.* นกเขา [nók kǎo]

phallic image (often made from wood)
n. ขิก [kìhk], ปลัดขิก [bpà lùt kìhk],
ไอ้ขิก ['âi kìhk]

phasing (as into a fraternity) *n.*
พี่รับน้อง [pêe rúp náwng]

phone number *n.* เบอร์ [ber]

physically fit *adj.* ฟิต [fíht]

to pick up (flirt) *v.* จีบ [jeep]

to pickpocket *v.* แซ้ง [sáeng]

Piece of shit! ระย่าคน [rá yum kohn],
ระย่าหมา [rá yum mǎh]

pimp *n.* แมงดา [maeng dah]

to piss *v.* เยี่ยว [yêeo],
ฉิ้งฉ่อง [chíng chàwng]

piss-drunk *v.* เมาดิบ [mao dìhp]

to piss someone off for fun *v.* กวนตีน
[guan dteen], กวนแข้ง [guan kâeng],
กวนส้นตีน [guan sôhm dteen]

pizza *n.* พิซซ่า [pít sâh]

to plan *v.* แพลน [plaen]

plans *n.* โปรแกรม [bproe graem]

plastic *n.* เงินพลาสติก [ngern plah sà dtìk]

to play truant *v.* โดดร่ม [dòet rôhm], โดด [dòet]

playboy *n.* เจ้าชู้ [jâo chóo], เจ้าชู้ประตูดิน [jâo chóo bprà dtoo din]

player *n.* เจ้าชู้ [jâo chóo]

please *part.* คราบ [krâhp], คร้าบ [kráhp], คับ [kúp], จ๊ะ [já], จ๋ะ [já], จ๋า [jǎh], หน่อยซิ [nòi síh], นะ [ná], นา [nah]

plain *adj.* ขี้เหล่ (ขี้เหร่) [kêe lày], ขี้ริ้วขี้เหร่ [kêe ríu kêe ràu]

plump *adj.* อวบ ['ùap]

plump (for women) *adj.* สบึม (สบึมส์) [sà buem]

plump (in a cute way) *adj.* อึ๋ม ['ǔem]

point of interest *n.* ช็อตเด็ด [cháwt dèht]

to poke (sexual) *v.* แทง [taeng]

to poke one's nose in *v.* ทะเล่อทะล่า [tá-lêr tá-lâh]

poker (cards) *n.* ไพ่ป๊อก [pâi bpáwk]

to pop a girl's cherry *v.* ฉีกทุเรียน [chèek tóo rian], เจาะไข่แดง [jàw kài daeng], เปิดซิง [bpèrt sing]

poop *n.* ขี้ [kêe]

to poop (poo) *v.* ขี้ [kêe]

poor (sucks) *adv.* หวย [hòoi], หวยแตก [hòoi dtàek]

poor man who takes a rich wife *n.* ตกถังข้าวสาร [dtòhk tǔng kôw sǎhn]

porn/pornography *n.* เอ็กซ์ ['èhk]

porn mag *n.* หนังสือโป๊ [nǔng sǔe bóe]

porn movie *n.* หนังโป๊ [nǔng bóe]

posh *adj.* ไฮโซ [hai soe]

position (rank) *n.* เก้าอี้ [gâo 'êe], ตำแหน่งแห่งหน [dtam nàeng hàeng hǒhn]

position (sex) *n.* ท่า [tâh]

positive *v.* ชัวร์ [chua]

post *n.* เก้าอี้ [gâo 'êe]

to pout *v.* ดูดี่ [dǒo dèe]

pox *n.* ซิฟิลิ [síh fíh líht]

to praise *v.* ชมเปาะ [chohm bpaw]

preference *n.* สเป็ค (สเป็ก) [sà bpèhk]

prefers the Western way of doing things *n./adj.* หัวนอก [hǔa nâwk]

to prematurely ejaculate *v.* ล่มปากอ่าว [lôhm bpàhk 'òw]

to prepare *v.* ชง [chohng]

(to) presume... *v.* ดิ๊งต่าง [dtǐhng dtàhng], ดิ๊งต่าง [dtíhng dtàhng], ดี่ต่าง [dtěe dtàhng]

to pretend *v.* สร้างภาพ [sâhng pâhp]

to pretend like you don't know what's going on *phr.* ตีลูกเซ่อ [dtee lôok sêr], ตีลูกซึม [dtee lôok suem], ทำไก [tam gǎi]

professional *n./adj.* เซียน [sian]

professor *n.* จารย์ [jahn]

profound *adj.* ถึงกึ๋น [tǔeng gǔen]

program *n.* โปรแกรม [bproe graem]

prominent (in laid back way) *adj.* ซ่า [sâh]

Prostitute! อีดอก ['ee dàwk], อีดอกทอง ['ee dàwk tawng]

prostitute *n.* กะหรี่ [gà rèe], ออหรี่ ['aw rèe], นางบำเรอ [nahng bam rer], นางฟ้าจำแลง [nahng fáh jam laeng], อีตัว ['ee dtua]

prostitute (who also has a normal job) *n.* ชั้นสูง [chún sǒong]

proud of your possessions *v.* เห่อของใหม่ [hèr kǎwng mài]

psyched (as in happy) *v.* ดี๊ด๊า [dée dáh], กระดี๊กระด๊า [grà dée grà dáh] pub *n.* ผับ [pùb]

pubes (pubic hair) *n.* หมอย [mŏi]

to puke *v.* อ้วก ['ûak]

to pull out (quickly) *v.* ชักออกเร็ว ๆ
[chúck àwk rayo rayo]

to punch *v.* เฉิ่ม [chèrm]

to push yourself *v.* ดันตัวเอง
[dun dtua 'ayng]

pussy/puss *n.* หี [hĕe], จิ๋ม [jĭhm], หอย
[hŏi], เต่า [dtào], นาผืนน้อย [nah
pŭen nói], อีโมะ ['ee móe], โมะ
[móe], อีเฉาะ ['ee chaw]

pussy (coward) *n.* หน้าตัวเมีย
[nâh dtua mia]

pussy lips *n.* แคม [kaem]

puzzled to boredom *adj.* เง๊ง [ngehng]

Q

queer *n.* เกย์ [gay], เต๊า [dtăo], แต๋ว
[dtóot], ถ้วด้ำ [tùa dam]

quick *adj.* ตีนหมา [dteen măh],
ซิ่ง [sîhng]

quickly *adv.* ฟุ๊บฟุ๊บ [fóop fúp]

quiet (untalkative) *v.* เฉาปาก
[chăo bpàhk]

to quit your position/rank *v.*
ถอดหัวโขน [tàwt hŭa kŏhn]

quite *adv.* ทีเดียว [tee deeo]

R

the race horse (gonorrhea) *n.*
หนองใน [năwng nai]

to rack yourself *v.* บีบไข่ [bèep kài]

radiating *adj.* ซู่ซ่า [sôo sâh]

to raise an issue *v.* ชูธง [choo tohng]

randomly *adv.* ดื้อ ๆ [dûe dûe]

rank *n.* ตำแหน่งแห่งหน [dtam nàeng
hàeng hŏhn], เก้าอี้ [gâo 'êe]

to rape *v.* ปล้ำ [bplâm], ปลุกปล้ำ
[bpòok bplâm]

to reach puberty *v.* แตกดังเปรี๊ยะ
[dtàek dung bpría]

real quick *adv.* แป๊บเดียว [bpáep deeo],
แป๊บนึง [bpáep nueng]

relaxed *adj.* มันส์ (มัน) [mun]

Ready! เอาละ ['ao lá]

realistic *adj.* ขวานผ่าซาก [kwăhn
pàh sâhk]

really *adj.* เชียว [cheeo], สุดตีน
[sòot dteen]

Really? เหรอ [rĕr], เหลอ [lĕr],
งั้นเหรอ [ngún rĕr], จริงเหรอ [jing
rĕr], จริงเหลอ [jing lĕr], เรอะ [rér]

really *part.* ซี้ [see], ซี่ [sêe]

really bad *adj.* เฮงซวย [hayng sooi]

really close (friendship) *adj.* ซี้ [sée],
ซี้ปึ้ก [sée bpùek]

really crappy *adv.* ห่วยแตก [hòoi dtàek]

redneck *adj.* บ้านนอก ๆ [bâhn náwk
bâhn nâwk]

to register *v.* ดีทะเบียน [dtee tá bian]

relationship oriented way *n.* กันเอง
[gun 'ayng]

repulsive *v./adj.* เป็นกะปิ [bpehn
gà bpìh]

retard *n.* ปัญญาอ่อน [bpun yah àwn]

retarded *adj./n.* ปัญญานิ่ม [bpun yah
nîhm], โง่ [ngôe], บา ๆ บอ ๆ [bâh
bâh baw baw], ไม่เต็มบาท [mâi
dtehm bàht]

rice whisky *n.* เหล้าขาว [lâo kŏw]

rich *adj.* มีกะตังค์ [mee gà dtung]

to ride for free *v.* เต๊า [dtăo]

the right *n.* ฝ่ายขวา [fài kwăh]

Right? ใช่มั้ย (ใช่มั้ย) [châi mái]

right thinking (as in conservative) *adj.*
เอียงขวา ['iang kwăh]

to roam around *v.* ตะลอน [dtà lawn]

to rob a house *v.* ตัดช่องย่องเบา
[dtùk châwng yâwng bao]

to role your eyes *v.* กรอกตา
[gràwk dtah]

romantic *adj.* โรแมนติค (โรแมนติก)
[roe maen dtík]

rotten look **n.** หน้าบึ้ง [nâh bûeng], หน้าบูด [nâh bòot]

rotten luck **adj.** ซวยกะลุดม้อ [sooi gà loot máh]

a rubber **n.** ปลอก [bplàwk], คอนด้อ [kawn dâwm], ถุงยาง [tǒong yahng]

Rubbish! ถุยส์ (ถุย) [tǒuie]

to ruin your reputation **v.** เสียหมา [sǐa mǎh]

to run a train (on someone) **v.** เรียงคิว [riang kiu]

run after two hares, catch neither **phr.** จับปลาสองมือ [jùp blah sǎwng mue]

to run like the wind **v.** ใส่ตีนหมา [sài dteen mǎh]

to run your mouth **v.** ชักยนต์ [chuck yohn]

to run for your life **v.** ก๋วย [gǒoi]

S

sad **adj.** จ๋อย [jǒi]

sadism **n.** ซาดิสม์ [sah dìht]

sadistic person **n.** ซาดิสม์ [sah dìht]

SAG **n.** คิง [kihng]

sag bags (breasts) **n.** นมยาน [nohm yahn]

the same **adj.** เซมเซม [saym saym]

sample **n.** แซมเปิ้ล [saem bpêrn]

satisfied (sexually) **v.** สำเร็จความใคร่ [sǎm réht kwahm krâi]

sauna **n.** เซาน่า [sao nâh]

savage **adj.** แสบ [sàep]

to save face **v.** กู้หน้า [gôo nâh]

savvy **adj.** ซิ่ง [sîhng]

Say! **interj.** เฮ้ย (เอ้ย) [héri], เฮ้ [háy], ไฮ้ [hái]

to say **v.** เซด [sâyt], ว่า [wâh]

to say nice things **v.** ชมเปาะ [chohm bpaw]

to say something stupid or offensive **v.** เกรียน [grian]

to say stupid shit **v.** เห่า [hào]

to say you're sorry but not really mean it **phr.** ฝืนไม่เลี้ยง [fun mâi líang]

to scam **v.** ต้ม [dtôhm], ต้มจนเปื่อย [dtôhm johm bpùeoi], ตุ๋น [dtǒon], ปอกลอ [bpàwk lâwk]

to scam a free ride **v.** ชักดาบ [chúk dàhp]

scantily clad **v.** แต่งตัววาบหวาน [dtàeng dua wâhp wǎhn], นุ่งน้อยห่มน้อย [nôong nói hòhm nói]

schedule **n.** โปรแกรม [bproe graem]

to scissor **v.** ตีฉิ่ง [dtee chìng]

to scold **v.** ว่า [wâh]

to score a goal in sports **v.** ทำประตู [tam brà dtoo]

Scram!/Scoot! ไปซะ [bpai sá]

to screw **v.** ฟัน [fun], ฟาด [fàht]

Screw him! ช่างหัวมัน [châhng hǔa mun], ชั่งหัวมัน [chùng hǔa mun]

Screw it! ช่างมัน [châhng mun], ช่างมันปะไร [châhng mun bpa rai], ช่างมันเป็นไร [châhng mun bpehn rai], ชั่งแม่ง [chùng màeng]

to screw over **v.** ฟัน [fun]

to seal the deal with a local girl **v.** ถึง [tǔeng]

seamstress in factory **n.** ฉันทนา [chǔn tá nah]

a second ago **adv.** ตะกี๊ (ตะกี้) [dtà gée]

secondhand **adj.** เซ็คกันแฮนด์ [séhk gun hâend]

secret **n.** ได [dtǎi]

secret partner **n.** กิ๊ก [geek]

seems innocent **adj.** ซีด [sêet]

seems to be a player **adj.** แซ่หลี [sâe lěe]

seen your share (of experiences) **n.** ชั่วโมงบิน [chûa moeng bin]

self-made person **v.** ได่เต่า [dtài dtâo]

to sell **v.** เซ้ง [sáyng]

to sell your body **v.** ทำประตู [tam brà dtoo]

semen *n.* ต๋อง [dtáwng], น้ำกาม [nám gahm], น้ำเงี่ยน [nám ngîan], น้ำรัก [nám rúk]

senselessly *adv.* ดื้อ ๆ [dûe dûe]

sensitive *adj.* เซ็นซิทิฟ [sehn síh tihn]

to separate *v.* ตัดเชือก [dtùt chûeak], ตัดเป็นตัดตาย [dtùt bpehn dtùt dtai], ตัดหางปล่อยวัด [dtùt hǎhng blòi wút]

serious *adj.* ซีเรียส [see rîat]

Serves you right! ช่วยไม่ได้ [chôoi mâi dâi]

servant *n.* เบ๋ [báy]

to serve somebody right *v.* สมน้ำหน้า [sǒhm nám nâh]

to service *v.* เซอร์วิส [ser wíht]

to service a man *v.* ทำประตู [tam brà dtoo]

to set *v.* เซ็ต [séht]

7-Eleven *n.* เซเว่ [say wâyn]

sex *n.* เซ็กซ์ (เซ็ก) [séhk]

sex crazed *adj.* บ้ากาม [bâh gahm]

sex with one's wife *n.* การบ้าน [gahn bâhn]

sexual perv (ert) *n.* กามวิตถาร [gahm wíht tǎhn]

sexy *adj.* เซ็กซี่ [séhk sêe]

shaved (as in pubic hair) *adj.* เกรียน [grian]

she (her) *pron.* ชี [chee], เค้า [káo], หล่อน [làwn], แก [gae], เธอ [ter], มัน [mun]

shirtless *v.* เซ็ตหนัง [chért nǔng]

shit *n.* ขี้ [kêe]

Shit! *interj.* ฉิบหาย [chìhp hǎi], วะ [wá]

to shit *v.* ขี้ [kêe], อึ ['ùe]

shit talk *n.* ปากหมา [bpàhk mǎh]

shocked *v.* ช็อก [cháwk]

to shoot a drink *v.* ดวด [dùat]

to shoot your load on contact *v.* ล่มปากอ่าว [lôhm bpàhk 'òw]

to shoot your load outside *v.* หลั่งข้างนอก [lùng kâhng nâwk]

to shoot up a drug *v.* โช้ก [chóhk]

to shop *v.* ช็อปปิ้ง [cháwp bpîng]

short a few coins *adj.* ไม่เต็มบาท [mâi dtehm bàht]

to shovel food into your mouth *v.* แดก [dàek]

show (concert) *n.* คอนเสิร์ต [kawn sert]

to show off *v.* แอ๊ค ['áek]

to show respect outwardly yet really dislike *phr.* หน้าไว้หลังหลอก [nâh wái lǔng làwk]

to show your stupidity *v.* ปล่อยไก่ [bplòi gài]

showy *adj.* ขี้โม้ [kêe móh], หวือหวา [wǔe wǎh]

Shush! *interj.* จุ๊ (จุ๊ ๆ) [jóo]

Sick! อี๊ (อี๋) ['ée]

Sick asshole! ท้วยส [tóoi]

sick of it *v.* ชะเบื่อ [sá bùea]

to sign *v.* เซ็น [sehn]

silly *adj.* ต๋อง [dtáwng], เบอะ [bér]

simple-minded *adj.* เชย [choei]

simply *adv.* แหละ [làe]

simply such and such *part.* นี่ [nêe]

sissy *n.* ตุ๊ด [dtóot]

69 position *n.* ท่าหกสิบเก้า [tâh hòhk sìhp gâo]

skilled *n./adj.* เซียน [sian]

skills *n.* น้ำยา [nám yah]

to skip class *v.* โดดรม [dòet rôhm], โดด [dòet], กระโดดรม [grà dòet rôhm]

to skip out *adv.* ชะแว่บ [chá wáep], ชะแว้บ [sá wáep]

to sleep with a hooker *v.* ตีกะหรี่ [dtee gà rèe]

to sleep with a lot of dudes *v.* มั่วผู้ชาย [mûa pôo chai]

to sleep your way to the top *v.* ใช้เต๋าได [chái dtâo dtài] sloppy *adj.* ชี้ช้ำ [sée súa]

sloshed (drunk) already *adj.* ดีมาแล้ว [dee mah láeo]

slow (stupid) *adj.* บื้อ [bûe]

slut *n.* แรด (แรด) [râet], ใก [gài]

to smack a kiss *v.* จูบ [jóop]

small boy *n.* ห่ำน้อย [hǎm nói]

smart looking *adj.* เท่ [tâh]

smashed (drunk) *v.* เมาดิบ [mao dìhp]

to smoke cigarette/tobacco *v.* ดูดบุหรี่ [dòot bòo rèe], ดูดยา [dòot yah]

to smoke opium *v.* เป่าปี่ [bpàa bpèe]

smooth *adj.* เท่ [tâh]

snacks eaten with booze *n.* กับแกล้ม [gùp gâem]

to snag (steal) *v.* อุ๊บอิ๊บ ['óop 'íp]

to snake (steal) *v.* ชิว [siu]

to snatch *v.* ชิว [siu]

to sneak into someone's house and rob them *v.* ตัดช่องย่องเบา [dtùk châwng yâwng bao]

to sneak off *v.* แวบ (แว้บ) [wâep]

to sniff kiss *v.* หอมแก้ม [hǎwm gâem]

so *conj.* ก้อ [gâw]

so *adv./adj.* เลย [leri], เล้ย [léri], เชียว [cheeo], งั้น [ngún]

so... *interj.* แล้ว [láeo]

so much *adv.* ชะ [sá]

so then... *interj.* แล้ว [láeo]

So what?/So... แล้วใง [láeo ngai]

so-so *adv.* เอาดี ['ao dee]

soap land *n.* อาบอบนวด ['àhp 'òhp nûat]

socialist leaning *adj.* เอียงซ้าย ['iang sái]

soda water *n.* โซดา [soe dah]

soft *adj.* มะเขือเผา [má kǔea pǎo]

to soil your reputation *v.* เสียหมา [sǐa mǎh]

some *adv.* มั่ง [mûng]

someone who acts too much like a Westerner *n.* ฝรั่งดอง [fà rùng dawng]

something just doesn't seem right *adj.* ดูไม่จืด [doo mâi jùet]

something like that *adv.* อะไรยังเนี้ย ['a rai yung nía]

sometimes/somewhat *adv.* มั่ง [mûng]

Son of a bitch! ฉิบหาย [chìhp hǎi], ไอ้เวร ['âi wayn]

sour face *n.* หน้าบูด [nâh bòot], หน้าบึ้ง [nâh bûeng]

spades (cards) *n.* โพดำ [poe dam], ไพ่โพดำ [pâi poe dam]

to speak *v.* อู้ ['ôo]

to speak carelessly *v.* พูดส่งเดช [pôot sòhng dàyt]

to speak straight *v.* พูดตรง [pôot dtrohng]

special K *n.* ยาเค [yah kay], เค [kay]

speech *n.* น้ำคำ [nám kam]

speechless *v.* ตันคอหอย [dtun kaw hǒi], อึ้งกิมกี่ ['ùeng gim gèe]

speed (cheep form) *n.* ยาบ้า [yah bâh]

spoiled *adj.* ปล่อยตัวปล่อยใจ [bplòi dtua bplòi jai], ปล่อยใจ [bplòi jai]

sponge (always borrows money) *n.* ดาวใถ [dow tǎi]

spoodge *n.* ต๋อง [dtáwng]

spooked *adj.* ตุ๊กกะใจ [dtóhk gà jai]

spoon position *n.* ท่านอนตะแคง [tâh nawn dtà kaeng]

spy *n.* สปาย [sà bpai]

Sorry! โทษที่ [tôet tee]

to stab (sexual) *v.* แทง [taeng]

to stall *v.* ดึงเกม [dueng gaym]

stamp *n.* แสตมป์ [sà dtaem]

standing out *adj.* ช้า [sâh]

to start shit *v.* ทำตัวงี่เง่า [tam dtua ngêe ngâo]

startled *adj.* ตาเหลือกตาปลิ้น [dtah lùeak stah bplîhn]

starting and stopping *adv.* ตุ๊กกะฉึก [dtóok gà chùek]

to starve *v.* ท้องแห้ง [táwng hâeng]

to stay up until dawn *adv./v.*
โต้รุ่ง [dtóe rôong]

to steal *v.* อุบอิ๊บ ['óop 'íp],
โอ๋โม ['oe moe], ซิว [siu]

stewardess *n.* นางฟ้า [nahng fáh]

to still be standing *v.* เตะปี๊บดัง [dtày
bpée dung]

to still have moves *v.* เตะปี๊บดัง
[dtày bpée dung]

stingy *adj.* ขี้เหนียว [kehm], เค็ม
[kehm], ทะเลเรียกพี่ [tá lay rîak pêe]

to stink *v./adj.* เป็นกะปิ [bpehn gà bpìh]

stock market/exchange *n.* ตลาดหุ้น
[dtà lath hôon]

stomach is making noises *phr.*
ท้องร้อง [táwng ráwng]

to stop talking *v.* รูดซิปปาก
[rôot síp bàhk]

straight-acting gay *n.* คิง [kihng]

strip club *n.* อะโกโก้ ['à goe gôe]

to strut *v.* ฉาย [chǎi]

stubbornly *adv.* ตะบัน [dtà bpun],
ตะบี้ตะบัน [dtà bêe dtà bpun]

stupid *adj.* โง่ [ngôe], งั่ง [ngûng],
งี่เง่า [ngêe ngâo], ซื่อบื้อ [sûe bûe],
เซ่อ [sêr], เซ่อซ่า [sêr sâh],
ทึ่ม [tûem], บื้อ [bûe]

Stupid idiot! *interj.* โง่เง่าเต่าตุ่น
[ngôe ngâo dtào dtòon]

stupid f—k *n.* ไอ้บ้า ['âi bâh]

stupid-looking *adj.* เบอะ [bér]

stupid person *n.* ควาย [kwai]

style *n.* สไตล์ [sà dtai]

style *cl./n.* ยัง [yung]

sucks *adj.* ส้ว [sùa], ระย่ำ [rá yum]

to suck dick *v.* โม้ก [móek]

sucks *adv.* ห่วย [hòoi], ห่วยแตก
[hòoi dtàek]

suddenly *adv.* พึ่บพึ่บ [fóop fúp]

sugar daddy *n.* ป๋า [bpǎh]

sullen *adj.* ขึ้งอน [kêe ngawn],
งอนตุบป่อง [ngawn dtóop bpàwng]

super *adj.* จ๋า [jǎh]

superb *adj.* เช็ด [chéht]

supermarket *n.* ซุปเปอร์ [sóop bper]

Sure! *interj.* ฮื่อ [hûe]

sure *v.* ชัวร์ [chua]

surely *part.* ซิ [síh], ซิ่ [sîh], ซี [see],
ซี่ [sêe]

to surf the internet *v.* โต้เซิร์ฟ [dtóe
sern], โต้ [dtóe]

superficial *adj.* เฟค (เฟก) [fáyk]

superficially *adv.* เผิน [pěr]

to support *v.* ซัพพอร์ต [súb páwt],
เชียร์ [chia]

suppose if… *adv.* ดิ๊งต่าง [dtíhng
dtàhng], ดี่ต่าง [dtěe dtàhng],
ดิ๊งต่าง [dtíhng dtàhng]

surprised *v.* ช็อก [cháwk],
ตาเหลือกตาปลิ้น
[dtah lùeak stah bplîhn]

to surprise the hell out of someone *v.*
ต๊กกะใจ [dtóhk gà jai]

sweat *n.* เหื่อ [hùea]

Sweet! *adj.* แจ๋ว [jǎeo],
เจ๋งเป้ง [jǎyng bpâyng]

sweet mouth/words *n.* ปากหวาน
[bpàhk wǎhn]

sweetie/sweet heart *n.* หวานใจ [wǎhn
jai], ที่รัก [têe rúk]

to swim up the red river *v.* ผ่าไฟแดง
[fàh fai daeng]

swims like a fish in the water *n.*
ฉลาม [chà lǎhm]

to swindle *v.* ปอกลอก [bpàwk lâwk],
ต้มตุ๋ [dtôhm dtǒom]

to swipe (steal) *v.* อุบอิ๊บ ['óop 'íp]

to switch back and forth *v.* ซิกแซ็ก
[síhk sâek]

synch *adj.* สบายมาก [sà bai mâk]

syphilis *n.* ซิฟิลิ [síh fíh líht],
โรคซิฟิลิ [rôek síh fíh líht]

T

to take *v.* เช็ด [chèrt]

to take a dump *v.* ขี้ [kêe]

to take a dump (want to really bad) *v.* ปวดขี้ [bpùat kêe]

to take a girl's virginity *v.* เปิดซิง [bpèrt sing], เจาะไขแดง [jàw kài daeng]

to take a wiz/leak *v.* ฉี่ [chèe], เยี่ยว [yêeo]

to take advantage of *v.* ต้ม [dtôhm], ต้มตุ๋ [dtôhm dtŏom]

to take and not return *v.* อม ['ohm]

to take care of *v.* เท็กแคร์ [téhk kae]

Take it! เอาซิ' ['ao sí]

to take it in the poop-shoot *v.* ตุย [dtŏuie]

to take over (business) *v.* เซ้ง [sáyng]

to talk *v.* อู้ ['ôo]

to talk a lot *v.* ฝอย [fŏi]

to talk about something that's already been talked about *v.* ฉายซ้ำ [chăi sám]

to talk nonstop *v.* ชักยนต์ [chuck yohn]

to talk little *v.* เฉาปาก [chăo bpàhk]

to talk shit *v.* เกรียน [grian], ทำตัวงี่เง่า [tam dtua ngêe ngâo], เห่า [hào]

to talk to a brick wall *phr.* ตักน้ำรดตอ [dtùk nám róht dtaw], ตักน้ำรดหัวตอ [dtùk nám róht hŭa dtaw], ตักน้ำรดหัวสาก [dtùk nám róht hŭa sàhk]

to taste *v.* เซี้ยบ ๆ [sérp sérp]

teach (teacher) *n.* จารย์ [jahn]

teenager *n.* วัยสะรุ่น [wai sà rôoo]

teenager always following the new trend *n.* เด็กแนว [dèhk naeo]

to tell it straight up *v.* พูดตรง [pôot dtrohng]

terrible luck *adj.* ซวยกะลุดม้อ [sooi gà loot máw]

to terrorize as a group *v.* รุมกินโต๊ะ [room gin dtóe]

to test *v.* เซี้ยบ ๆ [sérp sérp]

Thai dice game *n.* ไฮโล [hai loe]

Thai-ish *adj.* ไทๆไทย [tái tai]

Thai sake *n.* เหล้าขาว [lâo kŏw]

thanx *interj.* จ๊ะ [jâ], จ๊ะ [já], จ๋า [jǎh]

Thank you *part.* คับ [kúp], จ๋า [jǎh]

Thank you very much *part.* คราบ [krâhp], คร้าบ [kráhp]

that *adj.* งอน [ngôon], นู่น [nôon]

that *mod.* งั้น [ngún], งอน [ngóon], นู่น [nóon]

that chick *pron.* หล่อน [làwn]

that f—kin' guy *n.* ไอ้หมอนั้น ['âi măw nún]

that one *mod.* งั้น [ngún]

that one way over there *mod.* งอน [ngóon], นู่น [nóon]

that way *adj.* งั้น [ngún], ยังงั้น [yung ngúng], ยังโงน [yung ngóen]

that one right there *adj.* ไง [ngai]

That's the way it is! นั้นแหละ [nûn làe]

That's what you get! ช่วยไม่ได้ [chôoi mâi dâi]

then *conj.* ก้อ [gâw]

then *adv.* งั้น [ngún]

there *adj.* งอน [ngôon], นู่น [nôon]

There ya go! *phr.* นั่นแหละ [nûn làe]

therefore *adv.* งั้น [ngún]

There's no way! ไม่มีทาง [mâi mee tahng]

these (these ones) *mod.* งี้ [ngée]

they (them) *pron.* เค้า [káo], แก [gae], มัน [mun]

thingy (penis) *n.* เจ้าโลก [jâo lôek]

to think of it *v.* ถึงบางอ้อ [tŭeng bahn 'âw]

this *mod.* งี้ [ngée]

this *pron.* เนี่ย [nîa], นี่ [nêe]

this damn/freakin' one *n.* ไอ้นี่ ['âi nêe]

this one right here *adj.* ไง [ngai]

this way *adj.* ยังงี้ [yung ngée]

thoughts are wondering *adj.* ซึมกะทือ [suem gà tue]

to throw up *v.* อ้วก ['ûak]

tight-fitting *adj.* ฟิต [fíht]

time *n.* ที [tee]

times for having sex *cl.* ดอก [dàwk]

timid looking *adj.* ซีด [sêet]

tip *n.* ทิป [tíhp]

tired *adj.* เหงื่อตกกกืบ [ngùea dtòhk gèep]

tired as a bitch *adj.* เดี้ยง [dîang]

tits *n.* นม [nohm]

to each his own *adv.* ตัวใครตัวมัน [dtua krai dtua mun]

to the brim *adv.* เต็มคราบ [dtehm krâhp]

to the fullest *adv.* เต็มคราบ [dtehm krâhp]

tobacco *n.* ยา [yah], ยากาแร็ต [yah gah ráeht]

tomboy *n.* ทอมบอย [tawm boi]

a ton *adj./adv.* เยอะ (เยอะ ๆ) [yér], เยอะแยะ [yér yáe], อื้น ['uen]

a ton of something (like cash) *adv.* อู้ ['ôo]

too cool for school *adj.* ซ่า [sâh]

too much *adv.* เว่อร์ [wêr], โอเวอร์ ['oe wêr]

totally *adv./adj.* โคตร [kôht], เดี๊ยะ [día], ชิบหาย [chíhp hǎi], เต็มเปา [dtehm bpao], เต็มรัก [dtehm rúk], เต็มร้อย [dtehm rói], แน่ [nâe], เลย [leri], เล้ย [léri], จ๋า [jǎh]

totally awkward *adj.* เชยแหลก [choe làek]

totally Thai *adj.* ไท้ไทย [tái tai]

totally unlucky *adj.* เฮงซวย [hayng sooi]

traditionalist *n.* หัวโบราณ [hǔa boe rahn]

to trample *v.* ตื้บ [dtûep]

transgender *n.* กะเทย (กระเทย) [gà teri], ประเทือง [bpà tueang]

trash talk *n.* ปากหมา [bpàhk mǎh]

trendy *adj.* อินเทรนด์ ['in trehn]

trick *n.* ได [dtǎi]

to trick *v.* ตุ๋ม [dtôhm]

true bro *v.* ซี้แหง [sée hǎeng], เพื่อนซี้ [pûean sée], เพื่อนซี้ปี๊ก [pûean sée bpûek]

Truly? จริงเหรอ [jing rěr], จริงเหลอ [jing lěr]

Trust me! เชื่อหัวไอ้เรื่อง [chûea hǔa 'âi rueang]

truthfully *adj.* ซีเคร็ยด [see krîat]

truthfully *adv.* เอาจริงเอาจัง ['ao jihng 'ao jung]

to try *v.* เซิ้บ ๆ [sérp sérp]

Turkish bath *n.* อาบอบนวด ['àhp 'òhp nûat]

Turn about is fair play. ทีฮูทีอิด [tee hoo tee íht]

to be turned on *v.* เสียว [sěeo]

to tutor *v.* ติว [dtiu]

twat *n.* หอย [hǒi], จิ๋ม [jǐhm]

two-faced *n.* นกสองหัว [nóhk sǎwng hǔa]

type *n.* สเป็ค (สเป็ก) [sà bpèhk], สไตล์ [sà dtai]

type *cl./n.* ยัง [yung]

U

ugly *adj.* ขี้เหล่ (ขี้เหร่) [kêe lày], ขี้ริ้วขี้เหร่ [kêe ríu kêe rày]

Uhhh? *interj.* เอ ['ǎy]

Uh-huh, I get it! อื้อ ['ue]

uhmm *interj.* แล้ว [láeo]

ultra *adj.* จ๋า [jǎh]

unable to show your face in public *adj.* เอาปี๊บคลุมตัว ['ao bpéep kloom dtua]

unassuming *v./adj.* ถ่อมตัว [tà lòhm dtua]

unattractive *adj.* ขี้เหล่ (ขี้เหร่) [kêe lày], ขี้ริ้วขี้เหร่ [kêe ríu kêe rày]

uncircumcised *v.* ไม่ขลิบ [mâi kà lìhp]

uncultured villager *n.* ตาสีตาสา [dtah sěe dtah săh]

under the table *adv./n.* ใต้โต๊ะ [dtâi dtóh]

to understand *v.* เก็ท (เก็ต) [géht], รู้เรื่อง [róo rûeang]

To understand something, see where it came from ดูช้างให้ดูหาง ดูนางให้ดูแม่ [doo cháhng hâi doo hǎhng doo nahg hâi doo mâe], ดูวัวให้ดูหาง ดูนางให้ดูแม่ [doo wua hâi doo hǎhng doo nahg hâi doo mâe]

To understand something, witness it at the appropriate time ดูช้างดูหน้าหนาว ดูสาวดูหน้าร้อน [doo cháhng doo nâh nǒw doo sǒw doo nâh râwn]

underwear *n.* ก.ก.น. [gaw gaw naw], ชั้นใน [chún nai]

undisciplined cop *n.* ตำรวจนอกแถว [dtam rùat nâwk tǎeo]

unequal treatment *phr.* ฝนตกไม่ทั่วฟ้า [fǒhn dòhk mâi tûa nâh]

unemployed *adj.* นั่งตบยุง [nûng dtòhp young]

uni/university *n.* มหาลัย [má hǎh lai]

universal *adj.* อินเตอร์ ['in dter]

unlucky *adj.* ดวงจู๋ [duang jǒo]

unmarried women *n.* สาวขึ้นคาน [sǎo kûen kahn]

unpretentious *v./adj.* ถ่อมตัว [tà lòhm dtua]

unsatisfied feelings/pleasure *n.* อารมณ์ค้าง ['ah rohm káhng]

until dawn *adv./v.* โต้รุ่ง [dtóe rôong]

up-to-date *adj.* ซิ่ง [sîhng]

to use sex for career advancement *v.* ใช้เต้าใต้ [chái dtâo dtài]

to use something and not pay for it *v.* ชักดาบ [chúk dàhp]

to use your tongue *v.* ลงลิ้น [lohng lín]

useful *v.* เวิร์ก (เวิร์ค) [wérk]

V

vagina *n.* หี [hěe], เต๋า [dtào]

vagina lips *n.* แคม [kaem]

VD/venereal diseases *n.* กามโรค [gahm rôek], โรคซุกซน [rôek sóok sohn], โอกินาวา ['oe gìh nah wah]

to vent *v.* ระบาย [rá bai]

very *adj./adv.* สุดตีน [sòot dteen], จ๋า [jǎh], เหลือกิน [lǔea gin], เหลือเกิน [lǔea gern], เหลือแดก [lǔea dàek], แฮ [hae]

very short (as in pubic hair) *adj.* เกรียน [grian]

very hard (at work) *adv.* ตัวเป็นเกลียว [dtua bpehn gleeo], ตัวเป็นเกลียว หัวเป็นน็อต [dtua bpehn gleeo hǔa bpehn náwt]

very Thai *adj.* ไท้ไทย [tái tai]

Very well! *interj.* ดีละ [dee lá], ดีแล้ว [dee láeo]

to visit the brothel/bordello *v.* ตีกะหรี่ [dtee gà rèe], ซุกซน [sóok sohn], ไปเที่ยวช่อง [bpai têeo sâwng]

vivid *adj.* ซู่ซ่า [sôo sâh]

to vomit *v.* อ้วก ['ûak]

to voyeur *v.* แอบดี ['àep dee]

W

to wack off *v.* ขัดถูกล้อง [kùt tǒo glâwng], ชักจุ๊ฟ้า [chúk jǒo lah], ชักว่าว [chúk wôw], ทำร้ายตัวเอง [tam rái dtua ayng]

Wait! *interj.* อย่าเพิ่ง [yàh pêrng]

Wait, I mean... *interj.* เออ ['éri]

to walk like a flirt *v.* ฉาย [chǎi]

walks around like a playboy *adj.* แซ่หลี [sâe lěe]

to wander *v.* ตะเวน [dtà wayn]

to wander around aimlessly *v.* ตะลอน [dtà lawn]

to wanna jump for joy *v.* ดี๊ด๊า [dée dáh]

wasted already *adj.* ดีมาแล้ว [dee mah láeo]

way *n.* สไตล์ [sà dtai]

Way to go! ลุยเลย [louie leri]

we *pron.* เรา [rao]

weak *adj.* มะเขือเผา [má kŭea păo]

to wear whatever *v.* ปล่อยตัว [bplòi dtua]

weblog *n.* บล็อก [blàwk]

web-board *n.* เว็บบอร์ด [wéhp báwt]

weird *adj.* เซอร์ [ser], เบ๊อะ [bér]

Well! *interj.* อ้าว ['ôw], แล้ว [láeo]

West coast of Thailand *n.* ทะเลหน้านอก [tá lay nâh nâwk]

Western (in general) *adj.* อินเตอร์ ['in dter]

Western (exceedingly) *adj.* ฝรั่งจ๋า [fà rùng jăh], หรั่งจ๋า [rùng jăh]

Westerner *n.* ฝรั่ง [fà rùng]

Westerner with no cash and no clue *n.* ฝรั่งขี้นก [fà rùng kêe nóhk]

wet dream *n.* ฝันเปียก [fŭn bpìak]

Whadya say about… ไอ้ที่ว่า ['âi têe wâh]

Whahhht? *interj.* ว่า [wáh]

What? *adv.* ยังไง [yung ngai], ไง [ngai], ไร [rai]

What a shame/pity! โธ่ [tôe]

What, again?! เอาอีกแล้ว ['ao 'èek láeo]

What could/can? ได้ไง [dâi gnai], ได้ยังไง [dâi yung gnai]

What is your name? ชื่อเรียงเสียงไร [chùe riang síang rai]

What just happened? เป็นอะไรไป [bpehn 'a-rai bpai], เป็นไรไป [bpehn rai bpai]

What you just freakin said about… ไอ้ที่ว่า ['âi têe wâh]

What's new! ว่ายังไง [wâh yung-ngai]

What's this? อะไรเนี่ย ['a rai nîa]

What's up!/Wuz up! ว่าไง [wâh ngai]

when *adv.* ที่ไร [tee rai]

When? *adv.* เมื่อไร [mûe rai]

When a guy gets his turn, why then, he gets *his* turn! *n.* ที่สูที่อิด [tee hoo tee íht]

When in Rome do as the Romans do *phr.* เข้าเมืองตาหลิ่ว [kâo mueang dtah lìu]

whenever *adv.* ที่ไร [tee rai]

whew… *op.* เฮอ [her], เฮ่อ [hêr], เฮือก [hûeak]

wishy-washy *v.* ชักเข้าชักออก [chúk kâo chúk 'ăhk]

whisky *n.* วิสกี้ [wíh sà gêe], เหล้าวิสกี้ [lâo wíh sà gêe]

white and milky *adj.* แดงร่มใบ [dtaeng rôhm bai]

white-boy *n.* ฝรั่ง [fà rùng]

Whoa! *interj.* โอ้โห ['ôe hŏe], โอ้โฮ ['ôe hoe], โอ้โฮเฮะ ['ôe hoe háy]

Whore! *adj.* อีดอกทอง ['ee dàwk tawng], อีดอก ['ee dàwk]

whore *n.* กะหรี่ [gà rèe], ช๊อกการี [cháwk gah ree], นางบำเรอ [nahng bam rer], อีตัว ['ee dtua]

Why wouldn't it be like that? นะซิ [ná síh]

wicked (evil) *adj.* แสบ [sàep]

wicked (cool) *adj.* เจ๋งเป้ง [jăyng bpâyng]

wicked fun *adj.* ซี้ดปาก [séet bpàhk]

a widow that no guy wants to get with again *n.* แดงเถาตาย [dtaeng tăo dtai]

wife *n.* แฟน [faen]

will *adv.* กะลัง [gà lung]

to wish for the moon *phr.*
ชิ้นกบนปลายไม้
[chée nóhk bohn bplai mái]

with *prep.* กะ [gà]

withered *adj.* มะเขือเผา
[má kǔea pǎo]

withered penis *n.* หำเหี่ยว [hǎm hèeo]

to withhold back cash *v.* เม้มสตางค์
[máym sà dtāhng]

without end *adv.* ตอยหอย [dtòi hǒi]

without feeling *adv.* กินข้าวแกงจืด
[gin kôa gàeng jùet]

wolf eyes (like a pervert) *n.* หน้าหม้อ
[nâh mâw]

woman ticket-taker on bus *n.* กระป๋ี
[grà bpěe]

woman's period *n.* ไฟแดง [fai daeng]

woman's virginity *n.* ไข่แดง [kài daeng]

words *n.* น้ำคำ [nám kam]

to work (as in be useful) *v.* เวิร์ก
(เวิร์ค) [wérk]

to work your game *v.* จีบ [jeep]

workaholic *adj.* บ้างาน [bâh ngahn]

worn-out *adj.* เดี้ยง [dîang],
เหงื่อตกกีบ [ngùea dtòhk gèep]

Wow! *interj.* อู้ฮู [ʻôo hoo],
เออเฮอ [ʻer her]

Wow! *part.* แฮะ [háe]

wretched *adj.* ระย่า [rá yum]

X

xxx *n.* เอ็กซ์ [ʻèhk]

xxx mag *n.* หนังสือโป๊ [nǔng sǔe bóe]

xxx movie *n.* หนังโป๊ [nǔng bóe]

Y

Yeah? *Interj.* นะ [ná], เนอะ [nér]

yeah and... *phr.* แล้วไง [láeo ngai]

to yell at an old-timer *v.* ถอนหงอก
[tǎwn ngàwk]

yellow (coward) *adj.* แหยแฝน
[yǎe fàen]

Yep! *interj.* เออ [ʻer], อื้อ [hûe]

Yep, I get it! อื้อ [ʻue]

Yes, all right! เอาซี [ʻao sí]

...yet? *adv.* ยัง [yung], รึยัง [rúe yung]

Yo! *interj.* เฮ้ [háy], เฮ้ย (เฮีย) [héri],
ไฮ้ [hái], ไง [ngai]

you (y'all) *pron.* แก [gae], เอ็ง
[ʻehng], เธอ [ter], ตัว [dtua]

You f—k! ไอ้เหี้ย [ʻâi hîa], เหี้ย [hîa]

you get what you hate *phr.*
เกลียดแบบไหนได้แบบนั้น
[glìat bàep nǎi dâi bàep nún]

You win some, you lose some!
ตาดีก็ได้ ตาร้ายก็เสีย
[dtah dee gâw dâi dtah rái gâw sǐa]

Young/youthful *adj.* เอาะ [ʻáw],
มะ [má]

young dirty Western backpacker *n.*
ฝรั่งขี้นก [fà rùng kêe nóhk]

your johnson *n.* เจ้าหนู [jâo nǒo]

your own way *n.* ฟรีสไตล์ [free sà dtai]

Yuck! *interj.* อี๊ (อี๋) [ʻée]

Z

to zigzag *v.* ซิกแซ็ก [síhk sâek]

to zip up your mouth *v.* รูดซิปปาก
[rôot síp bàhk]